KEYS TO CHINESE
(Book II)

Keys to Chinese Language
(Book II)

漢語入門
(下冊)

By Jing-Heng Sheng Ma

馬盛靜恆 著

The Chinese University Press

Keys to Chinese Language (Book II)
   By Jing-Heng Sheng Ma

© Jing-Heng Sheng Ma, 2006

All rights reserved. No part of this publication may be reproduced or transmitted in any form or by any means, electronic or mechanical, including photocopying, recording, or any information storage and retrieval system, without permission in writing from the author.

ISBN 962–996–212–8

THE CHINESE UNIVERSITY PRESS
The Chinese University of Hong Kong
SHA TIN, N.T., HONG KONG
Fax: +852 2603 6692
      +852 2603 7355
E-mail: cup@cuhk.edu.hk
Web-site: www.chineseupress.com

Printed in Hong Kong

CONTENTS

Introduction	vii
Acknowledgements	ix
Abbreviations of Parts of Speech	xi
Cast of Characters	xii
18 Most Frequently-used Radicals	xiii

Lesson 11 Introducing friends — 1
  Pinyin Text — 3
  Chinese Character Text — 25

Lesson 12 An e-mail from a friend — 43
  Pinyin Text — 45
  Chinese Character Text — 63

Lesson 13 Reply to a friend's e-mail — 79
  Pinyin Text — 81
  Chinese Character Text — 99

Lesson 14 What plans do you have for vacation? — 113
  Pinyin Text — 115
  Chinese Character Text — 133

Lesson 15 I went to China — 147
  Pinyin Text — 149
  Chinese Character Text — 165

Lesson 16 I went to Japan — 177
  Pinyin Text — 179
  Chinese Character Text — 193

Lesson 17 Celebrating father's birthday — 205
  Pinyin Text — 207
  Chinese Character Text — 221

Lesson 18	Thanksgiving	233
	Pinyin Text	235
	Chinese Character Text	249
Lesson 19	Heart-to-heart talk	261
	Pinyin Text	263
	Chinese Character Text	277
Lesson 20	A picnic	289
	Pinyin Text	291
	Chinese Character Text	307
Lesson 21	I got sick	319
	Pinyin Text	321
	Chinese Character Text	339
Lesson 22	Plans for summer vacation	353
	Pinyin Text	355
	Chinese Character Text	371

Appendixes

Vocabulary Index	385
Sentence Pattern Index	403
Flash Cards	407

INTRODUCTION

Keys to Chinese Language is a comprehensive package of course material for elementary learners of Mandarin Chinese. It is a set of two volumes of textbooks, workbooks, and an interactive tutorial software (CD-ROM).

In each lesson of the textbooks, a pinyin text precedes a Chinese character text. All the lessons basically include (1) a short text (most of them are in the form of conversation); (2) an annotated vocabulary list with illustrated sentences; (3) sentence pattern drills; (4) a Sentence Building section; and (5) a Questions and Responses section.

In the pinyin texts of some of the lessons, extra sections — Cultural Notes and Fun Activity — are included. The Cultural Notes section is designed to explain some of the cultural difference between China and the western world. Interesting genres such as songs, word-play, and tongue-twisters are also introduced in the Fun Activity section, to enliven and vary the language experience.

In the Chinese character texts of each lesson, a reading section is included at the end. In this reading section some characters and expressions not covered in class are deliberately introduced, providing learners with an opportunity to take the initiative to learn outside class.

The pinyin text focuses on pronunciation, accuracy of intonation and fluency of speech, while the Chinese character text stresses character recognition and reading comprehension. Therefore, the pinyin text should be used prior to the Chinese character text.

A list of the 18 most frequently-used radicals and a set of flash cards (numbered with proper stroke order) are included for reference.

The workbooks contain different drillings, namely, (1) New Character Practice; (2) New Word and Expression Practice; (3) Grammar Practice; and (4) Reading and Writing Exercises. All of these exercises are designed in such a way that learners can revise what they have learnt efficiently.

An interactive tutorial software (CD-ROM) comes with the text. It is designed to help learners prepare class assignments. Each lesson consists of four sections: (1) Listening Comprehension; (2) Vocabulary (Chinese to English and English to Chinese translations); (3) Illustrative Sentences; and (4) Audio-Only Grammar Exercises (Sentence Patterns, Sentence Building and Questions and Responses.) In the Listening Comprehension section, one is asked to listen to a dialogue and complete a multiple-choice, self-correcting quiz. In the Vocabulary section, one will take part in an interactive flashcard game. The Illustrative Sentences section provides one with listening exercises combined with the Chinese characters for each sentence and images to aid in comprehension. The Audio-Only Grammar Exercise section allows one to listen to native speakers reading exercises while they follow along in their textbook. The tutorials give the language learner a concrete sense of accomplishment for work done on that lesson. What's more, through the online tutorials, one can receive immediate feedback and recognize their progress.

Traditional Chinese characters are used in *Keys to Chinese Language*. According to many experienced educators, it is easier for learners to begin with learning traditional Chinese characters, before switching to simplified Chinese characters. The phonetic transcription used in the book is the pinyin system adopted by the People's Republic of China after 1949.

There are ten lessons in *Keys to Chinese Language (Book I)*. Although only ten new characters are introduced in each lesson, one will actually be learning 20 to 30 compound words, idioms and / or expressions. One will have learned a total of 225 characters, 347 compound words/expressions, and 117 basic sentence patterns from *Keys to Chinese Language (Book I)*. When finishing the materials of this package, one should also be able to use familiar everyday expressions (e.g., greetings, self-introduction, requests, and preferences) and some basic phrases for making conversations, telephone conversations, letter and e-mail writing.

Keys to Chinese Language (Book II) consists of 12 lessons. A total of 120 new characters, 361 compound words/expressions, and 89 sentence patterns are introduced. With the successful completion of this set of materials, one will be able to report on events in the past, discuss plans for the future, make comparisons, express cause, effect and purpose, talk about holidays and birthday parties, ask permission, express emotion, give advice and make suggestions.

Keys to Chinese Language is based upon and constitutes a logical continuation of the introductory course materials *Keys to Chinese Character Writing*, in which a systematic instruction in the writing of Chinese characters is introduced. It is strongly recommended to use both of the texts together for more effective learning.

ACKNOWLEDGEMENTS

Many people have helped shape this project. This project would not have succeeded without institutional support, especially the technology resources from Wellesley College and many of my colleagues and students at Wellesley. My thanks go to my colleagues, Dai Chen and Weina Zhao, for their hard work on the reading section and grammar section of the workbook, respectively. My thanks also go to my colleagues, Dai Chen, Ann Huss, Haoming Liu, and my husband Wei-Yi Ma, for recording the texts. I would also like to express my gratitude to Li Yu and Minji Yao for the many hours they spent on typing the texts. Special thanks go to my student, Ee Cheng Ong — she has helped throughout the preparation of this project. My thanks also go to Stephani Cho for her wonderful illustrations and book cover designs.

Many people have helped develop the online tutorial program accompanying the texts. I am grateful to Kenneth B. Freundlich, Director, Instructional Technology, and Andrew W. Waldron, Director, Knapp Media & Media Technology Center; for their excellent technical support and advice. Special thanks must go out to Heather Elizabeth E. Woods, Project Leader, for her inspiration during the development of this project, her excellent technical advice and software design throughout the project. If not for the incredible effort Heather put into it — discussing the project with me for the past ten months, designing the Flash template, and organizing the students, the project would never have been achieved. Special thanks to Wellesley Knapp Instructional Technology Summer 2003 Interns, Jiayang Chien and Gowun Kim — lead designers for the project, Daphne Francois, Joyce Hsu, Tara McGovern, and Kate Tetreault. Chinese Department Interns Julia Zhang, Joyce Lo, Wen-chi Alice Tiao, and Minji Yao for the hundred of hours they devoted to the project; I am in awe of their technological skills! My deepest thanks and love go to my husband, Wei-yi Ma for his endless support.

I am indebted to the work of a number of linguists who have contributed to the study of the Chinese language, especially John DeFrancis, Charles N. Li, Sandra A. Thompson, Chao Yuen-ren and Wang Hai.

I am special grateful to my editor, Helene Schulman, for helping me shape the book and for her patience, support, and her detailed commentary. She has been invaluable to this project. My deepest gratitude go to the editors of The Chinese

University Press. They offered generous advice, assistance, and excellent editorial suggestions in the course of preparation of *Keys to Chinese Language*. Any remaining errors and infelicities are of course my own responsibility.

This project was generously funded by special gift contributions from Mrs. Elizabeth Tu Hoffman, her husband, Mr. Rowe Hoffman, and Mrs. Ann Munro. Their support was extremely valuable and no words can express my appreciation for their support and encouragement.

Jing-Heng Sheng Ma
Wellesley, Massachusetts
June 2006

ABBREVIATIONS OF PARTS OF SPEECH

Adj	Adjective	xíngróngcí	形容詞
Adv	Adverb	fùcí	副詞
As	Aspect Marker	tǐmào cíwěi	體貌詞尾
AV	Auxiliary Verb	zhùdòngcí	助動詞
Conj	Conjunction	liáncí	連詞
CV	Coverb	fǔdòngcí (jiècí)	輔動詞(介詞)
Det	Determinative	zhǐshìcí	指示詞
DO	Direct Object	zhíjiē bīnyǔ	直接賓語
EV	Equative Verb	duìděng dòngcí	對等動詞
IE	Idiomatic Expression	xíguàn yòngyǔ	習慣用語
IO	Indirect Object	jiànjiē bīnyǔ	間接賓語
IV	Intransitive Verb	bùjíwù dòngcí	不及物動詞
MA	Movable Adverb	kěyí fùcí	可移副詞
MW	Measure Word	liàngcí	量詞
N	Noun	míngcí	名詞
Neg	Negative	fǒudìngcí	否定詞
Nu	Number	shùcí	數詞
O	Object	bīnyǔ	賓語
Pron	Pronoun	dàimíngcí	代名詞
PW	Place Word	dìfāngcí	地方詞
QP	Question Particle	yíwènyǔ zhùcí	疑問語助詞
QW	Question Word	yíwèncí	疑問詞
S	Subject	zhǔyǔ	主語
SV	Stative Verb	jìngtài dòngcí	靜態動詞
TW	Time Word	shíjiāncí	時間詞
V	Verb	dòngcí	動詞
VO	Verb-Object	dòngbīn fùhécí	動賓複合詞

CAST OF CHARACTERS

Mǎ Sīwén
馬思文

Mǎ Àiwén
馬愛文

Mǎ xiānsheng
馬先生

Mǎ tàitai
馬太太

Xǔ Xiǎoměi
許小美

Lín Hǎiyīng
林海英

Mǎ Hóng
馬紅

Jīn Jiàn
金建

Wáng lǎoshī
王老師

18 MOST FREQUENTLY-USED RADICALS

Radical (部首)　　　　　Chinese Character (漢字)

Radical					
人/亻	他	們	今	大	來呢報姓從愛才是樂酒熱笨給花請跟進鉛
口	喝	問	哥	和	
土	土	地	坐	在	
女	媽	姐	妹	好	
彳	很	後	得	待	
心/忄	想	慢	快	怕	
手/扌	手	指	找	拿	
日	日	明	晚	早	
木	木	樹	林	本	
水/氵	水	汽	海	湯	
火/灬	火	煩	災	燙	
竹/⺮	竹	筆	第	等	
糸/纟	紙	紅	累	緊	
艹	草	茶	葉	菜	
言	許	誰	說	話	
足/⻊	足	跑	跳	路	
走/辶	近	遠	送	過	
金/金	金	錢	銀	錶	

第十一課　介紹朋友
Lesson 11　Introducing friends

Lesson 11
Pinyin Text

CONTENTS

*T*ext 4

*V*ocabulary and Illustrative Sentences 5
(diǎn, fēn, chē, shì, qíng, xiān, zài, zhōng, kè, ér)

*P*attern Drills 14
(yìdiǎnr, zài)

*S*entence Building 22
(jǐ diǎn zhōng, xiān chīfàn, yàodiǎn, yìdiǎnr)

*Q*uestions and Responses 22

*P*ronunciation Review 23

*S*upplementary Vocabulary 24

*C*ultural Notes 24

Text

Jièshào péngyou
Introducing Friends

Xīngqīliù wǎnshang qī diǎn shí fēn, Lín Hǎiyīng kāichē dào le Jīn Jiàn jiā. Jīn Jiàn gěi tā jièshào tā de nǚpéngyou.

At 7:10 on a Saturday night, Lin Haiying drives up to Jin Jian's house. Jin Jian introduces his girlfriend to Lin Haiying.

Jīn Jiàn	: Hǎiyīng, wǒ gěi nǐmen jièshào jièshào, zhè shì Mǎ Hóng, tā shì wǒ de tóngxué. Zhè shì Lín Hǎiyīng, wǒmen shì zhōngxué de tóngxué, tā shì wǒ zuìhǎo de péngyou.	Haiying, I will introduce you. This is Ma Hong, she is my classmate. This is Lin Haiying. We were high school classmates, and she is my best friend.
Lín Hǎiyīng:	Nǐ hǎo, Mǎ Hóng.	Hi, Ma Hong.
Mǎ Hóng	: Nǐ hǎo, Hǎiyīng. Jīn Jiàn gàosu wǒ hěn duō nǐmen zhōngxué shíhou de shìqing.	Hi, Haiying! Jin Jian has told me a lot about your high school years.
Lín Hǎiyīng:	Shì ma!	Really!
Mǎ Hóng	: Wǒmen jīntiān wǎnshang qù nǎr?	Where are we going tonight?
Jīn Jiàn	: Wǒmen kěyǐ chūqu chīfàn, kàn diànyǐng.	We can go out to dinner and watch a movie.
Lín Hǎiyīng:	Hǎo. Wǒmen shì xiān chīfàn zài qù kàn diànyǐng, háishì xiān kàn diànyǐng zài chīfàn?	Okay, should we eat first, then watch a movie, or should we watch a movie first, then eat?

Lesson 11 Introducing friends
第十一课 介绍朋友

Mǎ Hóng	: Wǒ xiǎng xiān chīfàn zài kàn diànyǐng.	I think we should eat first, then watch a movie.
Lín Hǎiyīng	: Wǒ tóngyì. Kàn diànyǐng yǐhòu, wǒ qǐng nǐmen chī diǎnxīn.	I agree. After the movie, I'll treat you to some snacks.
Jīn Jiàn	: Hǎo, nà wǒmen xiànzài jiù qù chīfàn ba.	All right then, let's go eat now.
Lín Hǎiyīng	: Wǒmen kàn jǐ diǎn zhōng de diànyǐng?	What time is the movie?
Jīn Jiàn	: Jiǔ diǎn sān kè de.	Nine fifteen.

🐾 Vocabulary and Illustrative Sentences

1. **diǎn**   **dot, point; drop (of liquid) (N); o'clock (MW)**

☞ jǐ diǎn   what time, when (QW)

(1) A: Qǐngwèn, xiànzài jǐ diǎn?   Excuse me, what time is it now?
    B: Wǒ yě méiyǒu biǎo.   I don't have a watch (either).

(2) A: Wǒmen jǐ diǎn jiàn?   What time will we meet up?
    B: Shí'èr diǎn wǔ fēn.   Five minutes past twelve.

☞ zǎodiǎn   breakfast (N)

(1) A: Nǐ chī zǎodiǎn de shíhou xǐhuan hē shénme?   What do you like to drink for breakfast?
    B: Wǒ xǐhuan hē hóng chá.   I like to drink red (black) tea.

(2) A: Nǐ jǐ diǎn chī zǎodiǎn?   What time do you have breakfast?
    B: Wǒ bù chī zǎodiǎn.   I don't eat breakfast.

☞ diǎnxīn   snacks (N)

(1) A: Nǐ xǐhuan chī Zhōngguó diǎnxīn háishì Měiguó diǎnxīn?
      Do you like Chinese snacks or American snacks?

    B: Wǒ xǐhuan chī Měiguó diǎnxīn.
      I like to eat American snacks.

(2) Wǒ bù chī diǎnxīn, yīnwèi chī le diǎnxīn yǐhòu, jiù bù xiǎng chīfàn le.
    I don't eat snacks because after (I) have snacks, (I) no longer want to have a decent meal.

☞ chádiǎn   tea and pastries, refreshments (N)

(1) Qǐng nǐmen wǎnshang qī diǎn lái kāihuì, wǒmen yǒu hěn duō chádiǎn.
    Please come to the meeting at seven o'clock tonight. We'll have a lot of refreshments.

(2) Yàoshì kāihuì yǒu chádiǎn, lái de rén jiù duō.
    If refreshments are available at a meeting, more people will come.

☞ diǎn cài   choose dishes from a menu, order dishes (in a restaurant) (VO)

(1) A: Xiǎojiě, nǐmen xiànzài yào diǎn cài ma?
      Miss, would you like to order now?

    B: Wǒmen xiān kànkan, děng yíhuìr zài diǎn.
      Give us a moment. We'll order in a while.

(2) A: Wǒ bú huì diǎn Zhōngguócài. Zhōngguócài de míngzi hěn nán. Nǐ diǎn ba.
      I don't know how to order Chinese dishes. Chinese dishes have complicated names. You order, please.

    B: Hǎo, wǒ shìshi.
      Okay, I will try.

☞ yàodiǎn   main points, essentials, gist, key point (N)

A: Lǎoshī jīntiān shuō de yàodiǎn shì shénme?
    What were the main points of the teacher's lecture today?

B: Wǒ yě bù zhīdào.
    I don't know (either).

Lesson 11 Introducing friends
第十一課 介紹朋友

☞ nándiǎn   difficult point, difficulty (N)

    Xué Zhōngwén de nándiǎn shì   The difficulty with learning
    Zhōngguózì tài duō, tài nán xiě.   Chinese is that there are too
        many characters and (they are)
        too difficult to write.

2. **fēn**   **divide, separate (V); minute (of time) (MW)**

    (1) A: Wǒ yǒu shí běn shū, qǐng   I have ten books. Please
          nǐ fēn gěi tāmen wǔ ge   distribute them among those five
          rén.   people.

       B: Hǎo, yí ge rén liǎng běn.   All right, each person can have
          two books.

    (2) A: Xiànzài shì liù diǎn jǐ fēn?   What time is it? Six something?

       B: Liù diǎn èrshí fēn.   6:20.

☞ xuéfēn   credit (official acceptance and record of a student's work in a particular course of study) (N)

    (1) A: Nǐ zhè xuéqī xuǎn le jǐ ge   How many credits are you taking
          xuéfēn?   this semester?

       B: Shíliù ge.   Sixteen.

    (2) Shàng xuéqī wǒ de shùxuékè   Last semester (I) didn't do well
       kǎo bù hǎo, méiyǒu dédào   in my math exam. (I) didn't get
       xuéfēn.   credit (for the course).

3. **chē**   **vehicle, wheeled machine (N)**

    A: Zhè ge chē shì nǐ de háishì   Is this car yours or your
       nǐ gēge de?   brother's?

    B: Shì wǒ gēge de.   It's my brother's.

☞ qìchē   automobile, car (N)

    A: Nǐ de qìchē shì nǎ nián de?   Which year was your car
       (introduced in the market)?

    B: Èrlínglíngèr nián de.   It's a 2002 model.

	diànchē	trolley, streetcar (N)	
		A: Nǐ yǒu-méiyǒu jiànguo diànchē?	Have you seen trolleys before?
		B: Jiànguo.	(I) have seen them before.
	huǒchē	train (N)	
		A: Nǐ xǐhuan zuò huǒchē háishì zuò qìchē?	Do you like to ride on a train or in a car?
		B: Wǒ xǐhuan zuò huǒchē.	I like to ride on a train.
	kāichē	drive or start a car, train, etc. (VO)	
		(1) Kāichē de shíhou, bù kěyǐ hē jiǔ.	One cannot drink when driving.
		(2) A: Nǐ huì kāichē ma?	Do you know how to drive?
		B: Wǒ zǎo jiù huì kāi le.	I have known how to drive for a long time.
4.	shì	**matter, affair, thing; business; trouble; job, work (N)**	
		A: Nǐ zhǎo wǒ yǒu shénme shì ma?	Is there a reason why you were looking for me?
		B: Wǒ xiǎng qǐng nǐ gěi wǒ zhǎo yí ge shìr.	I wanted to ask if you could find me a job.
	dàshì	great (or major) event, important matter, major issue (N)	
		(1) Zhè shì guójiā dàshì, wǒmen yīnggāi rènzhēn de xiǎng-yi-xiǎng.	This is a national issue. We should think about it seriously.
		(2) Nǐ jiā yǒu shénme dàshì?	Has something serious happened in your family?
	běnshi	skill; ability, capability (N)	
		A: Tā shì shénmeyàng de rén?	What kind of person is he?
		B: Tā shì yí ge hěn yǒu běnshi de rén.	He is a very capable person.

Lesson 11 Introducing friends
第十一課 介紹朋友

	yǒu shì	when problems crop up (VO); busy (N)	
		(1) Yàoshì tā méiyǒu shì, tā bú huì lái zhǎo wǒ.	He wouldn't come to see me if he didn't have a problem.
		(2) Wǒ jīntiān wǎnshang yǒu shì, bú qù kàn diànyǐng le.	I am busy tonight, (I) can't go to the movie.
	zhǎo shì	look (or hunt) for a job (VO); pick a quarrel (V)	
		Xiànzài hěn duō rén dōu méiyǒu gōngzuò, zhǎo shì zhēn nán.	Now many people are out of work; it is really difficult to get a job.
	méishì-zhǎoshì	ask for trouble, try hard to find fault (IE)	
		Zhège rén shéi dōu bù xǐhuan tā, yīnwèi tā lǎo méishìzhǎoshì.	Nobody likes this person because he is always asking for trouble.

5. qíng **feeling, sentiment; love (N)**

	shìqing	affair; matter; thing; business (N)	
		Yàoshì nǐ jīntiān wǎnshang méiyǒu shìqing, wǒmen qù kàn diànyǐng, hǎo ba?	If you haven't got anything to do tonight, how about going to watch a movie?
	àiqíng	love (romance) (N)	
		(1) Shénme shì "àiqíng," wǒ yě bù zhīdào.	What is "love," I don't know either.
		(2) Wǒ mèimei zuì xǐhuan kàn àiqíng de xiǎoshuō gēn àiqíng diànyǐng.	My little sister loves reading romances and watching romantic movies.
	qíngrén	sweetheart, lover (N)	
		Tā qíngrén shēngrì de shíhou, tā sòng tā hěn duō huār.	On her sweetheart's birthday, she gave him a lot of flowers.
	xīnqíng	frame of mind, mood (N)	
		(1) Zuìjìn wǒ de hǎopéngyou xīnqíng bù hǎo, yìtiāndàowǎn zài shēngqì.	These days my good friend is in a bad mood. She's always upset.

| | | (2) Wèishénme yǒu rén xīnqíng bù hǎo de shíhou jiù hē jiǔ? | Why do some people drink when they're in a bad mood? |

6. **xiān** — **earlier, before; first; in advance** (Adv)

  (1) Nǐ zuìhǎo xiān dǎ ge diànhuà kàn tā zài jiā bú zài jiā. — It's best to give him a call and find out whether he is home.

  (2) Wǒmen xué Zhōngwén shì xiān xué shuōhuà, zài xué rèn zì, xiě zì. — We learn to speak Chinese before learning to recognize and write Chinese characters.

☞ **xiānsheng** — teacher; mister (Mr.); gentleman, sir; husband (N)

  (1) Yè xiānsheng shì nǐ de lǎoshī ma? — Is Mr. Ye your teacher?

  (2) Xiānsheng, nǐ yào hē diǎnr shénme? — Sir, what would you like to drink?

  (3) Wǒ xiānsheng jīntiān bú zài jiā, qǐng nǐ míngtiān zài lái ba! — My husband is not home today. Please come again tomorrow!

☞ **xiānhòu** — altogether; priority, order, successively, one after another (Adv)

  A: Nǐ xiānhòu xuéguo jǐ ge yuè de Rìwén? — How many months did you study Japanese altogether?

  B: Wǒ xiānhòu xuéguo liù ge yuè. Qùnián zài Rìběn xuéguo liǎng ge yuè, jīnnián zài Měiguó xuéguo le sì ge yuè. — Altogether, I studied for six months. Two months in Japan last year and, four months in the States this year.

7. **zài** — **another time, again, once more** (Adv)

  (1) Qǐng nǐ zài shuō. — Please say it again.

  (2) Zài duō chī yìdiǎnr. — Eat a bit more.

  (3) Děng tā xīnqíng hǎo yìdiǎnr zài gēn tā shuō ba. — Tell him when he's in a better mood.

☞ **xiān ... zài** — first ... then (Conj)

  (1) Nǐ xiān shìshi kàn, yàoshi nǐ bú huì, zài lái wèn wǒ. — Try first. If you still don't understand, then come and ask me.

Lesson 11 Introducing friends
第十一課 介紹朋友

| | (2) Wǒmen děi xiān qù yínháng ná qián, zài qù kàn diànyǐng. | We must first go to the bank to get some money, then go watch the movie. |

☞ zàisān — over and over again, repeatedly (Adv)

(1) Wǒ zàisān gàosu tā kāichē de shíhou bú yào hē jiǔ, kěshì tā hái hē. — I have told him repeatedly not to drink and drive, but he still drinks.

(2) Māma zàisān gēn tā shuō nàge rén shì ge xǐhuan méishìzhǎoshì de rén, kěshì tā bú xìn. — Mother has told him over and over again that that person is a trouble-maker, but he doesn't believe her.

☞ zàishuō — put off until some time later; moreover (IE)

(1) Qù Zhōngguó de shì, yǐhòu zàishuō ba. — As for going to China, let's talk about it later.

(2) Zhège fànguǎnr de cài hěn hǎo, zàishuō fànguǎnr de rén yě hěn héqi. — The food in this restaurant is excellent. Moreover, the workers in the restaurant are very nice.

☞ zàijiàn — good-bye; see you again (V)

(1) Wǒmen shénme shíhou kěyǐ zàijiàn? — When can we see each other again?

(2) A: Shíhou bù zǎo le, wǒ děi qù shàng kè le, zàijiàn! — It's getting late, I have to get to class. Good-bye!

  B: Zàijiàn! — Good-bye!

8. zhōng — **clock; hour; time** (N)

(1) A: Xiànzài jǐ diǎn zhōng? — What time is it now?
   B: Qī diǎn sān kè. — 7:45.

(2) A: Zhège zhōng bù zǒu le? — Isn't this clock working?
   B: Nǐ méiyǒu biǎo ma? — Don't you have a watch?
   A: Méiyǒu. — No, I don't (have one).

9. kè — **a quarter of an hour; moment (MW); carve, engrave, cut (V)**

    (1) Shíwǔ fēnzhōng shì yí kè. Yí ge xiǎoshí shì jǐ kè? — Fifteen minutes is a quarter of an hour. How many quarters are there in an hour?

    (2) Sìshíwǔ fēn shì jǐ kè? — How many quarters are there in forty-five minutes?

☞ kè zì — carve (or engrave) characters on a seal, etc. (VO)

    A: Nǐ huì-bu-huì kè zì? — Do you know how to engrave characters?

    B: Wǒ bú huì, kěshì wǒ xiānsheng huì. — I don't know, but my husband does.

10. ér — **child, youngster, son; male (N); (suffix)**

☞ érnǚ — sons and daughters, children (N)

    A: Lǎoxiānsheng, nǐ yǒu-méiyǒu érnǚ? — Sir, do you have any children?

    B: Wǒ yǒu sān ge érzi, sì ge nǚ'ér. — Yes, I have three sons and four daughters.

☞ nǚ'ér — daughter, girl (N)

    Wǒ jiějie yǒu liǎng ge nǚ'ér, tāmen dōu zài Yīngguó shàngxué. — My elder sister has two daughters. They are both studying in England.

☞ nàr — there (PW)

    Nǐ kàn, nàr yǒu yí ge cháguǎnr. Wǒmen qù nàr hē diǎnr chá ba. — Look, there's a teahouse. Let's go there and have some tea.

☞ zhèr — here (PW)

    Nǐ kàn, zhèr yě yǒu yí ge cháguǎnr, wǒmen jiù zài zhège cháguǎnr hē ba! Jìn yìdiǎnr. — Look, there's also a teahouse here. Let's just have some tea here! It's closer.

Lesson 11 Introducing friends
第十一課 介紹朋友

☞ nǎr   where (QW)

    A: Nǐ xiǎng qù nǎr zhǎo shì?   Where do you want to find a job?

    B: Nǎr yào rén wǒ jiù qù nǎr zhǎo shì.   I'll look for a job wherever workers are needed.

☞ yǒu diǎnr   some, a bit; somewhat (IE)

    (1) Jīntiān de gōngkè yǒu diǎnr nán.   Today's homework is a bit difficult.

    (2) Tā nǚpéngyou yǒu diǎnr qián.   His girlfriend has some money.

☞ yìdiǎnr   a bit, a little (Adv)

    (1) A: Wǒ mā shuō Zhōngwén yìdiǎnr yě bù nán.   My mother says Chinese is not difficult at all.

       B: Nà shì yīnwèi tā shì Zhōngguórén.   That's because she's Chinese.

    (2) Zhège cài hěn hǎochī, duō chī yìdiǎnr.   This is a very tasty dish. Have some more.

☞ yíhuìr   soon, a little while, a moment; one moment (TW)

    (1) Wǒ yíhuìr jiù huílái.   I will be back soon.

    (2) Qǐng nǐ zài zhèr děng yíhuìr.   Please wait here for a little while.

Pattern Drills

11.1 CLOCK TIME

The three units for designating and measuring time by the clock are: <u>diǎn</u> "hour," <u>kè</u> "a quarter (of an hour)" and <u>fēn</u> "minute." These measures are preceded by appropriate numbers and followed by the noun <u>zhōng</u> "clock." Hours are expressed by the numbers one through twelve followed by the measure word <u>zhōng</u>. When the time expression contains <u>kè</u> or <u>fēn</u>, <u>zhōng</u> is often omitted.

yì diǎn zhōng	one o'clock
liǎng diǎn zhōng	two o'clock
shí'èr diǎn zhōng	twelve o'clock

We have already noted in Lesson 7 that the sequence of telling time in Chinese always begins with the largest unit followed by progressively smaller ones:

shí'èr diǎn èrshíwǔ fēn	12:25

Time before or after the hour is expressed with the verb <u>chà</u> "lacking" or <u>guò</u> "past":

yì diǎn chà wǔ fēn	five minutes to one
yì diǎn guò wǔ fēn	five minutes past one

<u>Guò</u> may be omitted before quarters and before minutes expressed in more than two syllables:

liǎng diǎn yí kè	2:15
liǎng diǎn èrshí fēn	2:20

Minute expressions with <u>chà</u> may be placed before or after the hour:

<u>chà</u> qī fen sān diǎn	seven minutes to three
sān diǎn <u>chà</u> qī fēn	seven minutes to three

Lesson 11 Introducing friends
第十一課 介紹朋友

11.1.1 Asking and answering in clock time

1. A: Shénme shíhou le?   What time is it?
   B: Liǎng diǎn yí kè.   Quarter past two.
2. A: Xiànzài jǐ diǎn zhōng?   What time is it now?
   B: Qī diǎn zhōng.   Seven o'clock.

11.1.2 Amounts of clock time

The noun <u>zhōngtóu</u> "hour," preceded by the measure word <u>ge</u>, is used when a quantity of time is referred to:

yí ge zhōngtóu	one hour
liǎng ge zhōngtóu	two hours
shí'èr ge zhōngtóu	twelve hours
wǔ ge duō zhōngtóu	more than five hours
wǔ-liù ge zhōngtóu	five or six hours
shíjǐ ge zhōngtóu	more than ten hours

The noun <u>zhōng</u> "hour," preceded by <u>fēn</u> "minute" and/or by <u>kè</u> "quarter," may denote a point in time or a quantity of time:

sān kè zhōng	three-quarters of an hour
sì ge zhōngtóu shí fēnzhōng	four hours and ten minutes
èrshíwǔ fēnzhōng	twenty-five minutes

11.2 FUNCTIONS OF TIME WORDS

Time words have two main functions.

11.2.1 As movable adverbs

As movable adverbs, time words may stand at the beginning of a sentence or before a verb or other adverb to form a time background for the verb.

A: Nǐ jīntiān qù shàng kè ma?
Are you going to class today?

B: Jīntiān wǒ bú qù shàng kè, míngtiān qù.
I am not going to class today. (I am) going tomorrow.

11.2.2 As nouns

As nouns, time words may function as the subject or object of a verb or modify another noun (with the particle **de**).

A: Jīntiān xīngqī jǐ?
What day (of the week) is today?

B: Jīntiān xīngqī'èr.
Today is Tuesday.

A: Nǐ kànjian jīntiān de bào le ma?
Have you read today's newspaper?

B: Méiyǒu.
No.

11.3 TIME EXPRESSIONS AND THEIR POSITIONS WITHIN THE SENTENCE

There are two types of time words in Chinese. Note the differences among the following kinds of time expressions and their positions within the sentence.

11.3.1 A particular point of time

Time expressions which indicate a particular point of time when an action takes place, such as <u>jīntiān</u> "today," <u>qùnián</u> "last year," <u>yǐqián</u> "before" or <u>yǐhòu</u> "in the future," come **before** the verb.

1. A: Nǐ shénme shíhou qù shàng kè?
   When are you going to class?

   B: Wǒ míngtiān zǎoshang bā diǎn qù shàng kè.
   I am going to class tomorrow morning at 8:00.

2. A: Nǐ míngnián qù Zhōngguó ma?
   Are you going to China next year?

   B: Míngnián bú qù, hòunián qù.
   (I) am not going next year; (I am) going the year after the next.

Lesson 11 Introducing friends
第十一課 介紹朋友

3. A: Nǐ yǐqián huì shuō Zhōngguóhuà ma? — Could you speak Chinese before?

   B: Wǒ yǐqián bú huì shuō, kěshì xiànzài huì le. — (No,) I couldn't speak Chinese before, but now I can.

11.3.2 Duration I

Time expressions which indicate the duration in which an action takes place, such as yí ge zhōngtóu "one hour," liǎng tiān "two days," or sān nián "three years," come **after** the verb in a sentence.

1. A: Mǎ Hóng yào zài Měiguó jǐ nián? — How many years does Ma Hong want to stay in the States?

   B: Tā yào zài zhèr liǎng-sān nián. — She wants to stay here for two or three years.

2. A: Mǎ Hóng yào xué jǐ nián Yīngwén? — How many years of English does Ma Hong want to study?

   B: Tā shuō tā yào xué liǎng nián Yīngwén. — She says she wants to study English for two years.

3. A: Nǐ xué le jǐ ge xuéqī de Zhōngwén le? — How many semesters have you studied Chinese?

   B: Wǒ xué le sì ge xuéqī de Zhōngwén le. — I have been studying Chinese for four semesters.

11.3.3 Duration II

Time expressions which indicate the duration in which an action does not take place comes **before** the verb in a sentence.

1. A: Jīn Jiàn qùnián xué Rìwén le méiyǒu? — Did Jin Jian take Japanese class last year?

   B: Tā yǐjīng liǎng nián méi xué Rìwén le. — He hasn't taken Japanese class for two years already.

2. A: Nǐ zuìjìn kàn diànyǐng le ma? — Have you watched a movie recently?
   B: Wǒ yǐjīng sān ge xīngqī méi kàn diànyǐng le. — It's already been three weeks since I last watched a movie.
3. A: Nǐ zěnme le? — What happened to you?
   B: Wǒ liǎng tiān méi chīfàn le. — I haven't eaten anything for two days.
   A: Wèishénme? — Why?
   B: Bù xiǎng chī. — (I) had no appetite.

11.4 THE PATTERN yìdiǎnr

11.4.1 When yìdiǎnr comes after a verb

When yìdiǎnr "a bit" (or its shortened form diǎnr) comes after a verb, it means "just a little or some."

S	V	yìdiǎnr	N / SV
Tā	yǒu	yìdiǎnr	qián.
He has a little / some money.			

1. Wǒ jiù huì shuō yìdiǎnr Zhōngguóhuà. — I can speak only a little Chinese.
2. Wǒ jīntiān yǒu diǎnr lèi. — I am a bit tired today.
3. Zuìjìn wǒ yǒu diǎnr máng. — I have been a bit busy lately.
4. Wǒ nǚpéngyou zuìjìn yǒu diǎnr bù gāoxìng. — My girlfriend has been a bit unhappy recently.

When yìdiǎnr is combined with the stative verb duō "more" or shǎo "less," yìdiǎnr comes after the main verb.

S	SV	V	yìdiǎnr	O
Nǐ	děi	duō	kàn	yìdiǎnr	shū.
You have to read some more books.				

1. Qǐng nǐ duō chī yìdiǎnr. Please eat a bit more.
2. Qǐng nǐ shàng Zhōngwénkè de shíhou, shǎo shuō yìdiǎnr Yīngwén. Please speak less English in the Chinese class.

11.4.2 Yìdiǎnr may come either before or after a verb

When yìdiǎnr is combined with kuài "fast," màn "slow," zǎo "early" or wǎn "late," the phrase may come either before the main verb, as in (A), or after the main verb, as in (B).

(A)	S	SV	yìdiǎnr	V
	(Nǐ)	kuài	yìdiǎnr	zǒu!
	Walk a little faster!			
(B)	S	V	SV	yìdiǎnr
	(Nǐ)	zǒu	kuài	yìdiǎnr!
	Walk a little faster!			

1. Qǐng nǐ kuài yìdiǎnr shuō! Please speak a little faster!
2. Qǐng nǐ màn yìdiǎnr zǒu. Please walk a little slower!
3. Nǐ xiǎng zǎo yìdiǎnr qù ma? Do you want to go there a bit earlier?
4. Wǒ míngtiān kěyǐ wǎn yìdiǎnr lái ma? May I come a little later tomorrow?

11.4.3 Yìdiǎnr yě and yìdiǎnr dōu

When yìdiǎnr yě or yìdiǎnr dōu modifies a negative stative verb, it conveys the idea "not at all."

S	yìdiǎnr yě/dōu	Neg	SV
Tā	yìdiǎnr yě/dōu	bù	hǎokàn.
She is not pretty at all.			

1. Jiějie shuō de huà, wǒ yìdiǎnr dōu bù xǐhuan. I didn't like what my elder sister said at all.
2. Zhōngwén yìdiǎnr yě bù nán. Chinese isn't difficult at all.

3. Tā xiě de shū, yìdiǎnr yìsi yě méiyǒu.   The book he wrote was not interesting at all.

11.5 THE PATTERN zài

11.5.1 Zài indicates a repetition of an event in the future

> The adverb zài "again, once more" indicates a repetition that has not yet occurred or a repetition of an event that will occur in the future.

1. Nǐ shénme shíhou zài qù Rìběn?   When are you going to Japan again?
2. Yè xiānsheng jīntiān bú zài jiā, nǐ míngtiān zài lái ba.   Mr. Ye is not at home. You'd better come again tomorrow.
3. Zài gěi tā yìdiǎnr qián ba!   Give him a little more money!
4. Qǐng nǐ zài shuō-yi-shuō zhè kè shū de yàodiǎn.   Please repeat the main points of this lesson.
5. Zài duō chī yìdiǎnr diǎnxīn.   Have some more snacks.
6. A: Nǐ shénme shíhou zài lái?   When will you come again?
   B: Wǒ wǎnshang zài lái.   I will be back in the evening.

11.5.2 Zài denotes two actions in sequence

> When the adverb zài comes in the second clause of a sentence, it indicates that the action will take place after the completion of the first action.

1. Děng wǒ xiě hǎo le zhège bàogào, wǒmen zài qù kàn diànyǐng, hǎo ma?   Wait until I finish this report, then we will go watch a movie, all right?
2. Tā lái le, wǒmen zài chīfàn.   We will eat when he arrives.
3. Wǒ yào xué hǎo le Zhōngwén zài xué Rìwén.   I want to master Chinese before I learn Japanese.

11.5.3 Xiān ... zài ... also denotes two actions in sequence

The pattern xiān ... zài ... "first (and) then..." also denotes two actions in sequence. Xiān always comes in the first clause of a sentence and zài at the beginning of the second clause. Both xiān and zài are adverbs, thus they always precede the verbs.

S	xiān	V	O	zài	V	
Nǐ	xiān	diǎn	cài	zài	tánhuà	ba!

Please order the food first, then we can chat!

1. Wǒmen kěyǐ xiān chīfàn zài zuò gōngkè ma? — Can we eat first and then do homework?

2. Wǒ děi xiān qù yínháng ná diǎnr qián zài qù fànguǎn chīfàn. — I have to go to the bank to get some money first before I go to the restaurant to eat.

3. Nǐ xiān gàosu wǒ ài-bu-ài wǒ, wǒ zài gàosu nǐ. — You tell me first whether you love me, then I'll tell you.

11.5.4 The pattern zài yě bù

Zài yě bù means "no matter what."

1. Wǒ zài yě bú qù nàge fànguǎnr chīfàn le. — Under no circumstances will I eat at that restaurant again.

2. Wǒ zài yě bú gēn tā shuōhuà le. — I will never talk to him again.

Sentence Building

1.
Jǐ diǎn zhōng?
Jǐ diǎn zhōng shàng kè?
Tiāntiān jǐ diǎn zhōng shàng kè?
Nǐmen tiāntiān jǐ diǎn zhōng shàng kè?
Wǒmen tiāntiān bā diǎn shí fēn shàng kè.

2.
Xiān chīfàn.
Xiān chīfàn zài kàn diànyǐng.
Zuìhǎo xiān chīfàn zài kàn diànyǐng.
Wǒmen zuìhǎo xiān chīfàn zài kàn diànyǐng.

3.
Yàodiǎn
Zhè kè shū de yàodiǎn
Zhè kè shū de yàodiǎn shì shénme?
Gàosu wǒ zhè kè shū de yàodiǎn shì shénme.
Shéi gàosu wǒ zhè kè shū de yàodiǎn shì shénme?

4.
Yìdiǎnr
Yǒu yìdiǎnr
Yǒu yìdiǎnr bùhǎoyìsi.
Tā lái wǎn de shíhou yǒu yìdiǎnr bùhǎoyìsi.

Questions and Responses

1. Nǐ jǐ diǎn zhōng chī zǎofàn?
   What time do you have your breakfast?

   Wǒ qī diǎn shíwǔ fēn chī zǎofàn.
   I have my breakfast at 7:15.

2. Wǒmen qù kàn jiǔ diǎn de diànyǐng, hǎo ma?
   Let's go to the show at nine o'clock, okay?

   Jiǔ diǎn de tài wǎn le. Kàn liù diǎn de ba.
   The nine o'clock show is too late. Let's go to the six o'clock one.

3. Wǒmen shì kāichē qù háishì zuò diànchē qù?
   Are we driving there or are we taking the trolley?

   Wǒmen kāichē qù ba.
   Let's drive there.

4. Nǐ kěyǐ kāichē lái jiē wǒ ma?
   Can you come pick me up?

   Kěyǐ. Wǔ diǎn sān kè nǐ zài jiā děng wǒ.
   I can. Wait for me at your home at 5:45.

5. Wǒmen xiān chī yìdiǎnr diǎnxīn zài kàn diànyǐng, hǎo ma?
   Is it okay if we get something to eat first, then go to the movie?

   Hǎo. Wǒmen kěyǐ zài nàge xiǎo cháguǎn chī yìdiǎnr chádiǎn.
   Okay. We can go to that little cafe and have some snacks.

6. Wǒmen qù kàn de shì shénme diànyǐng?
   What kind of movie are we going to watch?

   Shì yí ge àiqíng de diànyǐng.
   It's a love story.

7. Jīntiān bào shàng yǒu shénme dàshì ma?
   Was there any important event in the newspaper today?

   Méi shénme dàshì.
   Nothing really big happened.

8. Zhōngguórén xǐhuan érzi háishì nǚ'ér?
   Do the Chinese prefer sons or daughters?

   Wǒ xiǎng duōshù Zhōngguórén xǐhuan érzi.
   I think most Chinese prefer sons.

9. Wǒ zuìjìn xīnqíng bù hǎo, nǐ ne?
   I've been in a bad mood lately. What about you?

   Wǒ hái hǎo.
   I've been okay.

10. Nǐ xuéguo Rìwén ma?
    Have you studied Japanese before?

    Wǒ xiānhòu xuéguo sān nián.
    I studied (Japanese) for three years altogether.

🐾 Pronunciation Review

Differentiating Pairs

(a)	chuánshàng	chuángshàng	(e)	bùxín	bùxíng
(b)	rémín	rénmíng	(f)	tánqín	tánqíng
(c)	bàojǐn	bàojǐng	(g)	bùchén	bùchéng
(d)	jīnyú	jīngyú	(h)	chūshén	chūshéng

Supplementary Vocabulary

yǎnyuán	actor or actress	míngxīng	movie star
jīngjù	Beijing opera	gējù	opera
xǐjù	comedy	gējùyuàn	opera house
dǎoyǎn	to direct (a film, play, etc.)	gēxīng	singer
nǚzhǔjué	leading actress	pèijué	supporting role
zhǔjué	leading role	jùyuàn	theater
nánzhǔjué	leading actor	bēijù	tragedy
diànyǐng	movie		

Cultural Notes

Names

Although a majority of Chinese given names are made up of two characters, many people in mainland China favor one-character given names. As in other cultures, Chinese parents usually name their children with words which associate with favorable meanings, such as health, beauty and good fortune. Chinese people, even among close friends, rarely address each other by given names. In informal social context, youngsters tend to address each other directly by full names. However, the commonest practice is to refer to a person as lǎo (old) or xiǎo (small) followed by their family names. For example, one would refer to someone elder as Lǎo Chén or someone younger as Xiǎo Huáng, though relative age is not always the determining factor. Say, if there are two Yáos in the workplace, one may be refered to as Lǎo Yáo and the other Xiǎo Yáo, according to their age. However, if the younger one is in a senior position, it is highly unlikely for his inferiors to call him Xiǎo Yáo. Since the elderly always gain the respect in Chinese society, lǎoxiānsheng and lǎotàitai are the decent form of address.

第十一課
漢字本

內容

課文	26
生詞及例句 （點、分、車、事、情、先、再、鐘、刻、兒）	27
句型練習 （一點兒、再）	33
造句 （幾點鐘、先吃飯、要點、一點兒）	40
問答	40
閱讀練習 我是甚麼？	41

課文

介紹朋友

星期六晚上七點十分,林海英開車到了金建家。金建給她介紹他的女朋友。

金　建:海英,我給你們介紹介紹,這是馬紅,她是我的同學。這是林海英,我們是中學的同學,她是我最好的朋友。

林海英:你好,馬紅。

馬　紅:你好,海英。金建告訴我很多你們中學時候的事情。

林海英:是嗎!

馬　紅:我們今天晚上去哪兒?

金　建:我們可以出去吃飯,看電影。

林海英:好。我們是先吃飯再去看電影,還是先看電影再吃飯?

馬　紅:我想先吃飯再看電影。

林海英:我同意。看電影以後,我請你們吃點心。

金　建:好,那我們現在就去吃飯吧。

林海英:我們看幾點鐘的電影?

金　建:九點三刻的。

Lesson 11 Introducing friends
第十一課：介紹朋友

生詞及例句

1. **點**   dot, point; drop (of liquid) (N); o'clock (MW)

   幾點   what time, when (QW)
   (1) A: 請問，現在幾點？
       B: 我也沒有錶。

   (2) A: 我們幾點見？
       B: 十二點五分。

   早點   breakfast (N)
   (1) A: 你吃早點的時候喜歡喝甚麼？
       B: 我喜歡喝紅茶。

   (2) A: 你幾點吃早點？
       B: 我不吃早點。

   點心   snacks (N)
   (1) A: 你喜歡吃中國點心還是美國點心？
       B: 我喜歡吃美國點心。

   (2) 我不吃點心，因為吃了點心以後，就不想吃飯了。

   茶點   tea and pastries, refreshments (N)
   (1) 請你們晚上七點來開會，我們有很多茶點。

   (2) 要是開會有茶點，來的人就多。

   點菜   choose dishes from a menu, order dishes (in a restaurant) (VO)
   (1) A: 小姐，你們現在要點菜嗎？
       B: 我們先看看，等一會兒再點。

   (2) A: 我不會點中國菜。中國菜的名字很難。你點吧。
       B: 好，我試試。

☞ 要點　main points, essentials, gist, key point (N)
　　　　A: 老師今天說的要點是甚麼？
　　　　B: 我也不知道。

☞ 難點　difficult point, difficulty (N)
　　　　學中文的難點是中國字太多、太難寫。

2. 分　**divide, separate (V); minute (of time) (MW)**
　　　(1) A: 我有十本書，請你分給他們五個人。
　　　　　B: 好，一個人兩本。

　　　(2) A: 現在是六點幾分？
　　　　　B: 六點二十分。

☞ 學分　credit (official acceptance and record of a student's work in a particular course of study) (N)
　　　(1) A: 你這學期選了幾個學分？
　　　　　B: 十六個。

　　　(2) 上學期我的數學課考得不好，沒有得到學分。

3. 車　**vehicle, wheeled machine (N)**
　　　　A: 這個車是你的還是你哥哥的？
　　　　B: 是我哥哥的。

☞ 汽車　automobile, car (N)
　　　　A: 你的汽車是哪年的？
　　　　B: 二〇〇二年的。

☞ 電車　trolley, streetcar (N)
　　　　A: 你有沒有見過電車？
　　　　B: 見過。

Lesson 11 Introducing friends
第十一課 介紹朋友

☞ 火車   train (N)
　　　　　A: 你喜歡坐火車還是坐汽車？
　　　　　B: 我喜歡坐火車。

☞ 開車   drive or start a car, train, etc. (VO)
　　　　　(1) 開車的時候，不可以喝酒。
　　　　　(2) A: 你會開車嗎？
　　　　　　　 B: 我早就會開了。

4. 事   **matter, affair, thing; business; trouble; job, work (N)**
　　　　　A: 你找我有甚麼事嗎？
　　　　　B: 我想請你給我找一個事兒。

☞ 大事   great (or major) event, important matter, major issue (N)
　　　　　(1) 這是國家大事，我們應該認真地想一想。
　　　　　(2) 你家有甚麼大事？

☞ 本事   skill; ability, capability (N)
　　　　　A: 他是甚麼樣的人？
　　　　　B: 他是一個很有本事的人。

☞ 有事   when problems crop up (VO); busy (N)
　　　　　(1) 要是他沒有事，他不會來找我。
　　　　　(2) 我今天晚上有事，不去看電影了。

☞ 找事   look (or hunt) for a job (VO); pick a quarrel (V)
　　　　　現在很多人都沒有工作，找事真難。

☞ 沒事找事 ask for trouble, try hard to find fault (IE)
　　　　　這個人誰都不喜歡他，因為他老喜歡沒事找事。

5. 情　　**feeling, sentiment; love** (N)

☞ 事情　　affair; matter; thing; business (N)

要是你今天晚上沒有事情，我們去看電影，好吧？

☞ 愛情　　love (romance) (N)

(1) 甚麼是"愛情"，我也不知道。

(2) 我妹妹最喜歡看愛情的小說跟愛情電影。

☞ 情人　　sweetheart, lover (N)

她情人生日的時候，她送他很多花兒。

☞ 心情　　frame of mind, mood (N)

(1) 最近我的好朋友心情不好，一天到晚在生氣。

(2) 為甚麼有人心情不好的時候就喝酒？

6. 先　　**earlier, before; first; in advance** (Adv)

(1) 你最好先打個電話看他在家不在家。

(2) 我們學中文是先學說話，再學認字、寫字。

☞ 先生　　teacher; mister (Mr.); gentleman, sir; husband (N)

(1) 葉先生是你的老師嗎？

(2) 先生，你要喝點兒甚麼？

(3) 我先生今天不在家，請你明天再來吧！

☞ 先後　　altogether; priority, order, successively, one after another (Adv)

A: 你先後學過幾個月的日文？

B: 我先後學過六個月。去年在日本學過兩個月，今年在美國學過了四個月。

Lesson 11 Introducing friends
第十一課 介紹朋友

7. **再** — another time, again, once more (Adv)
   (1) 請你再說。
   (2) 再多吃一點兒。
   (3) 等他心情好一點兒再跟他說吧。

   ☞ 先……再 — first ... then (Conj)
   (1) 你先試試看，要是你不會，再來問我。
   (2) 我們得先去銀行拿錢，再去看電影。

   ☞ 再三 — over and over again, repeatedly (Adv)
   (1) 我再三告訴他開車的時候不要喝酒，可是他還喝。
   (2) 媽媽再三跟他說那個人是個喜歡沒事找事的人，可是他不信。

   ☞ 再說 — put off until some time later; moreover (IE)
   (1) 去中國的事，以後再說吧！
   (2) 這個飯館兒的菜很好，再說飯館兒的人也很和氣。

   ☞ 再見 — good-bye; see you again (V)
   (1) 我們甚麼時候可以再見？
   (2) A: 時候不早了，我得去上課了，再見！
      B: 再見！

8. **鐘** — clock; hour; time (N)
   (1) A: 現在幾點鐘？
      B: 七點三刻。
   (2) A: 這個鐘不走了？
      B: 你沒有錶嗎？
      A: 沒有。

9. **刻** **a quarter of an hour; moment (MW); carve, engrave, cut (V)**
   (1) 十五分鐘是一刻。一個小時是幾刻？
   (2) 四十五分是幾刻？

☞ 刻字　carve (or engrave) characters on a seal, etc. (VO)
   A: 你會不會刻字？
   B: 我不會，可是我先生會。

10. **兒** **child, youngster, son; male (N); (suffix)**
☞ 兒女　sons and daughters, children (N)
   A: 老先生，你有沒有兒女？
   B: 我有三個兒子，四個女兒。

☞ 女兒　daughter, girl (N)
   我姐姐有兩個女兒，他們都在英國上學。

☞ 那兒　there (PW)
   你看，那兒有一個茶館兒。我們去那兒喝點兒茶吧！

☞ 這兒　here (PW)
   你看，這兒也有一個茶館兒，我們就在這個茶館兒喝吧！近一點兒。

☞ 哪兒　where (QW)
   A: 你想去哪兒找事？
   B: 哪兒要人我就去哪兒找事。

☞ 有點兒　some, a bit; somewhat (IE)
   (1) 今天的功課有點兒難。
   (2) 他女朋友有點兒錢。

☞ 一點兒　a bit, a little (Adv)
   (1) A: 我媽說中文一點兒也不難。
       B: 那是因為她是中國人。

Lesson 11 Introducing friends
第十一課 介紹朋友

    (2) 這個菜很好吃，多吃一點兒。

☞ 一會兒 soon, a little while, a moment; one moment (TW)

    (1) 我一會兒就回來。

    (2) 請你在這兒等一會兒。

句型練習

11.1 CLOCK TIME

The three units for designating and measuring time by the clock are: 點 "hour," 刻 "a quarter (of an hour)," and 分 "minute." These measures are preceded by appropriate numbers and followed by the noun 鐘 "clock." Hours are expressed by the numbers one through twelve followed by the measure word 鐘. When the time expression contains 刻 or 分, 鐘 is often omitted.

    一點鐘
    兩點鐘
    十二點鐘

We have already noted in Lesson 7 that the sequence of telling time in Chinese always begins with the largest unit followed by progressively smaller ones:

    十二點二十五分

Time before or after the hour is expressed with the verb 差 "lacking" or 過 "past":

    一點差五分
    一點過五分

過 may be omitted before quarters and before minutes expressed in more than two syllables:

    兩點一刻
    兩點二十分

Minute expressions with 差 may be placed before or after the hour:

    差七分三點
    三點差七分

11.1.1 Asking and answering in clock time

1. A: 甚麼時候了？
   B: 兩點一刻。

2. A: 現在幾點鐘？
   B: 七點鐘。

11.1.2 Amounts of clock time

> The noun 鐘頭 "hour," preceded by the measure word 個, is used when a quantity of time is referred to:
>
> > 一個鐘頭
> > 兩個鐘頭
> > 十二個鐘頭
> > 五個多鐘頭
> > 五六個鐘頭
> > 十幾個鐘頭
>
> The noun 鐘 "hour," preceded by 分 "minute" and/or by 刻 "quarter," may denote a point in time or a quantity of time:
>
> > 三刻鐘
> > 四個鐘頭十分鐘
> > 二十五分鐘

11.2 FUNCTIONS OF TIME WORDS

Time words have two main functions.

11.2.1 As movable adverbs

As movable adverbs, time words may stand at the beginning of a sentence or before a verb or other adverb to form a time background for the verb.

A: 你今天去上課嗎？

B: 今天我不去上課，明天去。

11.2.2 As nouns

As nouns, time words may function as the subject or object of a verb or modify another noun (with the particle 的).

A: 今天星期幾？

B: 今天星期二。

A: 你看見今天的報了嗎？

B: 沒有。

11.3 TIME EXPRESSIONS AND THEIR POSITIONS WITHIN THE SENTENCE

There are two types of time words in Chinese. Note the differences among the following kinds of time expressions and their position within the sentence.

11.3.1 A particular point of time

Time expressions which indicate a particular point of time when an action takes place, such as 今天 "today," 去年 "last year," 以前 "before" or 以後 "in the future," come **before** the verb.

1. A: 你甚麼時候去上課？
   B: 我明天早上八點去上課。

2. A: 你明年去中國嗎？
   B: 明年不去，後年去。

3. A: 你以前會說中國話嗎？
   B: 我以前不會說，可是現在會了。

11.3.2 Duration I

Time expressions which indicate the duration in which an action takes place, such as 一個鐘頭 "one hour," 兩天 "two days," 三年 "three years," come **after** the verb in a sentence.

1. A: 馬紅要在美國幾年？
   B: 她要在這兒兩三年。

2. A: 馬紅要學幾年英文？
   B: 她說她要學兩年英文。

3. A: 你學了幾個學期的中文了？
   B: 我學了四個學期的中文了。

11.3.3 Duration II

Time expressions which indicate the duration in which an action does not take place comes **before** the verb in a sentence.

1. A: 金建去年學日文了沒有？
   B: 他已經兩年沒學日文了。

2. A: 你最近看電影了嗎？
   B: 我已經三個星期沒看電影了。

3. A: 你怎麼了？
   B: 我兩天沒吃飯了。
   A: 為甚麼？
   B: 不想吃。

11.4 THE PATTERN 一點兒

11.4.1 When 一點兒 comes after a verb

When 一點兒 "a bit" (or its shortened form 點兒) comes after a verb, it means "just a little or some."

```
S        V         一點兒      N / SV
他       有        一點兒       錢。
He has a little/some money.
```

1. 我就會說一點兒中國話。

2. 我今天有點兒累。

3. 最近我有點兒忙。

4. 我女朋友最近有點兒不高興。

When 一點兒 is combined with the stative verb 多 "more" or 少 "less," 一點兒 comes after the main verb.

```
S          SV    V     一點兒     O
你         得    多     一點兒     書。
You have to read some more books.
```

1. 請你多吃一點兒。

2. 請你上中文課的時候，少說一點兒英文。

11.4.2 一點兒 may come either before or after a verb

When 一點兒 is combined with 快 "fast," 慢 "slow," 早 "early" or 晚 "late," the phrase may come either before the main verb, as in (A), or after the main verb, as in (B).

```
(A)    S      SV     一點兒     V
       (你)   快     一點兒      走！
       Walk a little faster!

(B)    S      V      SV        一點兒
       (你)   走     快         一點兒！
       Walk a little faster!
```

1. 請你快一點兒說！
2. 請你慢一點兒走！
3. 你想早一點兒去嗎？
4. 我明天可以晚一點兒來嗎？

11.4.3 一點兒也 and 一點兒都

When 一點兒也 or 一點兒都 modifies a negative stative verb, it conveys the idea "not at all."

S	一點兒也/都	Neg	SV
她	一點兒也/都	不	好看。
She is not pretty at all.			

1. 姐姐說的話，我一點兒都不喜歡。
2. 中文一點兒也不難。
3. 他寫的書，一點兒意思也沒有。

11.5 THE PATTERN 再

11.5.1 再 indicates a repetition of an event in the future

The adverb 再 "again, once more" indicates a repetition that has not yet occurred or a repetition of an event that will occur in the future.

1. 你甚麼時候再去日本？
2. 葉先生今天不在家，你明天再來吧！
3. 再給他一點兒錢吧！
4. 請你再說一說這課書的要點。
5. 再多吃一點兒點心。

6. A: 你甚麼時候再來？
   B: 我晚上再來。

11.5.2 再 denotes two actions in sequence

When the adverb 再 comes in the second clause of a sentence, it indicates that the action will take place after the completion of the first action.

1. 等我寫好了這個報告，我們再去看電影，好嗎？
2. 他來了，我們再吃飯。
3. 我要學好了中文再學日文。

11.5.3 先……再…… also denotes two actions in sequence

The pattern 先……再…… "first (and) then ..." also denotes two actions in sequence. 先 always comes in the first clause of a sentence and 再 at the beginning of the second clause. Both 先 and 再 are adverbs, thus they always precede the verbs.

S	先	V	O	再	V	
你	先	點	菜	再	談話	吧！

Please order the food first, then we can chat!

1. 我們可以先吃飯再作功課嗎？
2. 我得先去銀行拿點兒錢再去飯館吃飯。
3. 你先告訴我愛不愛我，我再告訴你。

11.5.4 The pattern 再也不

再也不 means "no matter what."

1. 我再也不去那個飯館兒吃飯了。
2. 我再也不跟他說話了。

🌸 造句

1.
幾點鐘？
幾點鐘上課？
天天幾點鐘上課？
你們天天幾點鐘上課？
我們天天八點十分上課。

2.
先吃飯。
先吃飯再看電影。
最好先吃飯再看電影。
我們最好先吃飯再看電影。

3.
要點
這課書的要點
這課書的要點是甚麼？
告訴我這課書的要點是甚麼。
誰告訴我這課書的要點是甚麼？

4.
一點兒
有一點兒
有一點兒不好意思。
他來晚的時候有一點兒不好意思。

🌸 問答

1. 你幾點鐘吃早飯？ 我七點十五分吃早飯。
2. 我們去看九點的電影，好嗎？ 九點的太晚了。看六點的吧。
3. 我們是開車去還是坐電車去？ 我們開車去吧。
4. 你可以開車來接我嗎？ 可以。五點三刻你在家等我。
5. 我們先吃一點兒點心再看電影，好嗎？ 好。我們可以在那個小茶館吃一點兒茶點。
6. 我們去看的是甚麼電影？ 是一個愛情的電影。
7. 今天報上有甚麼大事嗎？ 沒甚麼大事。
8. 中國人喜歡兒子還是女兒？ 我想多數中國人喜歡兒子。
9. 我最近心情不好，你呢？ 我還好。
10. 你學過日文嗎？ 我先後學過三年。

Lesson 11 Introducing friends
第十一課 介紹朋友

閱讀練習

我是甚麼？

　　會寫字的人都認識我。人們常把我放在書房裏，汽車裏⋯⋯。我很有用。每天有學生用我作功課，寫字，畫畫兒。我幫他們很多忙。有的學生對我很好，用了我以後，就把我放進筆盒裏，也有很多人用了我以後，就用牙咬我。同學們，工人做我很不容易，請你們愛惜我。

請查生詞
Look up the following words in a dictionary.

幫⋯⋯忙	bāng ... máng	咬	yǎo
對	duì	容易	róngyì
筆盒	bǐhé	愛惜	àixī
牙	yá		

填 空
Fill in the blanks with the appropriate words from the story.

1. 我知道你是 _____ _____ 。我很 _____ _____ 你。我不用牙 _____ 你。

2. 我今天的功課不 _____ _____ ，請你 _____ 我一點兒 _____ 。

3. 老師 _____ 我很好，同學也 _____ 我很好。

4. 鉛筆很有 _____ 。我們天天 _____ 鉛筆作 _____ _____ 。

第十二課　朋友來的電子信
Lesson 12　　An e-mail from a friend

Lesson 12
Pinyin Text

CONTENTS

*T*ext   46

*V*ocabulary and Illustrative Sentences   47
   (zǐ, yòu, fāng, biàn, jì, bǐ, guì, nǎo, xià, qián)

*P*attern Drills   52
   (yòu and zài, yòu ... yòu, bǐ)

*S*entence Building   60
   (yòu, yòu ... yòu, bǐ, chīdexià)

*Q*uestions and Responses   60

*P*ronunciation Review   61

*S*upplementary Vocabulary   62

*C*ultural Notes   62

🐾 Text

Péngyou lái de diànzǐxìn
E-mail from a friend

Hǎiyīng:

    Wǒ hěn gāoxìng rènshi nǐ. Nǐ xǐhuan wǒmen qiántiān kàn de nàge diànyǐng ma? Wǒ hěn xǐhuan, kěshì Jīn Jiàn shuō nàge diànyǐng méishénme yìsi. Nǐ xǐhuan-bu-xǐhuan xiě diànzǐxìn? Sòng diànzǐxìn yòu kuài yòu fāngbiàn. Zàishuō, jì xìn bǐ sòng diànzǐxìn guì duō le. Zuìjìn wǒ māma sòng wǒ yí ge diànnǎo. Wǒ yí xià kè jiù dǎkāi diànnǎo. Xiě diànzǐxìn bǐ kànshū yǒu yìsi duō le. Wǒmen kěyǐ xiě Zhōngwén de diànzǐxìn. Zhèyàng, wǒmen de Zhōngwén yídìng huì jìnbùde hěn kuài. Nǐ tóngyì ma? Wǒ děng nǐ de huíxìn.

    Zhù
  hǎo!

Mǎ Hóng
Shíyuè sìrì

Dear Haiying,

    I'm very glad to have met you. Did you like the movie that we watched the day before yesterday? I liked it a lot, but Jin Jian said that the movie wasn't very interesting. Do you like writing e-mail? E-mail is fast and convenient. Furthermore, sending letter is much more expensive than sending e-mail. Recently, my mother has bought me a computer. I turn on my computer right after class. Writing e-mail is much funnier than reading. We can write e-mail in Chinese. This way, our Chinese will definitely improve rapidly. Do you agree? I will be waiting for your reply.

Best wishes,
Ma Hong
4 October

Lesson 12 *An e-mail from a friend*
第十二課 朋友來的電子信

✿ Vocabulary and Illustrative Sentences

1. zǐ   **son; child; person; seed; egg** (N)

   ☞ érzi   son (N)

        A: Xǔ xiānsheng Xǔ tàitai yǒu jǐ ge érzi?   How many sons do Mr. and Mrs. Xu have?

        B: Tāmen yǒu wǔ ge érzi.   They have five sons.

   ☞ zǐnǚ   sons and daughters, children (N)

        Tāmen jiā de zǐnǚ dōu hěn hǎo.   The children of their family are all very nice.

   ☞ běnzi   notebook (N)

        Zhège běnzi shì shéi de? Méiyǒu míngzi.   Whose notebook is this? There's no name (on it).

   ☞ diànzǐxìn   electronic-mail, e-mail (N)

        Xuésheng dōu xǐhuan xiě diànzǐxìn.   All students like to write e-mail.

2. yòu   **again** (Adv)

   (1) A: Nàge rén zǎoshang lái le, xiànzài yòu lái le.   That person came by this morning. Now he's here again.

        B: Tā zhǎo shéi?   Who is he looking for?

        A: Tā méi shuō.   He didn't say.

   (2) A: Nǐ jīntiān yòu hē jiǔ le, yǐhòu bú yào zài hē le, hǎo ma?   You drank again today. Don't do it again, okay?

        B: Wǒ yǐhòu zài yě bù hē le.   I will never drink again.

   ☞ yòu ... yòu   both ... and (Conj)

   (1) Diànzǐxìn yòu kuài yòu fāngbiàn.   E-mail is both fast and convenient.

	(2) Tā de nǚpéngyou **yòu** hǎokàn **yòu** yǒu qián.	His girlfriend is both pretty and rich.

3. **fāng** — **square** (Adj); **locality** (N)

☞ dìfang — place, space (N)

    Qǐng nǐ jièshào yíxià zhège **dìfang**. — Please tell us something about this place.

☞ sìfāng — square; the four directions (north, south, east, west); all sides (Adj)

    Zhōngguózì shì **sìfāng** de. — Chinese characters are square-shaped.

☞ duōfāng — in many ways, in every way, from various angles (Adj)

    Zhège shìqing wǒmen děi cóng **duōfāng** lái kàn. — We have to view this matter from various angles.

☞ duìfāng — the other (or opposite) side; the other party (N)

    Tā qǐng **duìfāng** duō gěi yìdiǎnr qián, kěshì **duìfāng** bù gěi. — She asked the other party to give a little more money, but he wouldn't (give).

☞ dàfāng — generous; poised and natural (SV)

    (1) Wǒ de péngyou hěn **dàfāng**, tiāntiān qǐng wǒ chīfàn, wǒ zhēn bùhǎoyìsi. — My friend is very generous. He invites me to dinner every day. I'm really embarrassed.

    (2) Nàge nǚxuésheng shuōhuà de shíhou hěn **dàfāng**. — When that (female) student speaks, she is very poised and natural.

4. **biàn** — **convenient, handy** (Adj)

☞ fāngbiàn — convenient (Adj)

    A: Cóng Zhōngguó dào Rìběn **fāngbiàn**-bu-**fāngbiàn**? — Is it convenient to travel from China to Japan?

    B: Xiànzài hěn **fāngbiàn** le. Jǐ ge xiǎoshí jiù kěyǐ dào le. — It's very convenient now. You can get there in just a few hours.

Lesson 12 An e-mail from a friend
第十二課 朋友來的電子信

☞ biànfàn — a simple meal (N)

    A: Míngtiān qǐng nǐ dào wǒ jiā lái chī biànfàn. — Tomorrow, please come to my house for a simple meal.

    B: Bùhǎoyìsi, nǐ lǎo qǐng wǒ chīfàn, míngtiān wǒ qǐng nǐ ba. — I feel embarrassed. You always treat me. Let me treat you tomorrow.

5. jì — **send, mail** (V)

    Jīntiān zǎoshang gēge jìgěi wǒ liǎng běn shū. — This morning my elder brother sent me two books.

☞ jì xìn — mail letters (VO)

    A: Wǒ méiyǒu qián le, wǒ děi mǎshàng jì xìn gěi wǒ māma. — I'm out of money, I have to write to my mother right away.

    B: Nǐ māma huì mǎshàng gěi nǐ jì qián lái ma? — Will your mother send you money right away?

    A: Wǒ xiǎng huì. — I think so.

☞ jìxìnrén — sender (N)

    A: Jīn Jiàn, nǐ yǒu xìn. — Jin Jian, you have mail.

    B: Shì shéi jì lái de? — Who sent it?

    A: Bù zhīdào shì shéi jì lái de, méiyǒu jìxìnrén de xìngmíng. — (I) don't know who sent it. There's no sender's name (on it).

6. bǐ — **compare, contrast, compete** (V)

    A: Nǐmen liǎng ge rén bǐ-yi-bǐ. Kàn shéi gāo. — Compare the two of you. See who's taller.

    B: Sīwén bǐ wǒ gāo yìdiǎnr. — Siwen is a little taller than I.

7. guì — **expensive, costly** (SV)

    A: Xiànzài shū zhēn guì. — Now books are really expensive.

    B: Kěbúshì ma! — That's true!

☞ guìxìng   what is your name (lit., honorable family name) (IE)

A: Lǎoxiānsheng, qǐngwèn nǐ guìxìng?	Sir, what is your (honorable) family name?
B: Wǒ xìng Zhù.	My family name is Zhu.
A: Xiǎomèimei, nǐ xìng shénme?	Little girl, what is your family name?
C: Wǒ xìng Jīn.	My family name is Jin.

☞ mínguì   famous and very valuable (Adj/SV)

Māma shēngrì de shíhou, wǒmen sòng tā yí ge hěn mínguì de biǎo, tā hěn xǐhuan.	For Mom's birthday, we gave her a very expensive watch. She liked it very much.

8. nǎo   **brain** (N)

☞ diànnǎo   computer (N)

A: Nǐ hái jìdé méiyǒu diànnǎo de rìzi ma?	Do you still remember the days when computers still did not come into existence?
B: Jìdé. Xiànzài yǒu diànnǎo xiě bàogào fāngbiàn duō le.	I remember. Now that there are computers, report-writing is much more convenient.

☞ nǎozi   brain (N)

A: Nǐ xiǎng diànnǎo bǐ rén de nǎozi kuài ma?	Do you think computers are faster than human brains?
B: Yǒude shíhou.	Sometimes.

9. xià   **below, under, underneath** (PW); **to descend, to get off** (V)

☞ xià kè   get out of class, finish class (VO)

(1) A: Nǐ jīntiān jǐ diǎn zhōng xià kè?	What time will your class end today?
B: Shí diǎn yí kè.	A quarter after ten.
(2) A: Xià kè yǐhòu nǐ qù nǎr?	Where are you going after class?

Lesson 12 An e-mail from a friend
第十二課 朋友來的電子信

		B: Gēn péngyou qù kàn diànyǐng.	I am going to watch a movie with my friends.
☞	xià chē	get off or out of a vehicle (VO)	
		(1) Dào le. Qǐng xià chē.	We are there. Please get off the car.
		(2) Xià chē de shíhou xiǎoxīn diǎnr.	Be careful when you get off the car.
☞	dìxia	on the ground (PW)	
		Dìxia yǒu hěn duō shuǐ, xiǎoxīn!	There is a lot of water on the ground. Be careful!
☞	chīdexià	be able to eat (RV)	
		A: Nǐ jiào zhème duō cài, wǒmen chīdexià ma?	You have ordered so many dishes. Will we be able to finish them all?
		B: Méishénme cài, qǐng chī!	There aren't that many dishes. Please enjoy!
☞	chībuxià	do not feel like eating; be unable to eat any more (RV)	
		(1) A: Māma, zhège cài tài nánchī le, wǒ chībuxià.	Mother, this dish is too unappetizing. I can't eat it.
		B: Chībuxià jiù bú yào chī le.	If you can't eat it, then you don't have to.
		(2) A: Zài duō chī diǎnr!	Eat a bit more!
		B: Wǒ chī de tài duō le, zhēnde chībuxià le.	I ate too much. I really can't eat any more.
☞	shàngxià- wén	context (N)	
		A: Lǎoshī, zhège zì shì shénme yìsi?	Teacher, what does this character mean?
		B: Nǐ kàn shàngxiàwén. Yǒu hěn duō Zhōngguózì yí kàn shàngxiàwén jiù zhīdào shì shénme yìsi le.	Look at the context. You can tell the meaning of many Chinese characters simply by looking at the context.

	qīshàng-bāxià	be agitated, be perturbed (IE)	
☞		Yào kǎoshì le. Wǒ hěn pà, wǒ de xīn qīshàngbāxià de tiào.	It's time for the exam. I am frightened. My heart's pounding so hard.

10. **qián** — **front; forward, ahead; before, preceding; former; first (Adv)**

	qiántiān	the day before yesterday (TW)	
☞		A: Nǐ qiántiān wǎnshang qù shénme dìfang le?	Where did you go the evening of the day before yesterday?
		B: Wǒ gēn péngyou qù tiàowǔ le.	I went to a dance with a friend.
☞	yǐqián	before; formerly, previously (Adv)	
		A: Nǐ yǐqián huì yòng diànnǎo ma?	Have you known how to use a computer before?
		B: Wǒ zài zhōngxué de shíhou jiù huì yòng diànnǎo le.	I've known how to use a computer since middle school.
☞	shìqián	before the event, in advance, beforehand (Adv)	
		Tā qù Zhōngguó, shìqián méiyǒu gàosu wǒ. Wǒ yìdiǎnr yě bù zhīdào.	He didn't tell me beforehand when he went to China. I didn't have a clue.

🐾 Pattern Drills

12.1 THE DIFFERENCES BETWEEN yòu AND zài

The adverbs **yòu** and **zài** have similar meanings but are used in different contexts. **Yòu** means "again, more, also," referring to a **past** action. **Zài** means the same but with respect to a **future** action.

1. Qǐng nǐ míngtiān zài lái. — Please come again tomorrow.
2. Nǐ shénme shíhou zài qù kàn tā? — When are you going to see him again?
3. Tā qùnián qù Zhōngguó le, jīnnián yòu qù le. — He went to China last year and he went there again this year.

4. Tā yòu gěi nǚpéngyou dǎ le yí ge diànbào. — He has sent another wire to his girlfriend.

> Zài is often used in commands and suggestions, situations where yòu cannot be used.

1. Qǐng nǐ zài chī yìdiǎnr. — Please eat a bit more.
2. Zài shuō! — Say it again!
3. Zài xiǎngxiǎng! — Think about it again!

> Zài cannot come before auxiliary verbs such as xiǎng "intend to" or yào "want to," whereas yòu can.

1. Tā yòu xiǎng chī Zhōngguófàn le. — He wanted to eat Chinese food again.
2. Nǐ yòu yào huí guó le ma? — Do you want to go back to your country again?

12.2 THE PATTERN yòu ... yòu

> Yòu ... yòu "both ... and" or negatively "neither ... nor" can be inserted before verbs, stative verbs or phrases to indicate the simultaneous existence of several actions, characteristics or conditions.

1. Mǎ Hóng yòu huì shuō Zhōngguóhuà yòu huì shuō Rìběnhuà. — Ma Hong can speak both Chinese and Japanese.
2. Zhè běn shū yòu guì yòu méiyìsi. — The book is both expensive and dull.
3. Jīn Jiàn yòu xǐhuan tiàowǔ yòu xǐhuan kàn diànyǐng. — Jin Jian likes to dance and he likes to watch movies too.
4. Nàge rén yòu méi qián yòu méi xuéwèn. — That person is neither rich nor educated.

12.3 THE PATTERN bǐ

12.3.1 A bǐ B SV

The coverb bǐ "compared to, compared with" is used in comparing two things. The sentence pattern — A bǐ B SV — is used to express the difference in states or conditions between the items being compared. For comparisons involving people, the SVs dà "big" and xiǎo "little, small" often mean "elder" and "younger" respectively.

A	bǐ	B	SV
Bàba	bǐ	māma	dà.
Father is elder than mother.			

1. A: Nǐ gēn nǐ mèimei shéi gāo?
   Who is taller? You or your younger sister?

   B: Mèimei bǐ wǒ gāo.
   My younger sister is taller than I am.

2. A: Zhōngwén bǐ Rìwén nán ma?
   Is Chinese more difficult than Japanese?

   B: Shìde. Wǒ xiǎng Zhōngwén bǐ Rìwén nán.
   Yes. I think Chinese is more difficult than Japanese.

3. A: Jīntiān lěng háishì qiántiān lěng?
   Is today or the day before yesterday colder?

   B: Jīntiān bǐ qiántiān lěng.
   Today is colder than the day before yesterday.

12.3.2 A bù bǐ B SV

The opposite form of pattern 12.3.1 is obtained by placing the negative marker bù before bǐ.

A	bù	bǐ	B	SV
Bàba	bù	bǐ	māma	dà.
Father is not elder than mother.				

1. A: Shuō Zhōngguóhuà bǐ xiě
   Zhōngguózì nán ma?

   Is it more difficult to speak Chinese than to write Chinese characters?

   B: Shuō Zhōngguóhuà bù bǐ xiě
   Zhōngguózì nán.

   Speaking Chinese is not harder than writing Chinese characters.

2. A: Měiguófàn bǐ Rìběnfàn hǎo chī.

   American food tastes better than Japanese food.

   B: Měiguófàn bù bǐ Rìběnfàn hǎo chī.

   American food does not taste better than Japanese food.

12.3.3 A bǐ B SV degree

There are two ways to express degrees of comparison in Chinese: one way is to express degrees adverbially. Adverbs such as hái "still more" or gèng "even more" placed before the main verb indicate degree.

A	bǐ	B	gèng/hái	SV
Zhèr	bǐ	nàr	gèng/hái	lěng.

The weather here is even colder than the weather there.

1. Nǐ bǐ wǒ gāo, tā bǐ nǐ gèng/hái gāo.

   You are taller than I, (but) he is even taller than you.

2. Zhōngwén shū guì, Rìwén shū gèng/hái guì.

   Chinese books are expensive, (but) Japanese books are even more expensive.

3. Jīntiān hěn lěng, míngtiān bǐ jīntiān gèng/hái yào lěng.

   Today is cold, (but) tomorrow will be even colder than today.

Comparison may also be made by using a predicate complement. In the degree complement, the interrogative of quantity duōshǎo may be used to ask a question, and an indefinite answer, yìdiǎnr "a little" or SV-de duō or duō le "much more" or a number-measure expression, is used in reply. Do not use hěn "very" in a comparison. To express "A is much more expensive than B," you have to say A bǐ B guìde duō, **not** A bǐ B hěn guì.

A	bǐ	B	SV	degree
Tā	bǐ	wǒ	gāo	yìdiǎnr.

She is a little taller than I.

1. A: Tā bǐ nǐ gāo duōshǎo? How much taller is he?
   B: Tā bǐ wǒ gāo yìdiǎnr. He is a little taller than I.
2. A: Zhège diànnǎo guì háishì nàge diànnǎo guì? Is this computer or that one more expensive?
   B: Zhège diànnǎo bǐ nàge diànnǎo guì duō le. This computer is much more expensive than that one.
3. A: Shuō Zhōngguóhuà nán háishì xiě Zhōngguózì nán? Is it more difficult to speak Chinese or to write Chinese characters?
   B: Xiě Zhōngguózì bǐ shuō Zhōngguóhuà nánde duō. Writing Chinese characters is much more difficult than speaking Chinese.

12.3.4 Comparison of manner of action between A and B

For a comparison of manner in which two actors perform an action, either pattern (A) or pattern (B) can be used.

(A)	A	bǐ	B	V-de	SV
	Nǐ	bǐ	wǒ	chīde	kuài.
You eat faster than I do.					

1. Xiǎoměi bǐ wǒ pǎode màn. Xiaomei ran slower than I.
2. Hǎiyīng bǐ Sīwén xiěde hǎo. Haiying writes better than Siwen.

(B)	A	V-de	bǐ	B	SV
	Nǐ	chīde	bǐ	wǒ	kuài.
You eat faster than I do.					

1. Xiǎoměi pǎode bǐ wǒ màn. Xiaomei ran slower than I.
2. Hǎiyīng xiěde bǐ Sīwén hǎo. Haiying writes better than Siwen.

12.3.5 Comparison of an action with an object between A and B

When the action verb followed by an expression of manner has an object, either pattern (A) or pattern (B) can be used.

Lesson 12 An e-mail from a friend
第十二課 朋友來的電子信

> (A)   A   V   O,   V-<u>de</u>   <u>bǐ</u>   B   SV
>   Nǐ   shuō   Zhōngguóhuà,   shuōde   bǐ   wǒ   hǎo.
>   You speak Chinese better than I do.

1. Wǒ dìdi kāichē, kāide bǐ wǒ kuài.   My younger brother drives faster than I do.

2. Māma zuò Zhōngguófàn, zuòde bǐ bàba hǎo.   My mom cooks Chinese food better than my dad does.

3. Mǎ Hóng yòng diànnǎo, yòngde bǐ wǒ duō.   Ma Hong uses a computer more often than I do.

> (B)   A   <u>de</u>   O,   V-<u>de</u>   <u>bǐ</u>   B   SV
>   Nǐ   de   Zhōngguóhuà,   shuōde   bǐ   wǒ   hǎo.
>   You speak Chinese better than I do.

1. Wǒ de Zhōngwén jìnbùde bǐ nǐ màn.   My Chinese has improved more slowly than yours.

2. Nǐ de bàogào xiěde bǐ wǒ cháng.   Your report is longer than mine.

3. Nǐmen kàn diànyǐng, kànde bǐ tā duō.   You watched more movies than he did.

12.4 RESULTATIVE VERB COMPOUNDS

> The resultative verb compounds (RVCs) are compound transitive verbs. An RVC is always made up of two elements, although the second element may be a compound itself, such as <u>chūlái</u> "come out." The first element in such a compound designates the action; the second element indicates the result – **actual** or **potential**.

> An **actual** result is expressed by a simple combination of the two verbs.
>
>   Wǒ kànjian tā le.   I saw him.
>   Wǒ zhǎodào le.   I found it.
>
> **Potential** resultative verbs, as distinguished from other verbs, have special forms for adding the meanings "be able" and "be unable." For "be able," <u>de</u> is inserted between the two verbs; for "be unable," <u>bù</u> is inserted.

> kànjian "see" → kàndejian   able to see, can see
> kànjian "see" → kànbujian   unable to see, can't see
>
> **Potential** verbs can be used with any of the question forms already introduced.
>
> Nǐ kàndejian kànbujian nàge rén?
> Nǐ kàndejiàn nàge rén ma?   Are you able to see that person?
> Nǐ kàndejiàn háishì kànbujiàn nàge rén?
>
> There are a great many RVCs that must be learned one by one because their meanings cannot be derived from those of their constituents plus the relationship between their compounds. Several RVCs were introduced (without analysis) in previous lessons: huílai/qu, zuòhǎo, xuéhuì, kàndào. We will discuss them in details in the next few lessons.

12.4.1 The verbs dào and jiàn

> When dào is used as a second element in an RVC, it means "arrive, succeed, attain," and is often used with verbs such as zhǎo "look for," zǒu "walk," pǎo "run," xiǎng "think," kàn "see, read," xué "learn," or sòng "send."

1. A: Nǐ zhǎodedào zhǎobudào Jīn Jiàn de jiā?   Can you find Jin Jian's home?

   B: Wǒ zhǎobudào. Qǐng nǐ gēn wǒ yìqǐ qù.   I can't find it (alone). Please come with me.

2. A: Nǐ shí fēnzhōng zǒudedào zǒubudào túshūguǎn?   Can you walk to the library in ten minutes?

   B: Yàoshì zǒude kuài jiù zǒudedào.   (I) can make it if (I) walk faster.

3. A: Nǐ xiǎngdedào xiǎngbudào tā yǐjīng shì māma le?   Can you believe that she is a mother already?

   B: Zhēn xiǎngbudào.   That's really a surprise.

4. A: Zhè xuéqī wǒmen xuédedào xuébudào dì-shísì kè?   Will we be able to finish up to Lesson 14 in this semester?

   B: Yěxǔ xuédedào.   Maybe we will be able to do so.

> When <u>jiàn</u> is used as a second element in an RVC, it means "perception (sensory)." <u>Jiàn</u> is often used with verbs such as <u>kàn</u> "to see," <u>tīng</u> "to listen," and <u>wén</u> "to smell." (The characters for <u>tīng</u> and <u>wén</u> have not been introduced in the text.)

1. A: Wǒ de biǎo bújiàn le, nǐ kànjian le ma? — I cannot find my watch. Have you seen it?
   B: Wǒ méi kànjian. — I haven't seen it.
2. A: Lǎoshī, nàge zì nǐ xiěde tài xiǎo le, wǒ kànbujian. — Teacher, the character you wrote is too small. I can't see it.
   B: Hǎo, wǒ xiě dà yìdiǎnr, xiànzài nǐ kàndejian le ma? — All right, I will write it a little bigger. Can you see it now?
   A: Xiànzài kàndejian le. — I can see it now.
3. A: Nǐ tīngjian wǒ shuō de huà le ma? — Did you hear what I said?
   B: Méi tīngjian. — I didn't hear it.
   A: Wèishénme? — Why?
   B: Yīnwèi wǒ tīngbujian. — Because I couldn't hear it.

12.4.2 The verb <u>xià</u>

> When <u>xià</u> is used as a second element in an RVC, it has no meaning in itself but only in its grammatical function in the forming of compounds. It only appears in <u>de</u> and <u>bù</u> combinations. The most frequent combinations are the following:
>
> | | |
> |---|---|
> | zuòdexià zuòbuxià? | able to fit? |
> | chīdexià chībuxià? | able to eat more? |
> | zhùdexià zhùbuxià? | able to accommodate? |

1. A: Nǐ de chē zuòdexià zuòbuxià liù ge rén? — Can six people fit into your car?
   B: Wǒ de chē tài xiǎo, zuòbuxià liù ge rén. — My car is so small that six people can't fit into it.
2. A: Qǐng zài duō chī yìdiǎnr! — Please eat a little more!
   B: Wǒ chīde tài duō le, zhēn de chībuxià le. — I have eaten too much. I really can't eat anymore.

🐾 Sentence Building

1.
Yòu
Yòu lái le.
Jīntiān yòu lái le.
Zěnme jīntiān yòu lái le?
Tā zěnme jīntiān yòu lái le?

2.
Yòu ... yòu
Yòu gāo yòu dà.
Nǚpéngyou yòu gāo yòu dà.
Gēge de nǚpéngyou yòu gāo yòu dà.
Gēge cóngqián de nǚpéngyou yòu gāo yòu dà.

3.
Bǐ
Xiě zì bǐ rèn zì
Xiě zì bǐ rèn zì nán.
Xiě zì bǐ rèn zì nán yìdiǎnr ma?
Xiě zì bǐ rèn zì nán duō le.

4.
Chīdexià
Chīdexià zhème duō cài.
Chīdexià zhème duō cài ma?
Nǐ chīdexià zhème duō cài ma?
Wǒ xiǎng wǒ chīdexià.

🐾 Questions and Responses

1. Wéishénme xuésheng xǐhuan xiě diànzǐxìn?
   Why do students like to write e-mail?

   Yīnwèi diànzǐxìn yòu kuài yòu fāngbiàn.
   Because e-mail is both fast and convenient.

2. Nǐ xǐhuan gěi péngyou dǎ diànhuà háishì xiě diànzǐxìn?
   Do you like to phone or e-mail your friends?

   Wǒ xǐhuan dǎ diànhuà.
   I like to phone them.

3. Yàoshì nǐ xiǎng zhīdào nǐ de lǎoshī xìng shénme, nǐ zěnme wèn tā?
   If you wanted to know your teacher's family name, how would you ask him?

   Wǒ shuō, "Qǐngwèn, lǎoshī nǐ guìxìng?"
   I would say, "Excuse me teacher, what is your (honorable) family name?"

4. "Mínguì" shì shénme yìsi?

   What does "minggui" mean?

   "Mínguì" shì yòu guì yòu yǒumíng de yìsi. Rolex de biǎo hěn mínguì.

   "Minggui" means something that is both very valuable and well-known. A Rolex watch is very "minggui."

5. Xià kè yǐhòu nǐ yào qù nǎr?
   Where are you going after class?

   Wǒ děi qù jì xìn.
   I have to mail a letter.

6. Nǐ lǎojiā de tiānqì gēn zhèr de yíyàng ma?

   Is the weather here the same as that in your hometown?

   Bù yíyàng. Wǒ lǎojiā de tiānqì bǐ zhèr lěng duō le.

   It's not the same. The weather in my hometown is much colder than the weather here.

7. Nǐmen Zhōngwén kèběn de míngzi shì shénme?

   What is the title of your Chinese textbook?

   Jiào *Shuō Zhōngguóhuà*.

   (It's) called *Speaking Chinese*.

8. "Dàfāng" de yìsi shì shénme?

   What does "dafang" mean?

   "Dàfāng" de yìsi yǒu liǎng ge. Nǐ děi kàn shàngxiàwén cái zhīdào.

   "Dafang" has two meanings. You'll have to look at the context to know.

Pronunciation Review

Differentiating ui – un

(a)	zhuī	zhūn	(e)	zuì	zùn
(b)	chuī	chūn	(f)	cuì	cùn
(c)	shuì	shùn	(g)	suī	sūn
(d)	ruì	rùn			

🌸 Supplementary Vocabulary

Vehicles

qìchē	automobile, car
jiǎotàchē (ROC)	bicycle, bike
zìxíngchē (PRC)	bicycle, bike
mótuōchē	motorcycle
xiàochē	school bus
chūzū(qì)chē (PRC)	taxi
jìchéngchē (ROC)	taxi
huǒchē	train

🌸 Cultural Notes

Privacy

Privacy is not something one expects or can always have in China. In fact, there is no exact equivalent of the term "privacy" in the Chinese language. "Privacy" is commonly translated as yǐnsī, which literally means "hide one's secrets" or "hidden affairs," and has the connotation of something shady or illicit. In general, family members and close friends are not supposed to keep secrets from one another. Of course, as in other societies, people do in fact keep secrets. But the pretense of openness is perhaps more common in China. And the concept of "invasion of privacy" is not widely accepted in China. Thus, it is not unusual for Chinese friends, neighbors, and other acquaintances to pay a visit without previous arrangement.

第十二課
漢字本

內容

課文   64

生詞及例句   65
    (子、又、方、便、寄、比、貴、腦、下、前)

句型練習   69
    (又和再、又……又、比)

造句   76
    (又、又……又、比、吃得下)

問答   76

閱讀練習   77
    我的好朋友

課文

朋友來的電子信

海英：

　　我很高興認識你。你喜歡我們前天看的那個電影嗎？我很喜歡，可是金建說那個電影沒甚麼意思。你喜歡不喜歡寫電子信？送電子信又快又方便。再說，寄信比送電子信貴多了。最近我媽媽送我一個電腦。我一下課就打開電腦。寫電子信比看書有意思多了。我們可以寫中文的電子信。這樣，我們的中文一定會進步得很快。你同意嗎？我等你的回信。

　　　　　　　　　　　　　祝

　　　　　　　　　　　　快樂！

　　　　　　　　　　　　　　　　　　馬紅
　　　　　　　　　　　　　　　　　　十月四日

Lesson 12 An e-mail from a friend
第十二課 朋友來的電子信

🌸 生詞及例句

1. **子** **son; child; person; seed; egg (N)**

   ☞ 兒子 son (N)
   A: 許先生、許太太有幾個兒子？
   B: 他們有五個兒子。

   ☞ 子女 sons and daughters, children (N)
   他們家的子女都很好。

   ☞ 本子 notebook (N)
   這個本子是誰的？沒有名字。

   ☞ 電子信 electronic-mail, e-mail (N)
   學生都喜歡寫電子信。

2. **又** **again (Adv)**

   (1) A: 那個人早上來了，現在又來了。
       B: 他找誰？
       A: 他沒說。

   (2) A: 你今天又喝酒了，以後不要再喝了，好嗎？
       B: 我以後再也不喝了。

   ☞ 又……又 both … and (Conj)
   (1) 電子信又快又方便。
   (2) 他的女朋友又好看又有錢。

3. **方** **square (Adj); locality (N)**

   ☞ 地方 place, space (N)
   請你介紹一下這個地方。

- ☞ 四方　square; the four directions (north, south, east, west); all sides (Adj)

  中國字是四方的。

- ☞ 多方　in many ways, in every way, from various angles (Adj)

  這個事情我們得從多方來看。

- ☞ 對方　the other (or opposite) side; the other party (N)

  她請對方多給一點兒錢，可是對方不給。

- ☞ 大方　generous; poised and natural (SV)

  (1) 我的朋友很大方，天天請我吃飯，我真不好意思。

  (2) 那個女學生說話的時候很大方。

4. 便 **convenient, handy (Adj)**

- ☞ 方便　convenient (Adj)

  A: 從中國到日本方便不方便？

  B: 現在很方便了。幾個小時就可以到了。

- ☞ 便飯　a simple meal (N)

  A: 明天請你到我家來吃便飯。

  B: 不好意思，你老請我吃飯，明天我請你吧。

5. 寄 **send, mail (V)**

  今天早上哥哥寄給我兩本書。

- ☞ 寄信　mail letters (VO)

  A: 我沒有錢了，我得馬上寄信給我媽媽。

  B: 你媽媽會馬上給你寄錢來嗎？

  A: 我想會。

- ☞ 寄信人　sender (N)

  A: 金建，你有信。

  B: 是誰寄來的？

  A: 不知道是誰寄來的，沒有寄信人的姓名。

Lesson 12 An e-mail from a friend
第十二課 朋友來的電子信

6. **比** bǐ **compare, contrast, compete** (V)

 A: 你們兩個人比一比。看誰高。

 B: 思文比我高一點兒。

7. **貴** guì **expensive, costly** (SV)

 A: 現在書真貴。

 B: 可不是嗎！

☞ 貴姓 what is your name (lit., honorable family name) (IE)

 A: 老先生，請問你貴姓？

 B: 我姓祝。

 A: 小妹妹，你姓甚麼？

 C: 我姓金。

☞ 名貴 famous and very valuable (Adj/SV)

 媽媽生日的時候，我們送她一個很名貴的錶，她很喜歡。

8. **腦** nǎo **brain** (N)

☞ 電腦 computer (N)

 A: 你還記得沒有電腦的日子嗎？

 B: 記得。現在有電腦寫報告方便多了。

☞ 腦子 brain (N)

 A: 你想電腦比人的腦子快嗎？

 B: 有的時候。

9. **下** **below, under, underneath** (PW); **to descend, to get off** (V)

☞ 下課 get out of class, finish class (VO)

 (1) A: 你今天幾點鐘下課？

 B: 十點一刻。

☞ (2) A: 下課以後你去哪兒？
　　　B: 跟朋友去看電影。

☞ 下車　get off or out of a vehicle (VO)
　　(1) 到了！請下車。
　　(2) 下車的時候小心點兒。

☞ 地下　on the ground (PW)
　　地下有很多水，小心！

☞ 吃得下　be able to eat (RV)
　　A: 你叫這麼多菜，我們吃得下嗎？
　　B: 沒甚麼菜，請吃！

☞ 吃不下　do not feel like eating; be unable to eat any more (RV)
　　(1) A: 媽媽，這個菜太難吃了，我吃不下。
　　　　B: 吃不下就不要吃了。
　　(2) A: 再多吃點兒！
　　　　B: 我吃得太多了，真的吃不下了。

☞ 上下文　context (N)
　　A: 老師，這個字是甚麼意思？
　　B: 你看上下文。有很多中國字一看上下文就知道是甚麼意思了。

☞ 七上八下　be agitated, be perturbed (IE)
　　要考試了。我很怕，我的心七上八下地跳。

10. 前 qián　front; forward, ahead; before; preceding; former; first (Adv)

☞ 前天　the day before yesterday (TW)
　　A: 你前天晚上去甚麼地方了？
　　B: 我跟朋友去跳舞了。

☞ 以前   before; formerly, previously (Adv)

A: 你以前會用電腦嗎？

B: 我在中學的時候就會用電腦了。

☞ 事前   before the event, in advance, beforehand (Adv)

他去中國，事前沒有告訴我。我一點兒也不知道。

句型練習

12.1 THE DIFFERENCES BETWEEN 又 AND 再

The adverbs 又 and 再 have similar meanings but are used in different contexts. 又 means "again, more, also," referring to a **past** action. 再 means the same but with respect to a **future** action.

1. 請你明天再來。
2. 你甚麼時候再去看他？
3. 他去年去中國了，今年又去了。
4. 他又給女朋友打了一個電報。

再 is often used in commands and suggestions, situations where 又 cannot be used.

1. 請你再吃一點兒。
2. 再說！
3. 再想想！

再 cannot come before auxiliary verbs such as 想 "intend to" or 要 "want to," whereas 又 can.

1. 他又想吃中國飯了。
2. 你又要回國了嗎？

12.2 THE PATTERN 又……又

又……又 "both ... and" or negatively "neither ... nor" can be inserted before verbs, stative verbs or phrases to indicate the simultaneous existence of several actions, characteristics or conditions.

1. 馬紅又會說中國話又會說日本話。
2. 這本書又貴又沒意思。
3. 金建又喜歡跳舞又喜歡看電影。
4. 那個人又沒錢又沒學問。

12.3 THE PATTERN 比

12.3.1 A 比 B SV

The coverb 比 "compared to, compared with" is used in comparing two things. The sentence pattern — A 比 B SV — is used to express the difference in states or conditions between the items being compared. For comparisons involving people, the SVs 大 "big" and 小 "little, small" often mean "elder" and "younger" respectively.

A	比	B	SV
爸爸	比	媽媽	大。
Father is elder than mother.			

1. A: 你跟你妹妹誰高？
   B: 妹妹比我高。

2. A: 中文比日文難嗎？
   B: 是的。我想中文比日文難。

3. A: 今天冷還是前天冷？
   B: 今天比前天冷。

12.3.2 A 不 比 B SV

The opposite form of pattern 12.3.1 is obtained by placing the negative marker 不 before 比。

A	不	比	B	SV
爸爸	不	比	媽媽	大。

Father is not elder than mother.

1. A: 說中國話比寫中國字難嗎？
   B: 說中國話不比寫中國字難。

2. A: 美國飯比日本飯好吃。
   B: 美國飯不比日本飯好吃。

12.3.3 A 比 B SV degree

There are two ways to express degrees of comparison in Chinese: one way is to express degrees adverbially. Adverbs such as 還 "still more" or 更 "even more" placed before the main verb indicate degree.

A	比	B	更/還	SV
這兒	比	那兒	更/還	冷。

The weather here is even colder than the weather there.

1. 你比我高，他比你更/還高。

2. 中文書貴，日文書更/還貴。

3. 今天很冷，明天比今天更/還要冷。

Comparison may also be made by using a predicate complement. In the degree complement, the interrogative of quantity 多少 may be used to ask a question, and an indefinite answer, 一點兒 "a little" or SV-得多 or 多了 "much more" or a number-measure expression, is used in reply. Do not use 很 "very" in a comparison. To express "A is much more expensive than B," you have to say A 比 B 貴得多, **not** A 比 B 很貴.

A	比	B	SV	degree
她	比	我	高	一點兒。

She is a little taller than I.

1. A: 他比你高多少？
   B: 他比我高一點兒。

2. A: 這個電腦貴還是那個電腦貴？
   B: 這個電腦比那個電腦貴多了。

3. A: 說中國話難還是寫中國字難？
   B: 寫中國字比說中國話難得多。

12.3.4 Comparison of manner of action between A and B

For a comparison of manner in which two actors perform an action, either pattern (A) or pattern (B) can be used.

(A)	A	比	B	V-得	SV
	你	比	我	吃得	快。

You eat faster than I do.

1. 小美比我跑得慢。

2. 海英比思文寫得好。

(B)	A	V-得	比	B	SV
	你	吃得	比	我	快。

You eat faster than I do.

1. 小美跑得比我慢。

2. 海英寫得比思文好。

Lesson 12 An e-mail from a friend
第十二課 朋友來的電子信

12.3.5 Comparison of an action with an object between A and B

When the action verb followed by an expression of manner has an object, either pattern (A) or pattern (B) can be used.

> (A) A   V   O,   V-得   比   B   SV
>   你   說   中國話，   說得   比   我   好。
> You speak Chinese better than I do.

1. 我弟弟開車，開得比我快。

2. 媽媽作中國飯，作得比爸爸好。

3. 馬紅用電腦，用得比我多。

> (B) A   的   O,   V-得   比   B   SV
>   你   的   中國話，   說得   比   我   好。
> You speak Chinese better than I do.

1. 我的中文進步得比你慢。

2. 你的報告寫得比我長。

3. 你們看電影，看得比他多。

12.4 RESULTATIVE VERB COMPOUNDS

The resultative verb compounds (RVCs) are compound transitive verbs. An RVC is always made up of two elements, although the second element may be a compound itself, such as 出來 "come out." The first element in such a compound designates the action; the second element indicates the result – **actual** or **potential**.

An **actual** result is expressed by a simple combination of the two verbs.

> 我看見他了。
> 我找到了。

Potential resultative verbs, as distinguished from other verbs, have special forms for adding the meanings "be able" and "be unable." For "be able," 得 is inserted between the two verbs; for "be unable," 不 is inserted.

看見 "see" → 看得見
看見 "see" → 看不見

Potential verbs can be used with any of the question forms already introduced.

你看得見看不見那個人？
你看得見那個人嗎？
你看得見還是看不見那個人？

There are a great many RVCs that must be learned one by one because their meanings cannot be derived from those of their constituents plus the relationship between their compounds. Several RVCs were introduced (without analysis) in previous lessons: 回來/去, 作好, 學會, 看到. We will discuss them in details in the next few lessons.

12.4.1 THE VERBS 到 AND 見

When 到 is used as a second element in an RVC, it means "arrive, succeed, attain," and is often used with verbs such as 找 "look for," 走 "walk," 跑 "run," 想 "think," 看 "see, read," 學 "learn," or 送 "send."

1. A: 你找得到找不到金建的家？

   B: 我找不到。請你跟我一起去。

2. A: 你十分鐘走得到走不到圖書館？

   B: 要是走得快就走得到。

3. A: 你想得到想不到她已經是媽媽了？
   B: 真想不到。

4. A: 這學期我們學得到學不到第十四課？
   B: 也許學得到。

Lesson 12 An e-mail from a friend
第十二課　朋友來的電子信

When 見 is used as a second element in an RVC, it means "perception (sensory)." 見 is often used with verbs such as 看 "to see," 聽 "to listen," and 聞 "to smell." (The characters for 聽 and 聞 have not been introduced in the text.)

1. A: 我的錶不見了，你看見了嗎？
   B: 我沒看見。

2. A: 老師，那個字你寫得太小了，我看不見。
   B: 好，我寫大一點兒，現在你看得見了嗎？
   A: 現在看得見了。

3. A: 你聽見我說的話了嗎？
   B: 沒聽見。
   A: 為甚麼？
   B: 因為我聽不見。

12.4.2 The verb 下

When 下 is used as a second element in an RVC, it has no meaning in itself but only in its grammatical function in the forming of compounds. It only appears in 得 and 不 combinations. The most frequent combinations are the following:

坐得下坐不下？
吃得下吃不下？
住得下住不下？

1. A: 你的車坐得下坐不下六個人？
   B: 我的車太小，坐不下六個人。

2. A: 請再多吃一點兒！
   B: 我吃得太多了，真的吃不下了。

造句

1.
又
又來了。
今天又來了。
怎麼今天又來了？
他怎麼今天又來了？

2.
又……又
又高又大。
女朋友又高又大。
哥哥的女朋友又高又大。
哥哥從前的女朋友又高又大。

3.
比
寫字比認字
寫字比認字難。
寫字比認字難一點兒嗎？
寫字比認字難多了。

4.
吃得下
吃得下這麼多菜。
吃得下這麼多菜嗎？
你吃得下這麼多菜嗎？
我想我吃得下。

問答

1. 為甚麼學生喜歡寫電子信？
因為電子信又快又方便。
2. 你喜歡給朋友打電話還是寫電子信？
我喜歡打電話。
3. 要是你想知道你的老師姓甚麼，你怎麼問他？
我說："請問，老師你貴姓？"
4. "名貴"是甚麼意思？
"名貴"是又貴又有名的意思。Rolex的錶很名貴。
5. 下課以後你要去哪兒？
我得去寄信。
6. 你老家的天氣跟這兒的一樣嗎？
不一樣。我老家的天氣比這兒冷多了。
7. 你們中文課本的名字是甚麼？
叫《説中國話》。
8. "大方"的意思是甚麼？
"大方"的意思有兩個，你得看上下文才知道。

Lesson 12 *An e-mail from a friend*
第十二課 朋友來的電子信

閱讀練習

我的好朋友

我的中文老師給我介紹了一個朋友。從那天以後他就是我的好朋友了。我們常常在一起學中文。

我看新的課文的時候,有不認識的字,我一打開我的朋友,我的朋友就會告訴我那個字的意思是甚麼。我的朋友幫我認識很多新的字。

我作中文功課的時候,我想知道一個英文字的中文意思,他就很快告訴我。我不能一天沒有他。你現在知道我的好朋友是誰嗎?你也要認識他嗎?你也要一個這樣的好朋友嗎?我可以給你們介紹介紹。

請查生詞

Look up the following words in a dictionary.

從……以後	cóng … yǐhòu
新	xīn
打開	dǎkāi
不能	bùnéng

填 空

Fill in the blanks with the appropriate words from the story.

1. 你的名字是 _____ 典。你 _____ 學外國話的人很 _____ 用。

2. 我 _____ 有了字典 _____ _____ ，就一天不能沒有 _____ _____ 。字典 _____ 了我很多忙。

3. 馬思文 _____ 學中文 _____ _____ ，就喜歡吃中國菜了。

4. 海英，來，我給你介紹介紹，這是我 _____ 認識的朋友。我們 _____ 認識 _____ _____ 就是好朋友了。有一個 _____ 朋友很不容 _____ 。

5. 這是媽媽給我的 _____ 筆盒，請你幫我 _____ _____ 。

6. 媽媽說，我還太小，_____ _____ 喝酒。

第十三課　回朋友的電子信
Lesson 13　Reply to a friend's e-mail

Lesson 13
Pinyin Text

CONTENTS

Text 82

Vocabulary and Illustrative Sentences 83
(xiè, dāng, rán, suī, tú, cháng, yòng, chū, suǒ, kòng)

Pattern Drills 90
(suīrán ... kěshì, liǎo, chūlai, méiyǒu bù ... de, xiān ... ránhòu,
děi ... yàoburán, dāng ... de shíhou, yīnwèi ... suǒyǐ)

Sentence Building
(jīngcháng, cháng, suīrán, zài ... ba) 94

Questions and Responses 95

Pronunciation Review 96

Fun Activity 96

Supplementary Vocabulary 97

Cultural Notes 97

❧ Text

Huí péngyou de diànzǐxìn
Reply to a friend's e-mail

Mǎ Hóng:

Xièxie nǐ de diànzǐxìn. Wǒ dāngrán xǐhuan xiě diànzǐxìn le. Wǒ xiǎng xiànzài de xuésheng méiyǒu bù xǐhuan xiě diànzǐxìn de. Wǒ gēn nǐ yíyàng, měitiān kàn diànzǐxìn. Suīrán wǒ méiyǒu diànnǎo, kěshì wǒ kěyǐ zài túshūguǎn kàn, yě hěn fāngbiàn. Qǐng nǐ chángcháng lái diànzǐxìn. Wǒ xiǎng wǒmen xiànzài yòng Yīngwén xiě, yīnwèi wǒmen de Zhōngwén hái bú tài hǎo, yǒude zì bú huì xiě, yǒude yìsi xiě bù chūlai, suǒyǐ wǒmen zuìhǎo děng jǐ ge xīngqī yǐhòu zài shìshi yòng Zhōngwén xiě ba. Nǐ zhège xīngqīliù yǒu kòngr ma? Wǒ gēn Jīn Jiàn xīngqīliù wǎnshang yào qù fànguǎn chīfàn ránhòu qù tiàowǔ. Nǐ kěyǐ gēn wǒmen qù ma? Qǐng huí xìn. Zàijiàn.

    Zhù
kuàilè!

Hǎiyīng
Shíyuè wǔrì

Ma Hong,

Thank you for your e-mail. Of course I like to write e-mail. I think there aren't any students nowadays who don't like writing e-mail. I'm like you. I check my e-mail (box) every day. Although I don't have a computer, I can check my e-mail at the library. It's quite convenient. Please e-mail me often. I think for now we'd better write in English, since our Chinese is still not very good. There are some characters that we don't know how to write and some meanings that we can't express. So, we'd better wait for a few weeks and then try to write in Chinese again. Are you free this Saturday? Jin Jian and I are going to dine at a restaurant and go dancing afterwards this Saturday evening. Can you come with us? Please reply. Goodbye.

Wishing you happiness,
Haiying
5 October

Lesson 13 Reply to a friend's e-mail
第十三課 回朋友的電子信

🌸 Vocabulary and Illustrative Sentences

1. **xiè** — **thank (V); surname**

   Xiè xiānsheng, nǐ bú yào xiè wǒ, nǐ xiè wǒ xiānsheng ba.
   Mr. Xie, please don't thank me. Thank my husband.

   ☞ **xièxie** — thanks, thank you (V)

   A: Zhè shì nǐ de shū ma?
   Is this your book?

   B: Shì. Xièxie. Nǐ zài nǎr zhǎodào de?
   Yes, thank you. Where did you find it?

   ☞ **duōxiè** — many thanks, thanks a lot (IE)

   A: Nǐ sòng wǒ zhème míngguì de biǎo. Duōxiè, duōxiè.
   You gave me such an expensive watch! Thank you very much.

   B: Méishénme. Xiǎoyìsi.
   It's nothing. Just a little something.

   ☞ **búxiè** — don't mention it, not at all (IE)

   A: Xièxie nǐ qǐng wǒ chīfàn.
   Thank you for treating me.

   B: Búxiè. Wǒ hěn gāoxìng nǐ kěyǐ lái.
   Don't mention it. I'm glad you could make it.

2. **dāng** — **just at (a time or place); serve as; should, must (V)**

   (1) A: Nǐ zhǎngdà yǐhòu, xiǎng dāng shénme?
   What do you want to be when you grow up?

   B: Wǒ xiǎng dāng lǎoshī.
   I want to be a teacher.

   (2) A: Dāng wǒ qù zhǎo tā de shíhou, tā zài chīfàn.
   When I went to look for him, he was eating.

   B: Tā méi qǐng nǐ chīfàn ma?
   Didn't he invite you to eat with him?

   A: Qǐng le, kěshì wǒ bùhǎoyìsi zài nàr chī.
   He did, but I felt uneasy about eating there.

3. rán — **but, nevertheless, however** (Conj)

☞ dāngrán — as it should be, without doubt, certainly, of course, naturally (Adv)

(1) A: Nǐ wèishénme lǎo shēng tā de qì?
Why are you always mad at him?

B: Yīnwèi tā lǎo méishìzhǎoshì, wǒ dāngrán shēngqì le.
Because he always tries to make trouble, naturally I'm mad at him.

(2) Xuésheng yǒu wèntí dāngrán děi qù wèn lǎoshī.
If a student has questions, of course he should ask his teacher.

☞ ránhòu — then, after that, afterwards (Conj)

Nǐ zuìhǎo xiān zuò gōngkè ránhòu zài qù kàn diànyǐng.
It's best to do your homework first, then go watch the movie.

☞ tiānrán — natural (Adj)

Zhè shì tiānrán de shuǐ, hěn hǎo hē.
This is spring water. It tastes great.

☞ yàoburán — otherwise, if not, or else (Conj)

Nǐ děi mǎshàng gěi tā qián, yàoburán tā jiù bú shì nǐ de péngyou le.
You have to give him the money immediately, otherwise he will not be your friend anymore.

☞ bùyǐwéirán — not approve (IE)

Nǐ shuō de huà, wǒ bùyǐwéirán. Wǒ bù tóngyì.
I don't approve of what you said. I don't agree.

4. suī — **though, although, even though** (Conj)

☞ suīrán — though, although (Conj)

(1) Nàge rén suīrán méi shàngguo xué, kěshì tā de xuéwèn hěn hǎo.
Although that person has never attended school, he is very learned.

(2) Suīrán wǒ huì shuō Zhōngguóhuà, kěshì wǒ bú huì kàn Zhōngguózì.
Even though I can speak Chinese, I cannot read Chinese.

Lesson 13 *Reply to a friend's e-mail*
第十三課 回朋友的電子信

5. tú — **picture, drawing, chart, map (N)**

☞ dìtú — map (N)

    A: Nǐ yǒu Zhōngguó dìtú ma? — Do you have a map of China?
    B: Yǒu. — (Yes, I) have (one).

☞ túbiǎo — chart, diagram, graph (N)

    Nǐ zuò bàogào de shíhou, zuìhǎo yǒu jǐ ge túbiǎo. — When you give your report, it's best to have several charts.

☞ túshū — books (N)

    Wǒ jiā yǒu hěn duō túshū. — There are many books in my house.

☞ túshūguǎn — library (PW)

    Wǒ hěn xǐhuan zài túshūguǎn zuò gōngkè. — I really like doing homework at the library.

6. cháng — **ordinary, common, normal; frequently, often (Adv)**

    A: Nǐ cháng gěi nǐ tàitai xiě xìn ma? — Do you write to your wife often?
    B: Wǒ bù cháng gěi tā xiě xìn, kěshì wǒ tiāntiān gěi tā dǎ diànhuà. — I don't write often, but I call her every day.

☞ chángcháng — frequently, often, usually (Adv)

    Xiè xiānsheng chángcháng gàosu wǒmen tā zài Měiguó de jīngyàn. — Mr. Xie frequently tells us about his experiences in the States.

☞ chángjiàn — commonplace (SV)

    Zhè yàng xiǎoqì de rén bù chángjiàn. — You don't see such narrow-minded/stingy person like him very often.

	chángshí	general knowledge, common sense (N)	
		Tā méi shàngguo dàxué, kěshì tā de chángshí bǐ shàngguo dàxué de rén hái duō.	He has never attended college, but he has even more common sense than people who have been to college.

	jīngcháng	daily; constantly, often (Adv)	
		(1) Wǒ bú pà kǎoshì, yīnwèi wǒmen jīngcháng kǎo.	I'm not afraid of taking tests because we have them often.
		(2) Tā bàba jīngcháng bú zài jiā.	His father is often not home.

	rìcháng	daily; commonplace (Adj)	
		Wǒ māma lái xìn gàosu wǒ jiā rìcháng de shìqing.	My mom's letter told me about our family's daily life.

	shícháng	often, frequently (Adv)	
		Wǒ de hǎopéngyou zuìjìn xīnqíng bù hǎo, shícháng shēngqì.	My best friend has been in a bad mood lately. She gets angry often.

7.	yòng	**use, employ** (V)	
		A: Nǐ huì yòng Zhōngwén xiě xìn ma?	Do you know how to write a letter in Chinese?
		B: Xiànzài hái bú huì.	As of now, I still don't know.

	rìyòng	daily expenses; for everyday use (Adj)	
		A: Nǐ māma gěi nǐ de rìyòng qián gòu-bu-gòu?	Is the money your mother gave you for daily expenses enough?
		B: Xiànzài gòu, yǐhòu jiù bù zhīdào le.	It's enough for now, (but I) am not sure about that later.

	chángyòng	in common use, commonly-used, often used (Adj)	
		Wǒ chángyòng diànnǎo xiě bàogào.	I often use the computer to write reports.

Lesson 13 Reply to a friend's e-mail
第十三課 回朋友的電子信

☞ **yòng rén**   choose a person for a job, make use of personnel (VO)

(1) Wǒ bàba shuō zuò jìnchūkǒu shēngyi **yòng rén** zuì nán. — My father says that in the import-export business the most difficult thing is to find the right personnel.

(2) Tā xǐhuan **yòng** rèxīn de **rén** gěi tā zuò shì. — He likes to have enthusiastic people to work for him.

☞ **yònggōng**   hardworking, diligent, studious (SV)

(1) Wǒ de xuésheng dōu hěn **yònggōng**, tāmen yìtiāndàowǎn kàn shū. — All my students are very diligent. They study all the time.

(2) **Yònggōng** de xuésheng, kǎoshì de shíhou bú pà. — Hardworking students aren't afraid of tests.

☞ **yòngxīn**   diligently; attentively, with concentrated attention (SV)

Nǐ zuò shì de shíhou yídìng děi **yòngxīn**, yàoburán jiù zuò bù hǎo. — When you're working, you must be attentive, or else you won't do well.

☞ **búyòng**   need not (IE)

Māma, wǒ de qián gòu yòng le, nǐ **búyòng** jì lái le. Xièxie nǐ. — Mother, I have enough money to spend. You don't have to send me any more. Thank you.

☞ **yòngbuliǎo**   have more than is needed, use less than, not use up (RV)

(1) Zhè běn shū **yòngbuliǎo** zhème duō qián. — This book doesn't cost that much money.

(2) Nǐmen jīntiān de kǎoshì **yòngbuliǎo** liǎng ge xiǎoshí. — Your test today will take less than two hours to complete.

(3) Tā de qián tài duō le. Tā yídìng **yòngbuliǎo**. — He has too much money. He definitely cannot use it all up.

☞ **xīnbúèryòng**   concentrate on one thing at a time (IE)

Wǒ zuò shì de shíhou cónglái shì **xīnbúèryòng**. — I always concentrate on one thing at a time when I work.

8. chū   **go or come out** (V)

☞ chūqu   go out; get out (V)

(1) Jīntiān tiānqì hěn hǎo, wǒmen yào chūqu mànpǎo ma?   The weather is great today. Shall we go out jogging?

(2) Chūqu! Wǒ bú yào zài kànjian nǐ.   Get out! I don't want to see you again.

☞ chūlai   come out (V)

(1) Chūlai! Wǒ yǒu huà yào gēn nǐ shuō.   Come out! I have something to tell you.

(2) Zhège zì shì shénme yìsi wǒ xiǎng chūlai le.   I have recalled the meaning of this word.

☞ chūmén   be away from home; go on a journey, go out (V)

(1) Nǐ yí ge rén chūmén, děi duō xiǎoxīn.   You're going away from home by yourself. You have to be careful.

(2) A: Nǐ shénme shíhou zài chūmén?   When are you going away again?

B: Zuìjìn yì-liǎng tiān.   In the next day or two.

(3) A: Wǒ māma yìtiāndàowǎn zài jiā bù chūmén.   My mom stays at home all the time every day.

B: Wèishénme?   Why?

A: Tā bú huì kāichē.   She doesn't know how to drive.

☞ chū guó   go abroad (VO)

Xiànzài hěn duō Zhōngguórén xiǎng chū guó.   Many Chinese people want to go abroad now.

☞ chūkǒu   exit (PW); export (V)

Wǒ zài túshūguǎn chūkǒu de dìfang děng nǐ.   I'll wait for you at the library exit.

☞ jìnchūkǒu   imports and exports; exits and entrances (Adj)

Wǒ bàba zuò jìnchūkǒu de shēngyi.   My father works in the import-export business.

Lesson 13 Reply to a friend's e-mail
第十三課 回朋友的電子信

9. suǒ — **place (N); (MW for houses)**

☞ suǒyǐ — so, therefore, as a result (Conj)

    A: Nǐ jīntiān wèishénme méi lái shàng kè? — Why didn't you come to class today?

    B: Yīnwèi wǒ jiā yǒu hěn yàojǐn de shìqing, suǒyǐ méi lái shàng kè. — Because there was something important at home, (so) I didn't come to class.

☞ suǒyǒu — all (Adj)

    (1) Zhèr suǒyǒu de qián dōu shì tā de. — All the money here is his.

    (2) A: Suǒyǒu xué Zhōngwén de xuésheng dōu qù kāihuì le, nǐ wèishénme méi qù? — All the students who study Chinese went to that meeting. Why didn't you go?

       B: Yīnwèi wǒ shìxiān bù zhīdào, suǒyǐ méi qù. — Because I didn't know there was a meeting, (that's why) I didn't go.

10. kòng — **leave empty or blank; unoccupied (Adj)**

Zhèr yǒu hěn duō kòngdì, wǒmen kěyǐ zài zhèr pǎobù. — Here is a lot of unoccupied land. We can jog here.

☞ kòngr — free time, spare time (IE); empty space (N)

    A: Wǒ xiǎng qù kàn nǐ, bù zhīdào nǐ shénme shíhou yǒu kòngr. — I'd like to see you, but I don't know when you are free.

    B: Wǒ jīntiān méi kòngr, míngtiān shénme shíhou dōu kěyǐ. — I am busy today, but anytime tomorrow will be fine.

Pattern Drills

13.1 THE PATTERN suīrán ... kěshì

Suīrán ... kěshì "although ... but" are two adverbial linking words. Suīrán is a movable adverb — it can be placed either in a clause-initial position or after the topic/subject. Kěshì is used to begin the second clause.

(A) Suīrán subject/topic clause, kěshì clause.
     Suīrán Zhōngwén hěn nán, kěshì wǒ hái yào xué.
     Although Chinese is very difficult, (but) I still want to learn it.

(B) Subject/topic suīrán clause, kěshì clause.
     Zhōngwén suīrán hěn nán, kěshì wǒ hái yào xué.
     Although Chinese is very difficult, (but) I still want to learn it.

1. Wǒ suīrán xǐhuan tiàowǔ, kěshì jīntiān wǎnshang bù xiǎng tiào. — Although I like to dance, I don't feel like dancing tonight.

2. Suīrán tā hěn yǒuqián, kěshì tā lǎo shuō ta méi qián. — Although she is very rich, she always says she doesn't have any money.

3. Suīrán wǒ hěn yònggōng, kěshì wǒ háishì kǎode bù hǎo. — Although I studied very hard, I still didn't do well in my test.

13.2 THE VERB liǎo

When liǎo is used as a second element in an RVC, it has two basic meanings: "be able to" or "be able to finish," depending on the context.

1. A: Jīntiān de gōngkè nǐ zuòdeliǎo ma? — Will you be able to finish today's homework?

   B: Zhème duō gōngkè wǒ yídìng zuòbuliǎo. — So much homework! I definitely can't finish it.

2. A: Nǐ zuòdeliǎo zhège gōngzuò ma? — Are you able to do this job?

   B: Zhège gōngzuò tài nán, wǒ xiǎng wǒ zuòbuliǎo. — This task is too difficult. I don't think I can do it.

3. A: Nǐ zuò zhème duō cài, wǒmen zěnme chīdeliǎo?
   You cooked so much food. How can we finish it?

   B: Chībuliǎo bú yàojǐn, wǒmen kěyǐ míngtiān chī.
   It doesn't matter if we can't finish it. We can eat it tomorrow.

13.3 THE COMPOUND VERB chūlai

13.3.1 As a second element in an RVC

Chūlai is a compound direction verb. It means "come out" (toward the direction of the speaker). Chūlai can serve as a second element in an RVC.

1. Qǐng chūlai!
   Please come out!

2. Wǒmen bú yào chūlai.
   We don't want to come out.

13.3.2 As a complement

When chūlai comes after another motion verb, it functions as a complement.

1. Xuésheng xià kè yǐhòu, dōu hěn kuàide pǎochūlai le.
   Students all leave in a hurry after class.

2. Nàge lǎorén mànmānde zǒuchūlai le.
   That old man walked out slowly.

13.3.3 As a resultative verb ending

When chūlai functions as a resultative verb ending, it indicates appearance, identification or achievement.

1. Wǒ xiǎng bù chūlai nàge rén de míngzi le.
   I can't recall that person's name anymore.

2. A: Shàng xuéqī xué de zì, nǐ hái xiědechūlai ma?
   Can you still write the characters that you learned last semester?

   B: Wǒ xiědechūlai.
   Yes, I can write them (out).

3. A: Nǐ yǒu shénme yìjiàn, qǐng nǐ shuō-chūlai. — If you have any ideas, please speak up.

   B: Wǒ yǒu yìjiàn, kěshì wǒ pà shuō-chūlai. — I have some ideas, but I am afraid to speak up.

4. A: Nǐ rèndechūlai wǒ shì shéi ma? — Are you able to figure out who I am?

   B: Dāngrán rèndechūlai, nǐ shì wǒ cóngqián de nǚpéngyou. — Of course I recognize you. You were my ex-girlfriend.

13.4 THE PATTERN méiyǒu bù ... de

Méiyǒu "don't have" and bù "not" together with the particle de form a double negative pattern, literally meaning "there is nothing not possible." It is a strong statement to show resolution.

1. Méiyǒu xué bú huì de shì. — There is nothing that one cannot master. (One can master anything.)

2. Yàoshi nǐ tiāntiān shàng kè, jiù méiyǒu kǎo bù hǎo de. — If you go to class every day, you won't do badly in your test. (You will do well in your exam if you attend class every day.)

3. Méiyǒu bú ài qián de rén. — There is no one who doesn't love money. (Everybody loves money.)

13.5 THE PATTERN xiān ... ránhòu

Xiān "first" and ránhòu "then, after that, afterwards" together express the sequence of two actions.

1. Wǒmen xiān qù túshūguǎn, ránhòu zài qù jì xìn. — We will go to the library first, then we will mail the letter.

2. Nǐ děi xiān huì kāichē, ránhòu wǒ zài gěi nǐ wǒ de chē. — First, you have to know how to drive, then I will give you my car.

3. Wǒmen zuìhǎo xiān diǎncài, ránhòu zài tán shēngyi. — It's better if we order the food first and then talk about business.

13.6 THE PATTERN děi ... yàoburán

> Děi "have to, must" is a nonmovable adverb. It has to stand before the verb, while yàoburán "otherwise" stands at the beginning of the second clause.

1. Nǐ děi gěi tā huí xìn, yàoburán tā huì hěn shēngqì de.

   You have to reply to his letter, otherwise he will get very angry.

2. Wǒmen děi kuài diǎnr zǒu, yàoburán jiù wǎn le.

   We have to go faster, otherwise we will be late.

3. Zhège zì de yìsi, nǐ děi kàn shàngxiàwén, yàoburán hěn nán zhīdào.

   You have to read the context to know the meaning of this character, otherwise it will be very difficult to understand.

4. Shàng kè de shíhou, nǐ děi xīnbúèryòng, yàoburán nǐ jiù bù zhīdào lǎoshī zài shuō shénme.

   You have to pay attention in class, otherwise you won't know what your teacher is saying.

13.7 THE PATTERN dāng ... de shíhou

> Dāng "during" is often placed at the beginning of a sentence to serve as an adverb of time and de shíhou "when, while" serves as an object of dāng. The dāng ... de shíhou pattern indicates the time at which something happens.

1. Dāng lǎoshī xiě zì de shíhou, nǐ děi yòngxīn kàn.

   When your teacher is writing characters, you have to observe carefully.

2. Dāng bàba zuò jìnchūkǒu shēngyi de shíhou, tā jīngcháng bú zài jiā.

   My dad was often not home when he was in the import-export business.

3. Dāng suǒyǒu de gōngkè dōu zuò hǎo de shíhou, wǒ zuì kāixīn.

   The happiest time for me is when I have finished all my homework.

13.8 THE LINKING ADVERBS yīnwèi ... suǒyǐ

> Yīnwèi ... suǒyǐ "because ... therefore" links two clauses in a sentence to express cause and effect or a reason. Yīnwèi can come either after the subject/topic or in a clause-initial position, while the second clause is started with suǒyǐ, as in (1) and (2) below. Sometimes either yīnwèi or suǒyǐ can be omitted from a sentence, as in (3) and (4) below.

1. Tā yīnwèi hěn lèi, suǒyǐ bú yào shàng kè.
   Because he is very tired, (therefore) he doesn't want to go to class.

2. Yīnwèi tā hěn lèi, suǒyǐ bú yào shàng kè.
   Because he is very tired, (therefore) he doesn't want to go to class.

3. Tā hěn lèi, suǒyǐ bú yào shàng kè.
   He is very tired, so he doesn't want to go to class.

4. Tā yīnwèi hěn lèi, bù yào shàng kè.
   Because he is very tired, he doesn't want to go to class.

Sentence Building

1.
Jīngcháng
Jīngcháng chūmén.
Zuìjìn jīngcháng chūmén.
Shéi zuìjìn jīngcháng chūmén?
Wǒ xiānsheng zuìjìn jīngcháng chūmén.

2.
Cháng
Cháng qù.
Cháng qù túshūguǎn.
Wǒ cháng qù túshūguǎn.
Wǒ cháng qù túshūguǎn zuò gōngkè.

3.
Suīrán
Suīrán wǒ méi kòngr
Suīrán wǒ méi kòngr, wǒ hái děi qù kàn tā.
Suīrán jīntiān wǒ méi kòngr, wǒ hái děi qù kàn tā.

4.
Zài ... ba
Xiān chīfàn zài qù túshūguǎn ba!
Zuìhǎo xiān chīfàn zài qù túshūguǎn ba!
Wǒmen zuìhǎo xiān chīfàn zài qù túshūguǎn ba!

Lesson 13 Reply to a friend's e-mail
第十三課 回朋友的電子信

🌸 Questions and Responses

1. Guóyīng, míngtiān qǐng nǐ dào wǒ jiā lái chī biànfàn, hǎo ma?
   Guoying, please come over to my house tomorrow for a simple meal, okay?

   Hǎo, xièxie, nǐ tài kèqi le.
   Okay, thank you. You're too kind.

2. Sīwén, nǐ xiǎng Hǎiyīng de māma ài tā ma?
   Siwen, do you think Haiying's mother loves her?

   Dāngrán ài tā. Wǒ xiǎng méiyǒu māma bú ài tāmen háizi de.
   Of course she loves her. I think there are no mothers who do not love their children.

3. Nǐmen zěnme nàme yònggōng? Yìtiāndàowǎn bù chūqu.
   Why are you so diligent? You never go out.

   Bú yònggōng kǎobuhǎo.
   If you don't work hard, you won't do well in your exams.

4. Sīwén wèishénme lǎo kǎo dì-yī míng?
   Why does Siwen always score the best in the exam?

   Yīnwèi tā zuò gōngkè de shíhou hěn yòngxīn.
   Because he concentrates when he does his homework.

5. Shíhou bù zǎo le, wǒmen kuài qù shàng kè ba. Yàoburán jiù tài wǎn le.
   It's getting late, let's get to class quickly! Otherwise, it'll be too late.

   Hǎo. Wǒ mǎshàng jiù lái.
   Okay. I'm coming right away.

6. Nǐ bàba zuò shénme shēngyi?
   What business is your father in?

   Tā yǐqián zuò jìnchūkǒu shēngyi, xiànzài bú zuò le.
   He used to run an import-export business, but not anymore.

7. Wǒ xiǎng qǐng nǐ qù tiàowǔ, nǐ shénme shíhou yǒu kòngr?
   I'd like to ask you out to a dance. When are you free?

   Wǒ zhè xīngqītiān méi shì, wǒmen wǎnshang bā diǎn zhōng kěyǐ qù.
   I am free this Sunday. We can go at 8:00 p.m.

8. Wǒ rènwéi wǒmen de kǎoshì tài duō le. Nǐ shuō ne?
   I think we have too many tests. What do you think?

   Suīrán kǎoshì hěn duō, kěshì wǒ rènwéi chángcháng kǎoshì hěn hǎo.
   Although we have many tests, I think having tests frequently is good.

9. Nǐ xiǎng wǒ shì xiān zài zhèr xué Zhōngwén hǎo háishì qù Zhōngguó yǐhòu zài xué Zhōngwén hǎo?
Do you think it's better for me to learn Chinese here or should I learn Chinese after I get to China?

Wǒ xiǎng zuìhǎo shì xiān zài zhèr xué yì-liǎng nián Zhōngwén, ránhòu zài qù Zhōngguó hao.
I think it would be better if you studied Chinese here for a year or two, then went to China.

10. Qiántiān shéi qù tā de cháhuì le?
Who has gone to his tea party the day before yesterday?

Tā suǒyǒu de péngyou dōu qù le.
All his friends have gone.

Pronunciation Review

Differentiating in – ing

(a)	nín	níng	(e)	bīn	bīng
(b)	lín	líng	(f)	xìn	xìng
(c)	mín	míng	(g)	jǐn	jǐng
(d)	yìn	yìng	(h)	qín	qíng

Fun Activity

Let's Learn a Chinese Children's Song

Pay attention to the rhymes.

Sān lún chē
Pedicab (Three-Wheeled Cart)

Sān lún chē, pǎo de kuài.	The pedicab runs very fast.
Shàngmiàn zuò yí ge lǎo tàitai.	On it sits an old lady.
Yào wǔ máo, gěi yí kuài.	A ride costs fifty cents. She pays one dollar.
Nǐ shuō qíguài bù qíguài?	Do you think it is strange or not?

Supplementary Vocabulary

Some well-known Chinese teas

hóng chá	red (black) tea
júhuā chá	chrysanthemum tea
lóngjǐng chá	Dragon Well tea (a famous green tea produced in Hangzhou)
tiěguānyīn	Goddess of Mercy tea (a type of Oolong tea produced in Fujian)
lǜ chá	green tea
xiāngpiàn (ROC)	jasmine tea
huā chá (PRC)	jasmine tea
wūlóng chá	Oolong tea (a famous green tea produced in Taiwan)
pǔ'ěr chá	Pu'er tea (produced in Yunnan)

Cultural Notes

Asking personal questions

Chinese people often ask their new or casual acquaintances questions such as: "How old are you?" "How much money do you make?" "Are you married or not?" "Do you have a girlfriend (or boyfriend)?" etc. They do not consider these questions too personal. In fact, asking such personal questions is meant to show one's concern or interest in the Chinese social context. This is how people get acquainted and establish the grounds of a relationship. Please do not get upset when a stranger on the train asks you these kinds of personal questions. (Of course, you do not have to reveal anything personal if you do not feel comfortable with answering such questions.)

第十三課
漢字本

內容

課文　　　　　　　　　　　　　　　　　　　　100

生詞及例句　　　　　　　　　　　　　　　　101
（謝、當、然、雖、圖、常、用、出、所、空）

句型練習　　　　　　　　　　　　　　　　　106
（雖然……可是、了、出來、沒有不……的、先……然後、
得……要不然、當……的時候、因為……所以）

造句　　　　　　　　　　　　　　　　　　　109
（經常、常、雖然、再……吧）

問答　　　　　　　　　　　　　　　　　　　110

閱讀練習　　　　　　　　　　　　　　　　　111
便飯

課文

回朋友的電子信

馬紅：

　　謝謝你的電子信。我當然喜歡寫電子信了。我想現在的學生沒有不喜歡寫電子信的。我跟你一樣，每天看電子信。雖然我沒有電腦，可是我可以在圖書館看，也很方便。請你常常來電子信。我想我們現在用英文寫，因為我們的中文還不太好，有的字不會寫，有的意思寫不出來，所以我們最好等幾個星期以後再試試用中文寫吧。你這個星期六有空兒嗎？我跟金建星期六晚上要去飯館吃飯然後去跳舞。你可以跟我們去嗎？請回信。再見。

　　祝

快樂！

海英
十月五日

生詞及例句

1. **謝** — **thank (V); surname**

   謝先生，你不要謝我，你謝我先生吧。

   ☞ 謝謝 — thanks, thank you (V)

   A: 這是你的書嗎？
   B: 是。謝謝。你在哪兒找到的？

   ☞ 多謝 — many thanks, thanks a lot (IE)

   A: 你送我這麼名貴的錶。多謝，多謝。
   B: 沒甚麼。小意思。

   ☞ 不謝 — don't mention it, not at all (IE)

   A: 謝謝你請我吃飯。
   B: 不謝。我很高興你可以來。

2. **當** — **just at (a time or place); serve as; should, must (V)**

   (1) A: 你長大以後，想當甚麼？
       B: 我想當老師。

   (2) A: 當我去找他的時候，他在吃飯。
       B: 他沒請你吃飯嗎？
       A: 請了，可是我不好意思在那兒吃。

3. **然** — **but, nevertheless, however (Conj)**

   ☞ 當然 — as it should be, without doubt, certainly, of course, naturally (Adv)

   (1) A: 你為甚麼老生他的氣？
       B: 因為他老沒事找事，我當然生氣了。

   (2) 學生有問題當然得去問老師。

   ☞ 然後 — then, after that, afterwards (Conj)

   你最好先作功課然後再去看電影。

☞ 天然　　　natural (Adj)

　　　　　　這是天然的水，很好喝。

☞ 要不然　　otherwise, if not, or else (Conj)

　　　　　　你得馬上給他錢，要不然他就不是你的朋友了。

☞ 不以為然　not approve (IE)

　　　　　　你說的話，我不以為然。我不同意。

4. 雖　　　　**though, although, even though (Conj)**

☞ 雖然　　　though, although (Conj)

　　　　　　(1) 那個人雖然沒上過學，可是他的學問很好。

　　　　　　(2) 雖然我會說中國話，可是我不會看中國字。

5. 圖　　　　**picture, drawing, chart, map (N)**

☞ 地圖　　　map (N)

　　　　　　A: 你有中國地圖嗎？

　　　　　　B: 有。

☞ 圖表　　　chart, diagram, graph (N)

　　　　　　你作報告的時候，最好有幾個圖表。

☞ 圖書　　　books (N)

　　　　　　我家有很多圖書。

☞ 圖書館　　library (PW)

　　　　　　我很喜歡在圖書館作功課。

6. 常　　　　**ordinary, common, normal; frequently, often (Adv)**

　　　　　　A: 你常給你太太寫信嗎？

　　　　　　B: 我不常給她寫信，可是我天天給她打電話。

☞ 常常　　　frequently, often, usually (Adv)

　　　　　　謝先生常常告訴我們他在美國的經驗。

Lesson 13 Reply to a friend's e-mail
第十三課 回朋友的電子信

☞ 常見   commonplace (SV)
           這樣小氣的人不常見。

☞ 常識   general knowledge, common sense (N)
           他沒上過大學，可是他的常識比上過大學的人還多。

☞ 經常   daily; constantly, often (Adv)
           (1) 我不怕考試，因為我們經常考。
           (2) 他爸爸經常不在家。

☞ 日常   daily; commonplace (Adj)
           我媽媽來信告訴我家日常的事情。

☞ 時常   often, frequently (Adv)
           我的好朋友最近心情不好，時常生氣。

7. 用   **use, employ** (V)
           A: 你會用中文寫信嗎？
           B: 現在還不會。

☞ 日用   daily expenses; for everyday use (Adj)
           A: 你媽媽給你的日用錢夠不夠？
           B: 現在夠，以後就不知道了。

☞ 常用   in common use, commonly-used, often used (Adj)
           我常用電腦寫報告。

☞ 用人   choose a person for a job, make use of personnel (VO)
           (1) 我爸爸說作進出口生意用人最難。
           (2) 他喜歡用熱心的人給他作事。

☞ 用功   hardworking, diligent, studious (SV)
           (1) 我的學生都很用功，他們一天到晚看書。
           (2) 用功的學生，考試的時候不怕。

☞ 用心　　　diligently; attentively, with concentrated attention (SV)

你作事的時候一定得用心，要不然就作不好。

☞ 不用　　　need not (IE)

媽媽，我的錢夠用了，你不用寄來了。謝謝你。

☞ 用不了　　have more than is needed, use less than, not use up (RV)

(1) 這本書用不了這麼多錢。

(2) 你們今天的考試用不了兩個小時。

(3) 他的錢太多了，他一定用不了。

☞ 心不二用　concentrate on one thing at a time (IE)

我作事的時候從來是心不二用。

8. 出　　**go or come out** (V)

☞ 出去　　　go out; get out (V)

(1) 今天天氣很好，我們要出去慢跑嗎？

(2) 出去！我不要再看見你。

☞ 出來　　　come out (V)

(1) 出來！我有話要跟你說。

(2) 這個字是甚麼意思我想出來了。

☞ 出門　　　be away from home; go on a journey, go out (V)

(1) 你一個人出門，得多小心。

(2) A: 你甚麼時候再出門？

　　 B: 最近一兩天。

(3) A: 我媽媽一天到晚在家不出門。

　　 B: 為甚麼？

　　 A: 她不會開車。

Lesson 13 *Reply to a friend's e-mail*
第十三課 回朋友的電子信

☞ 出國   go abroad (VO)
         現在很多中國人想出國。

☞ 出口   exit (PW); export (V)
         我在圖書館出口的地方等你。

☞ 進出口 imports and exports; exits and entrances (Adj)
         我爸爸作進出口的生意。

9. 所   **place** (N); (MW for houses)

☞ 所以   so, therefore, as a result (Conj)
         A: 你今天為甚麼沒來上課？
         B: 因為我家有很要緊的事情，所以沒來上課。

☞ 所有   all (Adj)
         (1) 這兒所有的錢都是他的。
         (2) A: 所有學中文的學生都去開會了，你為甚麼沒去？
             B: 因為我事先不知道，所以沒去。

10. 空   **leave empty or blank; unoccupied** (Adj)
         這兒有很多空地，我們可以在這兒跑步。

☞ 空兒   free time, spare time (IE); empty space (N)
         A: 我想去看你，不知道你甚麼時候有空兒。
         B: 我今天沒空兒，明天甚麼時候都可以。

句型練習

13.1 THE PATTERN 雖然……可是

雖然……可是 "although ... but" are two adverbial linking words. 雖然 is a movable adverb – it can be placed either in a clause-initial position or after the topic/subject. 可是 is used to begin the second clause.

(A) 雖然　　subject/topic　　clause,　　可是　　clause.
　　雖然　　中文　　　　　　很難，　　可是　　我還要學。
　　Although Chinese is very difficult, (but) I still want to learn it.

(B) Subject/topic　　雖然　　clause,　　可是　　clause.
　　中文　　　　　　雖然　　很難，　　可是　　我還要學。
　　Although Chinese is very difficult, (but) I still want to learn it.

1. 我雖然喜歡跳舞，可是今天晚上不想跳。

2. 雖然她很有錢，可是她老說她沒錢。

3. 雖然我很用功，可是我還是考得不好。

13.2 THE VERB 了

When 了 is used as a second element in an RVC, it has two basic meanings: "be able to" or "be able to finish," depending on the context.

1. A: 今天的功課你作得了嗎？
   B: 這麼多功課我一定作不了。

2. A: 你作得了這個工作嗎？
   B: 這個工作太難，我想我作不了。

3. A: 你作這麼多菜，我們怎麼吃得了？
   B: 吃不了不要緊，我們可以明天吃。

13.3 THE COMPOUND VERB 出來

13.3.1 As a second element in an RVC

出來 is a compound direction verb. It means "come out" (toward the direction of the speaker). 出來 can serve as a second element in an RVC.

1. 請出來！
2. 我們不要出來。

13.3.2 As a complement

When 出來 comes after another motion verb, it functions as a complement.

1. 學生下課以後，都很快地跑出來了。
2. 那個老人慢慢地走出來了。

13.3.3 As a resultative verb ending

When 出來 functions as a resultative verb ending, it indicates appearance, identification or achievement.

1. 我想不出來那個人的名字了。
2. A: 上學期學的字，你還寫得出來嗎？
   B: 我寫得出來。
3. A: 你有甚麼意見，請你說出來。
   B: 我有意見，可是我怕說出來。
4. A: 你認得出來我是誰嗎？
   B: 當然認得出來，你是我從前的女朋友。

13.4 THE PATTERN 沒有不……的

沒有 "don't have" and 不 "not" together with the particle 的 form a double negative pattern, literally meaning "there is nothing not possible." It is a strong statement to show resolution.

1. 沒有學不會的事。
2. 要是你天天上課,就沒有考不好的。
3. 沒有不愛錢的人。

13.5 THE PATTERN 先……然後

先 "first" and 然後 "then, after that, afterwards" together express the sequence of two actions.

1. 我們先去圖書館,然後再去寄信。
2. 你得先會開車,然後我再給你我的車。
3. 我們最好先點菜,然後再談生意。

13.6 THE PATTERN 得……要不然

得 "have to, must" is a nonmovable adverb. It has to stand before the verb, while 要不然 "otherwise" stands at the beginning of the second clause.

1. 你得給他回信,要不然他會很生氣的。
2. 我們得快點兒走,要不然就晚了。
3. 這個字的意思,你得看上下文,要不然很難知道。
4. 上課的時候,你得心不二用,要不然你就不知道老師在說甚麼。

13.7 THE PATTERN 當……的時候

當 "during" is often placed at the beginning of a sentence to serve as an adverb of time and 的時候 "when, while" serves as an object of 當. The 當……的時候 pattern indicates the time at which something happens.

1. 當老師寫字的時後,你得用心看。

2. 當爸爸作進出口生意的時後,他經常不在家。

3. 當所有的功課都作好的時後,我最開心。

13.8 THE LINKING ADVERBS 因為……所以

> 因為……所以 "because ... therefore" links two clauses in a sentence to express cause and effect or a reason. 因為 can come either after the subject/topic or in a clause-initial position, while the second clause is started with 所以, as in (1) and (2) below. Sometimes either 因為 or 所以 can be omitted from a sentence, as in (3) and (4) below.

1. 他因為很累,所以不要上課。

2. 因為他很累,所以不要上課。

3. 他很累,所以不要上課。

4. 他因為很累,不要上課。

造句

1.
經常 — daily
經常出門。
最近經常出門。
誰最近經常出門?
我先生最近經常出門。

2.
常
常去。
常去圖書館。
我常去圖書館。
我常去圖書館作功課。

3.
雖然
雖然我沒空兒
雖然我沒空兒,我還得去看他。
雖然今天我沒空兒,我還得去看他。

4.
再……吧
先吃飯再去圖書館吧!
最好先吃飯再去圖書館吧!
我們最好先吃飯再去圖書館吧!

❀ 問答

1. 國英,明天請你到我家來吃便飯,好嗎? —— 好,謝謝,你太客氣了。

2. 思文,你想海英的媽媽愛她嗎? —— 當然愛她。我想沒有媽媽不愛她們孩子的。

3. 你們怎麼那麼用功?一天到晚不出去。 —— 不用功考不好。

4. 思文為甚麼老考第一名? —— 因為他作功課的時候很用心。

5. 時候不早了,我們快去上課吧!要不然就太晚了。 —— 好。我馬上就來。

6. 你爸爸作甚麼生意? —— 他以前作進出口生意,現在不作了。

7. 我想請你去跳舞,你甚麼時候有空兒? —— 我這星期天沒事,我們晚上八點鐘可以去。

8. 我認為我們的考試太多了。你說呢? —— 雖然考試很多,可是我認為常常考試很好。

9. 你想我是先在這兒學中文好還是去中國以後再學中文好? —— 我想最好是先在這兒學一兩年中文,然後再去中國好。

10. 前天誰去他的茶會了? —— 他所有的朋友都去了。

Lesson 13 Reply to a friend's e-mail
第十三課 回朋友的電子信

🌸 閱讀練習

便 飯

　　有一天，小葉請老王跟他們的幾個中國朋友吃飯。小葉跟老王是在美國長大的中國人。他們懂中文，可是不太好。小葉知道中國人很客氣，常常用"小"說自己的東西，用"大"說別人的東西。我們知道請朋友吃飯的時候，說來吃"便飯"是客氣話，所以他想對老王更客氣一點兒。他吃飯的時候，就說，"今天的小便飯不太好，請你多吃一點兒。"老王一想小葉這麼客氣，我也應該更客氣一點兒，所以他就說，"你太客氣了，今天的大便飯太好吃了。我吃得太多了。"他們的中國朋友聽見以後就都笑了。你知道為甚麼嗎？

請查生詞

Look up the following words in a dictionary.

懂	dǒng	聽見	tīngjian
自己	zìjǐ	笑	xiào
東西	dōngxi	笑話	xiàohuà
別人	biérén	應該	yīnggāi
客氣	kèqi	注意	zhùyì
更	gèng		

填 空

Fill in the blanks with the appropriate words from the story.

1. 他說的 _____ _____ ，你聽 _____ 了沒有？

2. 我 _____ 見了，可是我 _____ 不 _____ ，所以沒有笑。這是不是不太 _____ _____ ？

第十四課　假期有甚麼打算？
Lesson 14　What plans do you have for vacation?

Lesson 14
Pinyin Text

CONTENTS

*T*ext   116

*V*ocabulary and Illustrative Sentences   117
(jiān, wán, fàng, jià, suàn, fù, qǐ, hào, lǚ, xíng)

*P*attern Drills   123
(yīhuìr, cóng, wèi, wán and hǎo, qǐ)

*S*entence Building   128
(cóng ... dào, dǎsuàn, yìqǐ, wán le)

*Q*uestions and Responses   128

*P*ronunciation Review   129

*F*un Activity   130

*S*upplementary Vocabulary   130

*C*ultural Notes   131

🌸 Text

Jiàqī yǒu shénme dǎsuàn?
What plans do you have for vacation?

Wáng lǎoshī: Shíjiān guòde zhēn kuài, míngtiān xīngqīwǔ, mǎshàng yì xīngqī jiù yào wán le, xià xīngqīyī yě fàng jià. Nǐmen dōu yǒu shénme dǎsuàn?

Time passes by so quickly and it's Friday tomorrow. Soon this week will be over and next Monday is also a holiday. What plans do you have for vacation?

Mǎ Sīwén: Wǒ xīngqīsì yǒu yí ge kǎoshì, xīngqīwǔ méiyǒu kè, suǒyǐ wǒ yì kǎowán jiù huí jiā. Huí jiā yǐhòu jiù qù kàn wǒ jiā fùjìn de péngyou.

I have an exam on Thursday and I don't have classes on Friday, so I will go home right after my exam. After I get home I will visit friends who live nearby.

Wáng lǎoshī: Mǎ Àiwén, nǐ ne?

Ma Aiwen, what about you?

Mǎ Àiwén: Wǒ gēn gēge yìqǐ huí jiā. Zhè yuè sān hào shì wǒ bàba de shēngrì, wǒmen yào qǐng hěn duō péngyou lái gěi tā guò shēngrì.

My brother and I are going home together. The third of this month is my father's birthday. We are going to invite a lot of friends to celebrate his birthday.

Wáng lǎoshī: Xǔ Xiǎoměi, nǐ dǎsuàn zuò shénme?

Xu Xiaomei, what do you plan to do?

Xǔ Xiǎoměi: Wǒ xīngqīsì yě yí xià kè jiù huí jiā, ránhòu gēn māma dìdi qù Zhōngguó kàn wǒ bàba. Tā xiànzài zài nàr zuò shēngyi. Wǒmen hěn xiǎng tā.

I will go home right after class on Thursday, then I will go to China with my mom and little brother to visit my dad. My dad is doing business there right now. We miss him so much.

Lesson 14 What plans do you have for vacation?
第十四課 假期有甚麼打算？

Wáng lǎoshī:	Lín Hǎiyīng, nǐ zài Rìběn hái yào lǚxíng ma?	Lin Haiying, do you plan to travel around when you are in Japan?
Lín Hǎiyīng:	Wǒ zài Rìběn de shíhou, bú qù shénme dìfang lǚxíng. Nǐ zhīdào wǒ māma shì Rìběnrén, wǒmen qù Rìběn kàn māma de jiārén.	I am not traveling around in Japan. You know that my mom is Japanese. We go to Japan to visit my mom's family.
Wáng lǎoshī:	Nǐmen de jiàqī yídìng huì hěn yǒu yìsi.	Your vacations will surely be very interesting.

Vocabulary and Illustrative Sentences

1. **jiān**   **between; among; within a definite time or space (N)**

☞ shíjiān   (concept of) time; (duration of) time; (a point of) time (N)

(1) A: Māma, nǐ xiànzài yǒu kòngr ma? Wǒ yǒu shì yào gēn nǐ shuō.   Mom, are you free now? I have something to tell you.

B: Wǒ xiànzài méi shíjiān. Děng yíhuìr, hǎo ma?   I don't have time now. Wait for a while, okay?

A: Bù xíng, děng yīhuìr jiù tài wǎn le.   No, it will be too late if (we) wait for a while.

(2) A: Wǒ xiǎng jīntiān wǎnshang qǐng nǐ qù kàn diànyǐng. Nǐ yǒu shíjiān ma?   I'd like to invite you to watch a movie this evening. Do you have time for it?

B: Yǒu. Shénme shíjiān jiàn?   I do. When should we meet?

A: Qī diǎn yí kè.   7:15.

B: Hǎo.   Okay.

☞ wǎnjiān   (in the) evening; (at) night (TW)

(1) Wǒ xǐhuan zài wǎnjiān zuò gōngkè. — I like to do my homework in the evening.

(2) Nǐmen wǎnjiān chūqu yào xiǎoxīn. — You should be careful when you go out at night.

☞ zhōngjiān   among; between; center, middle (PW)

(1) Nǐ rènshi-bu-rènshi zuò zài tāmen liǎng ge rén zhōngjiān de nàge rén? — Do you recognize the person sitting between those two people?

(2) Kàn diànyǐng de shíhou, wǒ xǐhuan zuò zài zhōngjiān. — When I watch movies, I like to sit in the middle.

2. wán   **use up; finish; complete; be over** (V/RV)

A: Nǐ chī wán wǎnfàn yào qù nǎr? — Where are you going after having dinner?

B: Wǒ xiǎng qù túshūguǎn yòng diànnǎo. — I want to go to the library to use the computer.

☞ wán le   come to an end, be over (V)

(1) Wǒ de qián kuài yòng wán le. — My money is almost completely used up.

(2) Nǐmen kǎo wán le jiù kěyǐ chūqu le. — After finishing your exam, you may leave.

☞ wánměi   perfect, flawless (SV)

(1) Wánměi de rén hěn nán zhǎodào. — It's very hard to find a perfect person.

(2) Tā xiǎng tā de háizi hěn wánměi. — She thinks her child is perfect.

3. fàng   **put, place; let go, set free; give up** (V)

A: Zhège diànnǎo fàng zài nǎr? — Where (should I) place this computer?

B: Fàng zài zhèr. — Put it here.

Lesson 14 What plans do you have for vacation?
第十四課 假期有甚麼打算？

☞ fàngxīn   set one's mind at rest, be at ease, rest assured, feel relieved (SV)

(1) Wǒ yí ge rén chūqu lǚxíng, māma hěn bú fàngxīn.	My mother is very uneasy when I travel alone.
(2) Fàngxīn ba, wǒmen huì hěn xiǎoxīn de.	Rest assured, we will be very careful.

☞ xiàfàng   sent down (Cadres, etc., in Communist China, were "sent down" to work at the grassroots level or to do manual labor in the countryside or in a factory.) (V)

Zài yījiǔliùqī nián dào yījiǔ-qīliù nián qījiān, yǒu hěn duō rén xiàfàng le.	In the period between 1967 and 1976, many people were sent down (to the countryside).

☞ fàngxué   classes are over (V)

A: Fàngxué yǐhòu, wǒmen qù kàn diànyǐng hǎo ma?	When classes are over, can we go to watch a movie?
B: Bù xíng, wǒ jīntiān yǒu hěn duō gōngkè děi zuò.	(I) can't. I have a lot of homework to do today.

4. jià   **holiday, vacation; leave of absence (N)**

☞ fàngjià   have a holiday or vacation; have a day off (VO)

Fàngjià de shíhou, wǒ yào gēn jiārén yìqǐ qù lǚxíng.	During vacation, I want to travel with my family.

☞ jiàqī   vacation; period of leave (N)

Nǐ jīnnián yǒu duōshǎo tiān jiàqī?	How many days of vacation do you have this year?

☞ jiàrì   holiday; day off (N)

Dàjiā dōu xǐhuan zài jiàrì de shíhou qù kàn péngyou.	Everyone likes to visit (his or her) friends on days off.

☞ niánjià   New Year's holiday; winter vacation (N)

Jīnnián de niánjià shì cóng shí'èr-yuè èrshísì hào dào míngnián yīyuè èrshíbā hào.	This year's winter vacation goes from 24 December until 28 January of next year.

☞ qǐng jià	ask for leave (VO)	
	Wáng lǎoshī zhè xīngqī qǐng le sān tiān jià.	Professor Wang asked for a three-day leave this week.

☞ shìjià	leave of absence (to attend to private affairs) (N)	
	A: Wáng lǎoshī, míngtiān wǒ jiā yǒu shì, wǒ děi qǐng yì tiān shìjià.	Professor Wang, tomorrow I have some family affairs to take care of. I have to ask for a day off.
	B: Hǎo, nǐ zhīdào míngtiān de gōngkè shì shénme ma?	Okay, do you know what the homework for tomorrow is?
	A: Wǒ zhīdào.	I know.

5. suàn **calculate, reckon; include; count; suppose (V)**

	A: Qǐng nǐ suàn-yi-suàn, wǒmen hái yǒu jǐ tiān fàngjià?	Could you please count how many days left before our vacation?
	B: Hái yǒu shísì tiān jiù fàngjià le.	There are fourteen more days to go before our vacation.

☞ dǎsuàn	plan; intend (V/N)	
	A: Nǐ de bàogào dǎsuàn xiě shénme?	What do you plan to write about for your report?
	B: Xiànzài hái bù yídìng. Yěxǔ xiě "xiàfàng" de shìqing.	Right now I'm not sure. Perhaps (I'll) write on the topic of "being sent down."

☞ suànshì	consider as (V)	
	(1) Xiànzài Zhōngguó suànshì hěn hǎo le.	China is considered to be very good now.
	(2) Zhège diànnǎo suànshì hěn kuài de le.	This computer is considered to be fast.

☞ suàn le	forget it; drop it (IE)	
	A: Wǒ zhǎobudào nǐ de xìn.	I can't find your letter.
	B: Zhǎobudào jiù suàn le.	If you can't find it, forget it.

6. fù — **get close to, be near; attach, enclose** (V)

fùjìn — nearby, neighboring, close to, in the vicinity of (PW)

A: Zhèr fùjìn yǒu hǎo fànguǎnr ma?
Are there any good restaurants nearby?

B: Zhèr fùjìn méiyǒu hǎo de Zhōngguó fànguǎnr, búguò yǒu jǐ ge hǎo de Rìběn fànguǎnr.
There isn't any good Chinese restaurant around here, but there are a couple of good Japanese restaurants.

fùshàng — enclosed herewith (V)

Wǒ gěi nǐ de xìn fùshàng le yì zhāng Měiguó dìtú.
I am enclosing in my letter a map of the United States (for your reference).

7. qǐ — **rise, get up, stand up; start, begin** (V)

qǐlai — stand up, sit up, get up; get out of bed (V)

A: Nǐ jīntiān zǎoshang jǐ diǎn zhōng qǐlai de?
What time did you get up this morning?

B: Wǒ jīntiān wǔ diǎn zhōng jiù qǐlai le.
Today I got up at five o'clock in the morning.

yìqǐ — in the same place, together, in the company of (Adv)

A: Wǒmen yìqǐ qù túshūguǎn zuò gōngkè hǎo ma?
Let's go to the library to study together, okay?

B: Dāngrán hǎo.
Yes, of course.

qǐjiàn — for the purpose of; in order to (N)

Wèi le dédào jīngyàn qǐjiàn, wǒ dǎsuàn fàngjià de shíhou qù zuò shì.
In order to get some experience, I plan to work during vacation.

qǐxiān — at first, in the beginning (Adv)

Wǒ xué Zhōngwén de shíhou, qǐxiān hěn nán, sān ge yuè yǐhòu jiù bù nán le.
When I was studying Chinese, it was hard at the beginning, but things get better after three months.

	kànbuqǐ	look down upon, scorn, despise (IE)	
		Tā kànbuqǐ méiyǒu xuéwèn de rén.	He looks down upon uneducated people.
	chīdeqǐ	can afford to eat (RV)	
		A: Tiāntiān chī fànguǎnr, nǐ chīdeqǐ chībuqǐ?	Can you afford to dine at restaurants every day?
		B: Wǒ chībuqǐ.	I can't afford it.
	qǐyīn	cause; origin (N)	
		A: Zhège shìqing de qǐyīn, nǐ zhīdào-bu-zhīdào?	Do you know the cause of this matter?
		B: Wǒ zhīdào yìdiǎnr. Qǐyīn shì yīnwèi tāmen liǎng ge rén de yìjiàn bù tóng.	I know a bit. That's because those two people have different opinions.

8. **hào**   **date; number; size** (N)

	jǐ hào	which day of the month; what number (QW)	
		(1) A: Jīntiān shì jǐ yuè jǐ hào?	What is today's date?
		B: Sānyuè shíwǔ hào.	Today is 15 March.
		(2) A: Nǐ de diànhuà shì jǐ hào?	What is your telephone number?
		B: Qībāyī-èrbāsān-wǔliùsìjiǔ.	781-283-5649.
	wènhào	question mark; unknown factor; unsolved problem (N)	
		(1) Nǐ shénme shíhou yòng wènhào?	When do you use a question mark?
		(2) Wǒmen míngnián kěyǐ-bu-kěyǐ qù Zhōngguó háishì yí ge wènhào.	Whether we can go to China next year is still unsettled.

9. **lǚ**   **travel; stay away from home** (V)

	lǚguǎn	hotel (N)

Lesson 14 *What plans do you have for vacation?*
第十四課 假期有甚麼打算？

	(1) Zhège lǚguǎn xíng-bu-xíng?	Is this hotel okay?
	(2) Xíng. Hěn hǎo.	Yes. It's very good.

10. **xíng** — **go; travel** (V); **all right, okay; capable** (SV)

☞ **lǚxíng** — travel; journey, tour (V)

    A: Wǒ zuì xǐhuan lǚxíng, kěshì lǚxíng hěn guì. — I particularly like traveling, but the cost of travel is very expensive.

    B: Nǐ jīnnián dǎsuàn qù nǎr lǚxíng? — Where are you going to travel this year?

    A: Hái bù yídìng. — I am not sure yet.

☞ **bùxíng** — won't do; be out of the question (IE)

    A: Bàba, wǒ jīntiān wǎnshang kěyǐ yòng nǐ de chē ma? — Dad, may I use your car tonight?

    B: Bùxíng. Wǒ jīntiān wǎnshang děi qù kāihuì. — No, I have to go for a meeting tonight.

☞ **bùxíng** — go on foot, walk (V)

    A: Nǐ jīntiān zěnme shì bùxíng lái de, méi kāichē? — Why did you walk here today? Didn't you drive?

    B: Jīntiān tiānqì hěn hǎo, wǒ xǐhuan zǒulù. — The weather is very nice today. I enjoy walking.

☞ **sòngxíng** — see somebody off; give a send-off party (V)

    Zhēn xièxie nǐmen gěi wǒ sòngxíng. Wǒ huì cháng gěi nǐmen xiě xìn de. — Thank you very much for seeing me off. I will write to you often.

🐾 Pattern Drills

14.1 THE TIME WORD yīhuìr

Yīhuìr "in a moment, a (little) while" can be used before a verb or after a verbal expression.

1. A: Tā shénme shíhou lái? — When is she coming?
   B: Tā yīhuìr jiù lái. — She will be here shortly.
2. A: Qǐng nǐ zài zhèr děng yīhuìr. — Please wait here for a while.
   B: Hǎo. Xièxie. — Okay. Thank you.
3. A: Zài duō zuò yīhuìr! — (Please) stay a little while.
   B: Bù zǎo le, wǒ děi zǒu le. — It's getting late. I have to go now.

14.2 SENTENCE PATTERNS WITH cóng

14.2.1 The pattern cóng ... dào

> The pattern cóng ... dào "from ... to" can indicate from one place to another or from one point of time to another point of time.

1. A: Cóng nǐ jiā dào wǒ jiā yuǎn-bu-yuǎn? — Is it far from your house to my house?
   B: Bú suàn yuǎn, shí fēnzhōng jiù dào le. — Not too far. You can get there in ten minutes.
2. A: Cóng Rìběn dào Zhōngguó hěn jìn ma? — Is it very close from Japan to China?
   B: Hěn jìn, liǎng ge duō zhōngtóu jiù dào le. — Very close. You can get there in around two hours.
3. A: Cóng lǚguǎn dào fàndiàn zěnme zǒu? — How do I get to the restaurant from the hotel?
   B: Hěn yuǎn. Nǐ zuìhǎo jiào yí ge chē qù. — It's very far. You'd better call a taxi.
4. A: Nǐ xīngqī jǐ yǒu kè? — On which days do you have classes?
   B: Cóng xīngqīyī dào xīngqīwǔ, wǒ dōu yǒu kè. — I have classes from Monday to Friday.
5. A: Nǐ kàn le jǐ ge zhōngtóu de shū le? — How many hours have you been reading?
   B: Wǒ cóng zǎoshang bā diǎn kàndào xiànzài. — I've been reading from eight o'clock in the morning till now.

6. A: Cóng fàngjià dào xiànzài, wǒ méi shuōguo Zhōngguóhuà.
   B: Zhēnde!

   I haven't spoken any Chinese since the beginning of the vacation.
   Really!

7. Wǒ cóng yījiǔjiǔbā nián dào èrlínglínglíng nián zài Zhōngguó xué Zhōngwén.

   I studied Chinese in China from 1998 to 2000.

14.2.2 The pattern cóng ... qǐ

The pattern cóng ... qǐ "since, as of" indicates a duration of time.

1. Cóng míngtiān qǐ, wǒ jiù bú zuò shì le.
   I am not working anymore from tomorrow onwards.

2. Cóng fàngjià qǐ, wǒ tiāntiān kàn yì běn Zhōngwén xiǎoshuō.
   I have been reading one Chinese short story each day since vacation started.

3. Cóng xīngqī'èr qǐ, wǒ zài fùjìn túshūguǎn gōngzuò.
   I'll be working at the local library from Tuesday onwards.

14.3 SENTENCE PATTERNS WITH wèi

14.3.1 The verb wèi

The verb wèi indicates the object of one's action or intention.

1. Bàba māma wèi wǒmen zuò hěn duō shì.
   Dad and Mom have done a lot of things for us.

2. Tā wèi nǐ zuò nàme duō shì, nǐ yīnggāi xièxie tā.
   She has done so much for you. You should thank her.

14.3.2 The pattern wèi le ... qǐjiàn

When wèi le is accompanied by qǐjiàn, it means "in order to, for the purpose of."

1. Wèi le xué Zhōngwén qǐjiàn, wǒ dǎsuàn dào Zhōngguó qù.
   In order to study Chinese, I plan to go to China.

2. **Wèi le** jiào māma fàngxīn **qǐjiàn**, wǒ tiāntiān gěi tā dǎ yí ge diànhuà.

    I call my mom every day so that she won't worry about me.

3. **Wèi le** jiàqī kěyǐ qù lǚxíng **qǐjiàn**, wǒ děi qù zuò shì.

    In order to be able to go on a trip during vacation, I must work.

14.4 Wán AND hǎo

The words wán "finish, complete, end" and hǎo "satisfaction, completion" as the second element in an RVC convey the completion and/or achievement described by the first element introduced.

1. A: Wǒmen jiào zhème duō cài, chīde**wán** ma?

    We have ordered so many dishes. Can we finish eating them?

    B: Zhème duō rén dāngrán chīde**wán**.

    There are so many of us. We are sure to finish everything.

2. A: Jīntiān de shìqing nǐ zuòde**wán** ma?

    Can you finish today's work?

    B: Yídìng děi zuò**wán**.

    (I) definitely have to finish it.

3. A: Nǐ māma gěi nǐ nàme duō qián, nǐ yòngde**wán** ma?

    Your mother gave you so much money. Can you spend it all?

    B: Dāngrán yòngde**wán**, nǐ zhīdào xiànzài shū hěn guì.

    Of course I can spend all the money. You know, books are very expensive nowadays.

4. A: Nǐ de bàogào xiě**hǎo** le ma?

    Have you finished writing your report?

    B: Zǎo yǐjīng xiě**hǎo** le.

    I have already finished writing it for some time.

5. A: Nǐ lǚxíng yǐqián, shìqing zuòde**hǎo** zuòbu**hǎo**?

    Can you finish the job before you go on vacation?

    B: Māma shuō shìqing zuòbu**hǎo**, jiù bù néng qù lǚxíng.

    Mother said that I can't go on vacation if I can't finish the job.

6. A: Nǐ xiǎng tā xiěde**hǎo** zhè běn xiǎoshuō ma?

    Do you think he can write this novel well?

    B: Wǒ xiǎng tā xiěde**hǎo**. Tā hěn huì xiě xiǎoshuō.

    I think he can. He writes novels well.

14.5 THE VERB qǐ

When the verb qǐ "up" is used as a second element in an RVC, it means "afford to." Qǐ can only be used in potential form and must be accompanied by -de or -bu. For example, the question "Can you afford to buy a car?" in Chinese will be nǐ mǎideqǐ qìchē ma? **but not** nǐ mǎiqǐ qìchē ma? The following are some commonly-used expressions:

chīdeqǐ	can afford to eat
chībuqǐ	cannot afford to eat
chuāndeqǐ	can afford to wear
chuānbuqǐ	cannot afford to wear
mǎideqǐ	can afford to buy
mǎibuqǐ	cannot afford to buy
zhùdeqǐ	can afford to live
zhùbuqǐ	cannot afford to live

1. A: Tā zěnme mǎideqǐ nàme guì de chē? — How can he afford to buy such an expensive car?

   B: Tā jiā hěn yǒu qián. — His family is very rich.

2. A: Tiāntiān zài fànguǎn chīfàn, chīdeqǐ chībuqǐ? — Can one afford to eat at a restaurant everyday?

   B: Yǒude rén chīdeqǐ, yǒude rén chībuqǐ. — Some people can, but some people can't?

The following usages of qǐ are idiomatic expressions:

duìdeqǐ	not let somebody down; treat somebody fairly
duìbuqǐ	sorry, excuse me, beg your pardon
kàndeqǐ	think highly of (someone)
kànbuqǐ	look down on, despise (someone)

1. A: Nǐ bù yīnggāi kànbuqǐ tā. — You shouldn't look down on him.

   B: Wǒ cónglái méi kànbuqǐ tā. — I've never looked down on him.

2. A: Duìbuqǐ, wǒ lái wǎn le. — Sorry, I am late.

   B: Méishénme. — It doesn't matter.

3. A: Duìbuqǐ, nǐ shuō shénme? Wǒ méi tīngjian.
   Pardon me, what did you say? I didn't hear you.

   B: Méi tīngjian jiù suàn le.
   If you didn't hear it, forget it.

(Note that some of the vocabulary in this lesson, such as <u>chuān</u> "to wear," <u>zhù</u> "to live," and <u>duì</u> "to face," have not been introduced in the text.)

Sentence Building

1.
Cóng ... dào
Cóng zhèr dào nàr.
Cóng zhèr dào nàr yuǎn-bu-yuǎn?
Bú tài yuǎn, hěn jìn.

2.
Dǎsuàn
Yǒu shénme dǎsuàn?
Jiàqī yǒu shénme dǎsuàn?
Nǐ jiàqī yǒu shénme dǎsuàn?

3.
Yìqǐ
Yìqǐ qù lǚxíng.
Yìqǐ qù lǚxíng yǒuyìsi.
Yìqǐ qù lǚxíng yǒu-méiyǒu yìsi?
Gēn péngyou yìqǐ qù lǚxíng yǒu-méiyǒu yìsi?

4.
Wán le
Kǎoshì wán le.
Kǎoshì wán le zuò shénme?
Kǎoshì wán le jiù qù kàn diànyǐng.
Wǒmen kǎoshì wán le jiù qù kàn diànyǐng.

Questions and Responses

1. Nǐ cóng nǎ nián dào nǎ nián zài Měiguó?
   From which year to which year were you in the United States?
   Wǒ cóng yìjiǔbāqī nián dào yìjiǔjiǔsì nián zài Měiguó.
   From 1987 to 1994, I was in the United States.

2. Nǐmen jǐ yuè jǐ hào fàngjià?
   When will you go on vacation?
   Wǒmen shí'èryuè èrshísān hào fàngjià.
   We will start our vacation on 23 December.

3. Nǐ jiā fùjìn yǒu-méiyǒu túshūguǎn?
   Is there a library near your house?
   Wǒ jiā fùjìn cóngqián yǒu yí ge xiǎo túshūguǎn, kěshì xiànzài méiyǒu le.
   There was a small library near my house once, but now it's gone.

Lesson 14 *What plans do you have for vacation?*
第十四課 假期有甚麼打算？

4. Nǐ dǎsuàn shénme shíhou chū guó? Zhè xuéqī yì wán wǒ jiù chū guó.
   When do you plan to go abroad? Once this term is over, I will go abroad.

5. Nǐ cháng gēn shéi yìqǐ qù kàn diànyǐng? Dāngrán shì gēn wǒ de nǚpéngyou le.
   With whom do you often go to watch movies? Of course, I go with my girlfriend.

6. Nǐ wèishénme qǐng jià? Yīnwèi wǒ jiā jīntiān yǒu shì.
   Why did you ask for a day off? Because I've got some family matters to take care of today.

7. Nǐ chīwán wǎnfàn dào wǒ jiā lái, hǎo ma? Jīntiān wǎnshang bùxíng. Míngtiān kěyǐ.
   Come over to my place after dinner, okay? Tonight I can't. Tomorrow is okay.

8. Nǐ xǐhuan qù nǎr lǚxíng? Nǎr yǒu yìsi wǒ xǐhuan qù nǎr lǚxíng.
   Where do you wish to go traveling? I like to go wherever there is fun.

9. Lǎoshī gēn nǐ shuō de huà, nǐ tīngjian le méiyǒu? Tīng shì tīngjian le, kěshì wǒ tīngbudǒng.
   Did you hear what the teacher told you? I heard it all right, but I didn't understand it.

10. Zhè shì jīntiān de bàozhǐ ma? Bú shì, shì qiántiān de.
    Is this today's newspaper? No. It's the day before yesterday's.

Pronunciation Review

(1) Tonal Shifts in Stressed bù and yī

(a) bù-dā   (e) yìtiān
(b) bù-dá   (f) yìmáo
(c) bù-dǎ   (g) yìběn
(d) bú-dà   (h) yíkuài

(2) Differentiating Toned and Toneless Second Syllables

(a) dōngxī   dōngxi   (c) mǎimǎ   mǎima
(b) kuàilè   kuàile   (d) lǎomā   lǎoma

🐾 Fun Activity

Let's Learn a Chinese Children's Song

| Dà Tóu |
Big Head
Dà tóu, dà tóu,   Big head, big head.
Xià yǔ bù chóu.   There is nothing to dread when it rains.
Nǐ yǒu yǔsǎn,   You have an umbrella,
Wǒ yǒu dà tóu.   I have my big head.

🐾 Supplementary Vocabulary

American Soft Drinks and Fast Food

Kěkǒukělè	Coca-Cola	règǒu	hot dog
shǔtiáo	French fries	Bǎishìkělè	Pepsi
zhájī	fried chicken	písà	pizza
hànbǎobǎo	hamburger	Qīxǐ	Seven-up

🐾 Cultural Notes

Response to compliments — nǎlǐ, nǎlǐ

Traditionally, Chinese people do not say "thank you" in response to a personal compliment of any kind. Rather, some sort of demurral is used as a response. Chinese people often turn away compliments as a way of expressing modesty. Accepting a personal compliment might sound conceited to Chinese people. Thus, it is customary for Chinese people to respond to compliments with expressions such as nǎlǐ, nǎlǐ which means "where, where?" literally. Figuratively, nǎlǐ, nǎlǐ means, "I have done nothing to deserve your compliment."

Therefore, if someone comments that your Chinese is very good, you should respond with nǎlǐ, nǎlǐ or bùhǎo, bùhǎo. Don't say xièxie "thank you" in response to a personal compliment, it may mean "thank you for your kind compliment" to a Westerner, but to a Chinese, xièxie means "I agree with your assessment."

第十四課
漢字本

內容

課文   134

生詞及例句   135
(間、完、放、假、算、附、起、號、旅、行)

句型練習   140
(一會兒、從、為、完和好、起)

造句   143
(從……到、打算、一起、完了)

問答   144

閱讀練習   144
你給你孩子吃甚麼？

課文

假期有甚麼打算？

王老師：時間過得真快，明天星期五，馬上一星期就要完了，下星期一也放假。你們都有甚麼打算？

馬思文：我星期四有一個考試，星期五沒有課，所以我一考完就回家。回家以後就去看我家附近的朋友。

王老師：馬愛文，你呢？

馬愛文：我跟哥哥一起回家。這月三號是我爸爸的生日，我們要請很多朋友來給他過生日。

王老師：許小美，你打算作甚麼？

許小美：我星期四也一下課就回家，然後跟媽媽弟弟去中國看我爸爸。他現在在那兒作生意。我們很想他。

王老師：林海英，你在日本還要旅行嗎？

林海英：我在日本的時候，不去甚麼地方旅行。你知道我媽媽是日本人，我們去日本看媽媽的家人。

王老師：你們的假期一定會很有意思。

Lesson 14 What plans do you have for vacation?
第十四課 假期有甚麼打算？

生詞及例句

1. **間**   **between; among; within a definite time or space (N)**

   ☞ 時間   (concept of) time; (duration of) time; (a point of) time (N)

   (1) A: 媽媽，你現在有空兒嗎？我有事要跟你說。
       B: 我現在沒時間。等一會兒，好嗎？
       A: 不行，等一會兒就太晚了。

   (2) A: 我想今天晚上請你去看電影。你有時間嗎？
       B: 有。甚麼時間見？
       A: 七點一刻。
       B: 好。

   ☞ 晚間   (in the) evening; (at) night (TW)

   (1) 我喜歡在晚間作功課。
   (2) 你們晚間出去要小心。

   ☞ 中間   among; between; center, middle (PW)

   (1) 你認不認識坐在他們兩個人中間的那個人？
   (2) 看電影的時候，我喜歡坐在中間。

2. **完**   **use up; finish; complete; be over (V/RV)**

   A: 你吃完晚飯要去哪兒？
   B: 我想去圖書館用電腦。

   ☞ 完了   come to an end, be over (V)

   (1) 我的錢快用完了。
   (2) 你們考完了就可以出去了。

   ☞ 完美   perfect, flawless (SV)

   (1) 完美的人很難找到。
   (2) 她想她的孩子很完美。

3. 放　**put, place; let go, set free; give up** (V)

A: 這個電腦放在哪兒?

B: 放在這兒。

☞ 放心　set one's mind at rest, be at ease, rest assured, feel relieved (SV)

(1) 我一個人出去旅行,媽媽很不放心。

(2) 放心吧,我們會很小心的。

☞ 下放　sent down (Cadres, etc., in Communist China, were "sent down" to work at the grassroots level or to do manual labor in the countryside or in a factory.) (V)

在一九六七年到一九七六年期間,有很多人下放了。

☞ 放學　classes are over (V)

A: 放學以後,我們去看電影好嗎?

B: 不行,我今天有很多功課得作。

4. 假　**holiday, vacation; leave of absence** (N)

☞ 放假　have a holiday or vacation; have a day off (VO)

放假的時候,我要跟家人一起去旅行。

☞ 假期　vacation; period of leave (N)

你今年有多少天假期?

☞ 假日　holiday; day off (N)

大家都喜歡在假日的時候去看朋友。

☞ 年假　New Year's holiday; winter vacation (N)

今年的年假是從十二月二十四號到明年一月二十八號。

☞ 請假　ask for leave (VO)

王老師這星期請了三天假。

Lesson 14 What plans do you have for vacation?
第十四課 假期有甚麼打算？   137

☞ 事假   leave of absence (to attend to private affairs) (N)
            A: 王老師，明天我家有事，我得請一天事假。
            B: 好，你知道明天的功課是甚麼嗎？
            A: 我知道。

5. 算   **calculate, reckon; include; count; suppose** (V)
            A: 請你算一算，我們還有幾天放假？
            B: 還有十四天就放假了。

☞ 打算   plan; intend (V/N)
            A: 你的報告打算寫甚麼？
            B: 現在還不一定。也許寫"下放"的事情。

☞ 算是   consider as (V)
            (1) 現在中國算是很好了。
            (2) 這個電腦算是很快的了。

☞ 算了   forget it; drop it (IE)
            A: 我找不到你的信。
            B: 找不到就算了。

6. 附   **get close to, be near; attach, enclose** (V)
☞ 附近   nearby, neighboring, close to, in the vicinity of (PW)
            A: 這兒附近有好飯館兒嗎？
            B: 這兒附近沒有好的中國飯館兒，不過有幾個好的日本飯館兒。

☞ 附上   enclosed herewith (V)
            我給你的信附上了一張美國地圖。

7. **起** **rise, get up, stand up; start, begin** (V)

☞ 起來　stand up, sit up, get up; get out of bed (V)

A: 你今天早上幾點鐘起來的？

B: 我今天五點鐘就起來了。

☞ 一起　in the same place, together, in the company of (Adv)

A: 我們一起去圖書館作功課好嗎？

B: 當然好。

☞ 起見　for the purpose of; in order to (N)

為了得到經驗起見，我打算放假的時候去作事。

☞ 起先　at first, in the beginning (Adv)

我學中文的時候，起先很難，三個月以後就不難了。

☞ 看不起　look down upon, scorn, despise (IE)

他看不起沒有學問的人。

☞ 吃得起　can afford to eat (RV)

A: 天天吃飯館兒，你吃得起吃不起？

B: 我吃不起。

☞ 起因　cause; origin (N)

A: 這個事情的起因，你知道不知道？

B: 我知道一點兒。起因是因為他們兩個人的意見不同。

8. **號** **date; number; size** (N)

☞ 幾號　which day of the month; what number (QW)

(1) A: 今天是幾月幾號？

　　B: 三月十五號。

(2) A: 你的電話是幾號？

　　B: 七八一－二八三－五六四九。

Lesson 14 What plans do you have for vacation?
第十四課 假期有甚麼打算？

☞ 問號   question mark; unknown factor; unsolved problem (N)

(1) 你甚麼時候用問號？

(2) 我們明年可以不可以去中國還是一個問號。

9. 旅   **travel; stay away from home** (V)

☞ 旅館   hotel (N)

A: 這個旅館行不行？

B: 行。很好。

為了… 起見
zhong wen   *wǒ chū zhong guo.*

10. 行   **go; travel** (V); **all right, okay; capable** (SV)

☞ 旅行   travel; journey, tour (V)

A: 我最喜歡旅行，可是旅行很貴。

B: 你今年打算去哪兒旅行？

A: 還不一定。

V得起 V不得起
↳ able to afford.

☞ 不行   won't do; be out of the question (IE)

A: 爸爸，我今天晚上可以用你的車嗎？

B: 不行。我今天晚上得去開會。

☞ 步行   go on foot, walk (V)

A: 你今天怎麼是步行來的，沒開車？

B: 今天天氣很好，我喜歡走路。

☞ 送行   see somebody off; give a send-off party (V)

真謝謝你們給我送行。我會常給你們寫信的。

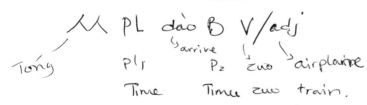

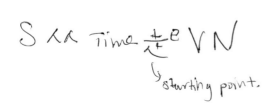

句型練習

14.1 THE TIME WORD 一會兒

一會兒 "in a moment, a (little) while" can be used before a verb or after a verbal expression.

1. A: 她甚麼時候來？
   B: 她一會兒就來。

2. A: 請你在這兒等一會兒。
   B: 好。謝謝。

3. A: 再多坐一會兒！
   B: 不早了，我得走了。

14.2 SENTENCE PATTERNS WITH 從

14.2.1 The pattern 從……到

The pattern 從……到 "from ... to" can indicate from one place to another or from one point of time to another point of time.

1. A: 從你家到我家遠不遠？
   B: 不算遠，十分鐘就到了。

2. A: 從日本到中國很近嗎？
   B: 很近，兩個多鐘頭就到了。

3. A: 從旅館到飯店怎麼走？
   B: 很遠。你最好叫一個車去。

4. A: 你星期幾有課？
   B: 從星期一到星期五，我都有課。

5. A: 你看了幾個鐘頭的書了？
   B: 我從早上八點看到現在。

6. A: 從放假到現在,我沒說過中國話。
   B: 真的!

7. 我從一九九八年到二〇〇〇年在中國學中文。

14.2.2 The pattern 從……起

The pattern 從……起 "since, as of" indicates a duration of time.

1. 從明天起,我就不作事了。
2. 從放假起,我天天看一本中文小說。
3. 從星期二起,我在附近圖書館工作。

14.3 SENTENCE PATTERNS WITH 為

14.3.1 The verb 為

The verb 為 indicates the object of one's action or intention.

1. 爸爸媽媽為我們作很多事。
2. 她為你作那麼多事,你應該謝謝她。

14.3.2 The pattern 為了……起見

When 為了 is accompanied by 起見, it means "in order to, for the purpose of."

1. 為了學中文起見,我打算到中國去。
2. 為了叫媽媽放心起見,我天天給她打一個電話。
3. 為了假期可以去旅行起見,我得去作事。

14.4 完 AND 好

The words 完 "finish, complete, end" and 好 "satisfaction, completion" as the second element in an RVC convey the completion and/or achievement described by the first element introduced.

1. A: 我們叫這麼多菜,吃得完嗎?
   B: 這麼多人當然吃得完。

2. A: 今天的事情你作得完嗎?
   B: 一定得作完。

3. A: 你媽媽給你那麼多錢,你用得完嗎?
   B: 當然用得完,你知道現在書很貴。

4. A: 你的報告寫好了嗎?
   B: 早已經寫好了。

5. A: 你旅行以前,事情作得好作不好?
   B: 媽媽說事情作不好,就不能去旅行。

6. A: 你想他寫得好這本小說嗎?
   B: 我想他寫得好。他很會寫小說。

14.5 THE VERB 起

When the verb 起 "up" is used as a second element in an RVC, it means "afford to." 起 can only be used in potential form and must be accompanied by -得 or -不. For example, the question "Can you afford to buy a car?" in Chinese will be 你買得起汽車嗎? **but not** 你買起汽車嗎? The following are some commonly-used expressions:

吃得起
吃不起
穿得起
穿不起
買得起
買不起
住得起
住不起

Lesson 14 What plans do you have for vacation?
第十四課 假期有甚麼打算？

1. A: 他怎麼買得起那麼貴的車？
   B: 他家很有錢。

2. A: 天天在飯館吃飯，吃得起吃不起？
   B: 有的人吃得起，有的人吃不起。

The following usages of 起 are idiomatic expressions:

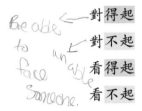

1. A: 你不應該看不起他。
   B: 我從來沒看不起他。

2. A: 對不起，我來晚了。
   B: 沒甚麼。

3. A: 對不起，你說甚麼？我沒聽見。
   B: 沒聽見就算了。

(Note that some of the vocabulary in this lesson, such as 穿 "to wear," 住 "to live," and 對 "to face," have not been introduced in the text.)

造句

1. 從……到
   從這兒到那兒。
   從這兒到那兒遠不遠？
   不太遠，很近。

2. 打算
   有甚麼打算？
   假期有甚麼打算？
   你假期有甚麼打算？

3.

一起

一起去旅行。

一起去旅行有意思。

一起去旅行有沒有意思？

跟朋友一起去旅行有沒有意思？

4.

完了

考試完了。

考試完了作甚麼？

考試完了就去看電影。

我們考試完了就去看電影。

問答

1. 你從哪年到哪年在美國？ 我從一九八七年到一九九四年在美國。
2. 你們幾月幾號放假？ 我們十二月二十三號放假。
3. 你家附近有沒有圖書館？ 我家附近從前有一個小圖書館，可是現在沒有了。
4. 你打算甚麼時候出國？ 這學期一完我就出國。
5. 你常跟誰一起去看電影？ 當然是跟我的女朋友了。
6. 你為甚麼請假？ 因為我家今天有事。
7. 你吃完晚飯到我家來，好嗎？ 今天晚上不行。明天可以。
8. 你喜歡去哪兒旅行？ 哪兒有意思我喜歡去哪兒旅行。
9. 老師跟你說的話，你聽見了沒有？ 聽是聽見了，可是我聽不懂。
10. 這是今天的報紙嗎？ 不是，是前天的。

閱讀練習

你給你孩子吃甚麼？

有一天，一個美國人跟她的孩子在公園裏坐著，一個中國老太太問那個美國人，你的孩子長得真好，你都給他吃甚麼好東西？那個美國人說，我不給他甚麼好的東西吃，我就給他吃我的牛奶。那

Lesson 14 What plans do you have for vacation?
第十四課 假期有甚麼打算？

個老太太聽了就大笑起來了。可是那個美國人不知道為甚麼那個老太太大笑。你可以告訴她嗎？這個笑話，是要學外國話的人注意甚麼？

請查生詞

Look up the following words in a dictionary.

着	zhe	真	zhēn
孩子	háizi	牛奶	niúnǎi
公園	gōngyuán	注意	zhùyì
長	zhǎng		

填空

Fill in the blanks with the appropriate words from the story.

1. 那個美國_____ _____跟他媽媽在_____ _____裏坐_____。

2. 那個_____ _____長_____真好。

3. 一個中國老_____ _____問那個美國人給他孩子吃甚麼_____ _____。

4. Milk 中國話是牛的奶，不是人的_____，所以說人的奶是_____的_____就是一個笑_____了。

第十五課　我去中國了
Lesson 15　　I went to China

Lesson 15
Pinyin Text

CONTENTS

Text — 150

Vocabulary and Illustrative Sentences — 151
(zū, fēi, jī, chǎng, huàn, běi, jīng, zhe, chéng, nán)

Pattern Drills — 156
(zhe, cái and jiù, yòu and zài)

Sentence Building
(děng, yòu, jīhuì, cái) — 160

Questions and Responses — 161

Pronunciation Review — 162

Supplementary Vocabulary — 162

Cultural Notes — 162

Text

Wǒ qù Zhōngguó le
I went to China

Xǔ Xiǎoměi :	Shàng ge xīngqī xià le kè wǒ jiù huíjiā le. Dì-èr tiān zǎoshang māma, dìdi hé wǒ zuò chūzūchē qù fēijīchǎng. Fēijī jiǔ diǎn yí kè qǐfēi. Wǒmen fēi le shí jǐ ge xiǎoshí cái dào Rìběn. Zài Rìběn huàn le fēijī, liǎng ge duō xiǎoshí jiù dào Běijīng le. Wǒmen yì chū jīchǎng jiù kànjian bàba yǐjing zài nàr děng zhe wǒmen le. Wǒmen zhēn gāoxìng yòu kànjian bàba le.	Last week, I went home after class. The next morning my mother, my younger brother and I took a cab to the airport. The plane took off at a quarter past nine. After a ten-hour flight, we finally arrived in Japan. In Japan, we took a connecting flight and it took us around two hours to get to Beijing. As soon as we walked out of the airport, we saw our father already there waiting for us. We were really happy to see our father again.
Lín Hǎiyīng :	Nǐ zài fēijī shàng zuò shénme le?	What did you do on the plane?
Xǔ Xiǎoměi :	Wǒ kàn shū, gēn rén tánhuà, hái kàn le liǎng ge diànyǐng.	I read books, chatted with people and watched two movies.
Mǎ Sīwén :	Nǐ zài Běijīng dōu zuò le shénme le?	What did you do in Beijing?
Xǔ Xiǎoměi :	Wǒmen qù fànguǎn chīfàn, kàn péngyou, kàn Zhōngguó diànyǐng, qù le hěn duō yǒumíng de dìfang, qù le Chángchéng, hái qù le Nánjīng.	We ate at restaurants, visited friends, watched Chinese movies, went to many famous places, went to the Great Wall, and also went to Nanjing.

Lesson 15 I went to China
第十五課 我去中國了

Mǎ Àiwén :	Běijīng de tiānqi zěnmeyàng?	How's the weather in Beijing?
Xǔ Xiǎoměi :	Wǒmen zài nàr de nà jǐ tiān zhēn hǎo, bù lěng yě bú rè.	The weather was very nice when we were there. It was neither too cold nor too hot.
Wáng lǎoshī:	Nǐ zài Zhōngguó de shíhou yǒu-méiyǒu yòng nǐ xuéguo de Zhōngguóhuà?	While you were in China, did you use the Chinese you had learned?
Xǔ Xiǎoměi :	Yǒu. Wǒmen tiāntiān shuō Zhōngguóhuà, kàn Zhōngguózì. Wǒ xiǎng wǒ de Zhōngwén jìnbù le hěn duō.	Yes, I did. We spoke and read Chinese every day. I think my Chinese has improved a lot.

❦ Vocabulary and Illustrative Sentences

1. **zū** **rent, lease; land tax** (V)

   Wǒ yào **zū** yí ge chē.   I would like to rent a car.

   ☞ **chūzū**   hire (V)
   出租
   A: Qǐng nǐ gěi wǒ jiào ge **chūzū**chē.   Please get a cab for me.

   B: Nǐ qù nǎr?   Where are you going?

   A: Qù fēijīchǎng.   To the airport.

2. **fēi**   **fly** (V)
   飞
   A: Yàoshì wǒ huì **fēi** jiù hǎo le.   It would be great if I could fly.

   B: Nǐ zuò **fēi**jī bú jiùshì "**fēi**" ma?   Isn't taking the airplane flying?

   ☞ **fēikuài**   very fast, at lightning speed (Adj)
   飞快
   Nǐ kàn, nàge huǒchē **fēikuài**de guòqu le.   Look! That train went by so quickly.

☞ fēiwǔ   dance in the air; flutter (V)

Shùyè zài tiānkōng fēiwǔ, zhēn měi. — The leaves are dancing in the air. It's beautiful.

☞ yuǎnzǒu-gāofēi   flee; run away (IE)

A: Tā méiyǒu érnǚ ma? Zěnme méiyǒu rén lái kàn tā? — Doesn't he have any children? Why is there nobody to visit him?

B: Yǒu. Kěshì tāmen zhǎngdà le, dōu yuǎnzǒugāofēi le, hěn shǎo huílái. — He has children, but they have grown up and left. They rarely come home.

3. jī   **machine, engine** (N)

☞ fēijī   aircraft, plane (N)

A: Qǐng wèn, fēijī jǐ diǎn qǐfēi? — Excuse me, what time will the plane take off?

B: Zài guò èrshí fēnzhōng jiù qǐfēi le. — The plane will take off in twenty minutes.

☞ jīhuì   chance, opportunity (N)

A: Wǒ bù zhīdào yǒu-méiyǒu qù Zhōngguó de jīhuì. — I don't know if there will be an opportunity to go to China.

B: Yídìng yǒu. — Of course there will be.

☞ bānjī   airline; flight (N)

A: Qù Rìběn de bānjī duō-bu-duō? — Are there many flights to China?

B: Bú tài duō. Yì tiān sān bān. — Not too many. (There are) three daily flights.

☞ diànjī   electrical engineering (N)

A: Wǒ dìdi shì xué diànjī de. — My younger brother is studying electrical engineering.

B: Diànjī shì hěn rèmén de kè. — Electrical engineering is a very popular course.

Lesson 15 I went to China

☞ shíjī — an advantageous time or opportunity (N)

时机

A: Nǐ shénme shíhou gàosu tā nǐ yào zǒu le? — When are you going to tell him that you are leaving?

B: Shíjī hái méi dào, xiànzài wǒ bù yào gàosu tā. — That's not the time yet. I won't tell him now.

4. chǎng — **a level open space** (PW)

☞ fēijīchǎng — airport (PW)

飞机场

A: Fēijīchǎng yuǎn-bu-yuǎn? — Is the airport far away?

B: Hěn yuǎn, wǒmen děi zǎo yìdiǎnr qù. — It is very far away, we have to set off (a little) early.

☞ chǎngdì — space, place, site (PW)

场地

A: Wǒmen děi zhǎo yí ge chǎngdì kāi wǔhuì. — We have to find a venue for the dance party.

B: Zhège chǎngdì zěnmeyàng? Hěn dà. — How about this place? It's very big.

☞ chǎngsuǒ — place, arena (PW)

A: Wǒ bù xǐhuan rén tài duō de chǎngsuǒ. — I don't like places that are too crowded.

B: Wǒ yě shì. — Neither do I.

☞ càichǎng — food market (PW)

菜场

Zhōngguórén xǐhuan tiāntiān qù càichǎng mǎi cài. — The Chinese like to buy vegetables at the food market every day.

5. huàn — **exchange; change** (V)

换

A: Zhège lǚguǎn tài guì le. Wǒ zhùbuqǐ. — This hotel is too expensive. I can't afford to stay here.

B: Nà nǐ jiù huàn yí ge ba. — In that case, you may change to another hotel.

☞ huàn qián   change money (VO)

换钱

A: Wǒmen shénme shíhou huàn qián?

When are we going to change our money?

B: Yí dào Běijīng jīchǎng jiù děi huàn qián. Yàoburán jiù bù néng gěi chūzūchē qián le.

As soon as we arrive at the Beijing airport, we have to change our money. Otherwise, we won't be able to pay the cab fare.

☞ huàn chē   change trains or buses (VO)

换车

A: Cóng fēijīchǎng dào lǚguǎn yào-bu-yào huàn chē?

Do we need to change buses from the airport to the hotel?

B: Děi huàn chē.

We have to change buses.

☞ huàn fēijī   take a connecting flight (VO)

换飞机

A: Nǐmen cóng Měiguó dào Shànghǎi huàn fēijī ma?

Did you take a connecting flight when you traveled from America to Shanghai?

B: Wǒmen děi zài Rìběn huàn jī.

We had to take a connecting flight in Japan.

6. běi 北 **north** (Adj)

☞ Héběi   Hebei (province in China) (PW)

A: Nǐ qùguo Héběi ma?

Have you ever been to Hebei?

B: Qùguo. Běijīng jiù zài Héběi.

I've been there before. Beijing is in Hebei.

7. jīng   **the capital of a country** (PW)

☞ Běijīng   Beijing (Peking) (PW)

北京

A: Nǐ yǐqián yǒu-méiyǒu láiguo Běijīng?

Have you ever been to Beijing?

B: Láiguo.

(Yes,) I've been to Beijing before.

8. zhe 著

(indicating an action in progress; stressing the tone in an imperative sentence; used after a verb to form a preposition) (As)

A: Qǐng nǐ zài zhèr zuòzhe děng wǒ. Wǒ qù jiào chūzūchē.
Please sit here and wait for me. I'm going to call a cab.

B: Xièxie.
Thank you.

☞ kànzhe 看著

see, look at (V)

A: Nǐmen kànzhe wǒ zěnme xiě zhège zì, hǎo ma?
See how I write this character, all right?

B: Hǎo.
All right.

☞ děngzhe

waiting (V)

A: Bàba zài nǎr děngzhe wǒmen ne?
Where is Dad waiting for us?

B: Tā zài nàr děngzhe wǒmen ne.
He is waiting for us over there.

☞ zuòzhe 坐著

sitting (V)

A: Mèimei zài nàr zuò shénme ne?
What is younger sister doing there?

B: Tā zài nàr zuòzhe kàn shū ne.
She is sitting there reading.

☞ mángzhe 忙著

busy (SV); fully occupied (V)

A: Māma zài zuò shénme ne?
What is mother doing?

B: Tā zài mángzhe gěi wǒmen zuò diǎnxīn chī ne.
She is busy preparing some snacks for us.

9. chéng 城市

city wall; wall; city; town (N)

Tā jīntiān méiyǒu lái. Tā jìn chéng le.
He didn't come today. He went into the town.

☞ Chángchéng

the Great Wall (PW)

Dìdi shàng xīngqī qù Chángchéng, zhè xīngqī yòu xiǎng qù Chángchéng le.
My younger brother went to the Great Wall last week and he wants to go there again this week.

10. nán **south** (Adj)

☞ Nánjīng Nanjing (capital of Jiangsu province) (PW)

 A: Shì Běijīng de rénkǒu duō háishì Nánjīng de rénkǒu duō? Which place has a larger population? Beijing or Nanjing?

 B: Běijīng de rénkǒu bǐ Nánjīng de duō duō le. The population in Beijing is a lot bigger than the population in Nanjing.

☞ Hé'nán Henan (province in China) (PW)

 A: Nǐ shì Hé'nánrén háishì Héběirén? Are you from Henan or Hebei?

 B: Wǒ shì zài Hé'nán chūshēng de, kěshì zài Héběi zhǎngdà de. I was born in Henan, but I grew up in Hebei.

Pattern Drills

15.1 THE MARKER zhe

The character **zhe** has several pronunciations. When it is used as a marker, it is pronounced in its neutral tone. **Zhe** can function as a durative marker or as an adverbial marker.

15.1.1 Zhe as a durative marker

When **zhe** functions as a durative marker indicating an ongoing situation, the ongoing situation may be a dynamic process, a static position, or a temporary state that is the result of the action expressed by the verb. The verb to which **zhe** is attached determines the type of ongoing situation. The marker **ne** often comes at the end of a sentence containing **zhe**.

When **zhe** is associated with a motion verb, such as **pǎo** "run" or **zǒu** "walk," it indicates a dynamic ongoing situation. **Zhe** is optional in association with motion verbs and **ne** often comes at the end of the sentence.

Lesson 15 I went to China

S	V(__zhe__)	O	__ne__
Māma	shuō(zhe)	huà	ne.
Mother is talking.			

1. Mǎ Hóng gēn Jīn Jiàn tiào(zhe) wǔ ne.   Ma Hong and Jin Jian are dancing.
2. Tāmen xiànzài hē(zhe) chá ne.   They are now having tea.

> When __zhe__ comes with verbs of activity, such as __chī__ "to eat" or __xiě__ "to write," it also indicates an ongoing activity. The coverbs __zài__ and __ne__ often come with __zhe__.

S	__zài__	V(__zhe__)	O	__ne__
Wǒ de péngyou	zài	hē(zhe)	jiǔ	ne.
My friends are drinking.				

1. A: Nǐ zài zuò(zhe) shénme ne?   What are you doing?
   B: Wǒ zài zuò(zhe) fàn ne.   I am cooking.
2. A: Nǐ zài xiě(zhe) shénme ne?   What are you writing?
   B: Wǒ zài xiě(zhe) xìn ne.   I'm writing a letter.

> When __zhe__ is associated with a verb of posture, such as __zuò__ "sit," __zhàn__ "stand" or __tǎng__ "lie," the sentence depicts the static posture of an animate subject. __Zhe__ is required in the sentence. Without __zhe__, the sentence is grammatically incorrect. (__Zhàn__ and __tǎng__ have not been introduced in the text.)

S	__zài__	*place*	V-__zhe__	__ne__
Māma	zài	fēijīchǎng	zuòzhe	ne.
Mother is sitting in the airport.				

1. Xiǎoměi zài fēijīchǎng ménkǒu zhànzhe ne.   Xiaomei is standing at the entrance of the airport.
2. Nǐ de péngyou dōu zài fànguǎn zuòzhe ne.   All your friends are sitting in the restaurant.

When <u>zhe</u> is associated with verbs of placement, such as <u>fàng</u> "to put, to place," <u>tíng</u> "to park" or <u>cún</u> "to save or deposit," it describes the state resulting from an action. <u>Zhe</u> is required with placement verbs to indicate an ongoing situation. (<u>Tíng</u> and <u>cún</u> have not been introduced in the text.)

S		zài	place	V-<u>zhe</u>	ne
Wǒ de qián		zài	yínháng	fàngzhe	ne.
My money is in the bank.					

1. Jīntiān de bào zài tā nàr fàngzhe ne. Today's newspaper is at his place.
2. A: Nǐ de chē zài nǎr ne? Where is your car?
   B: Wǒ de chē zài fēijīchǎng tíngzhe ne. My car is parked at the airport.

15.1.2 <u>Zhe</u> as an adverbial marker

When <u>zhe</u> appears in a complex sentence (a sentence consisting of two verbs with <u>zhe</u> suffixed to the first verb), it functions as an adverbial marker. It changes the first verbal expression into an adverbial phrase and modifies the following verbal expression.

When the first verb in a complex <u>zhe</u> sentence is a verb that describes a state, the verbal expression with <u>zhe</u> portrays the manner in which the main action verb is performed by the subject in the sentence.

S	Aux	V-<u>zhe</u>	(O)	V	(O)
Wáng lǎoshī	xǐhuan	zuòzhe		jiāo	shū.
Professor Wang prefers sitting while teaching.					

1. Wǒ bù xǐhuan zhànzhe chīfàn. I don't like to stand when I eat.
2. Bàba gēn péngyou zài nàr zhànzhe shuōhuà. Dad and his friends are standing there chatting.

When both verbs in a complex <u>zhe</u> sentence are action verbs, the first verbal expression with <u>zhe</u> not only describes how the activity is being carried out, but also indicates that the subject is performing two activities simultaneously.

Lesson 15 I went to China
第十五課 我去中國了

S	V-zhe	O	V (O)
Wǒmen	chīzhe	fàn	shuōhuà.
We talked while we ate.			

1. Gēge xǐhuan dǎzhe diànhuà kāichē. My elder brother likes to talk on the phone while driving.

2. Māma bù xǔ wǒ gēn péngyou shuōzhe huà zuò gōngkè. Mother doesn't allow me to talk on the phone with friends while doing homework.

Since zhe denotes duration or process, verbs involving neither motion nor movement are not compatible with zhe. Thus, verbs such as shì "is," zhīdào "know," huì "know how," etc. cannot be combined with the marker zhe.

15.2 THE ADVERBS cái AND jiù

Cái is a nonmovable adverb. It has many functions. Cái and jiù share an autonomous relationship with respect to time and expectation. Without an overt time expression, jiù indicates a future event and cái always indicates a past event, as in the following examples.

1. Jīn Jiàn jiù lái. Jin Jian will be here soon.
2. Jīn Jiàn cái lái. Jin Jian just got here.

When there is an overt future time expression, jiù implies that the speaker feels that the matter in question will happen soon, while cái implies that the matter in question will happen later than expected, as in the following examples.

1. Mǎ Hóng míngnián jiù kěyǐ qù Zhōngguó le. Ma Hong will be able to go to China (as soon as) next year.
2. Mǎ Hóng míngnián cái kěyǐ qù Zhōngguó ne. Ma Hong won't be able to go to China until next year.

The combination of cái ... ne always specifies a **future** event, as in the first example, whereas the cái ... de combination always indicates a **past** event, as in the second example.

1. Wǒ zuòhǎo gōngkè cái chīfàn ne. I won't eat until I finish my homework.
2. Wǒ zuòhǎo gōngkè cái chīfàn de. I didn't eat until I finished my homework.

15.3 THE ADVERBS yòu AND zài

Both the adverbs yòu and zài mean "again" in English. However, yòu indicates that the repetition of an action has become a fact, as in the first example; whereas zài indicates that a repetition has not yet taken place, as in the second example.

1. Lín Hǎiyīng shàng xuéqī qù Rìběn le, zhè xuéqī yòu qù le. Lin Haiying went to Japan last semester, and she went there again this semester.
2. Lín Hǎiyīng shàng xuéqī qù Rìběn le, zhè xuéqī yào zài qù. Lin Haiying went to Japan last semester, and she wants to go there again this semester.

Sentence Building

1.
Děng
Děng fēijī.
Děng le jǐ ge xiǎoshí de fēijī?
Děng le sān ge xiǎoshí de fēijī.

2.
Yòu
Yòu qù le.
Yòu qù le shénme dìfang?
Yòu qù le Nánjīng.

3.
Jīhuì
Qù Zhōngguó de jīhuì.
Qù Zhōngguó xuéxí de jīhuì.
Qù Zhōngguó xuéxí de jīhuì duō-bu-duō?

4.
Cái
Fēijī cái lái.
Fēijī cái lái jǐ fēnzhōng?
Fēijī cái lái shí jǐ fēnzhōng.

Lesson 15 I went to China
第十五課 我去中國了

🐾 Questions and Responses

1. Nǐmen de fēijī shénme shíhou qǐfēi?
   When will your plane take off?

   Mǎshàng jiù yào qǐfēi le.
   It is taking off very soon.

2. Nǐmen dào Běijīng de shíhou, yǒu rén lái jiē nǐmen ma?
   When you arrive in Beijing, will anyone be picking you up (at the airport)?

   Wǒ bàba huì lái jiē wǒmen.
   My father will pick us up (at the airport).

3. Nǐmen zài nǎr huàn fēijī?
   Where did you take a connecting flight?

   Wǒmen zài Rìběn huàn fēijī.
   We took a connecting flight in Japan.

4. Nǐmen zài Rìběn děng le jǐ ge xiǎoshí?
   How long did you wait in Japan?

   Wǒmen děng le liǎng ge duō xiǎoshí.
   We waited for more than two hours.

5. Nǐ zài Zhōngguó kěyǐ yòng Měijīn ma?
   Can you use American currency in China?

   Bù kěyǐ. Wǒmen děi yòng Zhōngguó qián "Rénmínbì."
   No, you can't. We have to use Chinese currency "Renminbi."

6. Nǐmen shénme shíhou huàn qián?
   When did you change your money?

   Māma shuō wǒmen dào Zhōngguó yǐhòu cái huàn qián.
   My mother said we should change our money after we arrived in China.

7. Nǐmen dào Zhōngguó yǐhòu, zài nǎr huàn qián?
   After you arrived in China, where did you change your money?

   Wǒ bàba shuō wǒmen kěyǐ zài fēijīchǎng huàn qián.
   My father said we could change our money at the airport.

8. Zài Zhōngguó fēijīchǎng kěyǐ jiào chūzūchē ma?
   In China, can you get a taxi at the airport?

   Dāngrán kěyǐ. Zhōngguó gēn Měiguó yíyàng, fēijīchǎng yǒu hěn duō chūzūchē.
   Of course you can. China and America are alike. There are many taxis at the airport.

9. Jiào chūzūchē guì-bu-guì?
   Is it expensive to take a taxi?

   Měiguó de chūzūchē bǐ Zhōngguó de guì duō le.
   Taking a taxi in America is a lot more expensive than in China.

10. Nǐ gēn nǐ bàba shuō Zhōngguóhuà háishì shuō Yīngwén?
Do you speak in Chinese or English with your father?

Wǒmen yǒushíhou shuō Zhōngwén, yǒushíhou shuō Yīngwén.
Sometimes we speak Chinese, and sometimes we speak English.

Pronunciation Review

Differentiating Pairs

(a)	chūbù	cūbù	(f)	yícì	yúcì
(b)	zhīdào	chīdào	(g)	bùyuǎn	bùyǎn
(c)	chīcǎo	chīzǎo	(h)	yànzǐ	yuànzǐ
(d)	zhàojiù	zàojiù	(i)	qiántiān	yuántiān
(e)	yìjiàn	yùjiàn	(j)	búqù	búqì

Supplementary Vocabulary

huìlǜ	exchange rate
Gǎngbì	Hong Kong currency
Táibì	Taiwan currency
Rénmínbì	PRC currency
Měijīn/Měiyuán	U.S. currency
Rìbì/Rìyuán	Japanese currency

Cultural Notes

Changcheng (The Great Wall of China)

During the Shang (1550–1030 B.C.) and Zhou (1030–256 B.C.) dynasties, various rulers constructed high walls across those valleys and mountain passes through which many raiders came from the north. These walls extended for around 31,000 *li*. During the Qin dynasty in 221 B.C., the Emperor Qin Shi Huang ordered a construction program to join these walls together into a one long "Great Wall" that could be defended against attackers. The Great Wall has been one of the primary symbols of Chinese civilization, a monument to the perseverance, diligence and ability of the Chinese people. Some have seen the Great Wall from a relatively negative perspective, regarding the Great Wall as reflecting the unrestrained power of despotic rulers to harness the energies of an oppressed population. Nevertheless, the Great Wall has been China's most famous and most frequently-visited scenic spot.

quān 关
open.

① A 在 B 的 direction.
      ↳
      B place

② S V 著 N one. → doing something now.
   S V 著 → something exist
      ↳ zuò
      ※ quān

   S V 著 (N) V N
   ↳ hē   jiǔ kāi chē

③ (一) V N, 就 V N
   ↓   jiù
   as soon
   hy   S V N 才 V N
         cài
   zuò wán gōng kè   wǒ xià kè cài huí jiā.
   làm xong bài   ↳
                             hy song.

④ S shì ~~年~~ year liǎ nián lái Brandeis de.

⑤ S shì qù nián cái lái Brandeis de.
              jiù

loss

第十五課
漢字本

內容

課文　　　　　　　　　　　　　　　　　　　166

生詞及例句　　　　　　　　　　　　　　　167
（租、飛、機、場、換、北、京、著、城、南）

句型練習　　　　　　　　　　　　　　　　171
（著、才和就、又和再）

造句　　　　　　　　　　　　　　　　　　174
（等、又、機會、才）

問答　　　　　　　　　　　　　　　　　　175

閱讀練習　　　　　　　　　　　　　　　　176
　　我吃小的

課文

我去中國了

許小美：上個星期下了課我就回家了。第二天早上媽媽、弟弟和我坐出租車去飛機場。飛機九點一刻起飛。我們飛了十幾個小時才到日本。在日本換了飛機，兩個多小時就到北京了。我們一出機場就看見爸爸已經在那兒等著我們了。我們真高興又看見爸爸了。

林海英：你在飛機上作甚麼了？

許小美：我看書、跟人談話、還看了兩個電影。

馬思文：你在北京都作了甚麼了？

許小美：我們去飯館吃飯、看朋友、看中國電影、去了很多有名的地方、去了長城、還去了南京。

馬愛文：北京的天氣怎麼樣？

許小美：我們在那兒的那幾天真好，不冷也不熱。

王老師：你在中國的時候有沒有用你學過的中國話？

許小美：有。我們天天說中國話、看中國字。我想我的中文進步了很多。

生詞及例句

1. **租** **rent, lease; land tax (V)**
   我要租一個車。

   ☞ 出租 hire (V)
   A: 請你給我叫個出租車。
   B: 你去哪兒?
   A: 去飛機場。

2. **飛** **fly (V)**
   A: 要是我會飛就好了。
   B: 你坐飛機不就是"飛"嗎?

   ☞ 飛快 very fast, at lightning speed (Adj)
   你看,那個火車飛快地過去了。

   ☞ 飛舞 dance in the air; flutter (V)
   樹葉在天空飛舞,真美。

   ☞ 遠走高飛 flee; run away (IE)
   A: 他沒有兒女嗎?怎麼沒有人來看他?
   B: 有。可是他們長大了,都遠走高飛了,很少回來。

3. **機** **machine, engine (N)**

   ☞ 飛機 aircraft, plane (N)
   A: 請問,飛機幾點起飛?
   B: 再過二十分鐘就起飛了。

   ☞ 機會 chance, opportunity (N)
   A: 我不知道有沒有去中國的機會。
   B: 一定有。

☞ 班機　　airline; flight (N)

A: 去日本的班機多不多？

B: 不太多。一天三班。

☞ 電機　　electrical engineering (N)

A: 我弟弟是學電機的。

B: 電機是很熱門的課。

☞ 時機　　an advantageous time or opportunity (N)

A: 你甚麼時候告訴他你要走了？

B: 時機還沒到，現在我不要告訴他。

4. **場**　　**a level open space** (PW)

☞ 飛機場　airport (PW)

A: 飛機場遠不遠？

B: 很遠，我們得早一點兒去。

☞ 場地　　space, place, site (PW)

A: 我們得找一個場地開舞會。

B: 這個場地怎麼樣？很大。

☞ 場所　　place, arena (PW)

A: 我不喜歡人太多的場所。

B: 我也是。

☞ 菜場　　food market (PW)

中國人喜歡天天去菜場買菜。

5. **換**　　**exchange; change** (V)

A: 這個旅館太貴了。我住不起。

B: 那你就換一個吧。

Lesson 15 I went to China
第十五課 我去中國了

☞ 換錢　　change money (VO)
　　　　　A: 我們甚麼時候換錢？
　　　　　B: 一到北京機場就得換錢。要不然就不能給出租車錢了。

☞ 換車　　change trains or buses (VO)
　　　　　A: 從飛機場到旅館要不要換車？
　　　　　B: 得換車。

☞ 換飛機　take a connecting flight (VO)
　　　　　A: 你們從美國到上海換飛機嗎？
　　　　　B: 我們得在日本換機。

6. 北　　**north (Adj)**
☞ 河北　　Hebei (province in China) (PW)
　　　　　A: 你去過河北嗎？
　　　　　B: 去過。北京就在河北。

7. 京　　**the capital of a country (PW)**
☞ 北京　　Beijing (Peking) (PW)
　　　　　A: 你以前有沒有來過北京？
　　　　　B: 來過。

8. 著　　(indicating an action in progress; stressing the tone in an imperative sentence; used after a verb to form a preposition) (As)
　　　　　A: 請你在這兒坐著等我。我去叫出租車。
　　　　　B: 謝謝。

☞ 看著　　see, look at (V)
　　　　　A: 你們看著我怎麼寫這個字，好嗎？
　　　　　B: 好。

☞ 等著   waiting (V)

A: 爸爸在哪兒等著我們呢？

B: 他在那兒等著我們呢。

☞ 坐著   sitting (V)

A: 妹妹在那兒作甚麼呢？

B: 她在那兒坐著看書呢。

☞ 忙著   busy (SV); fully occupied (V)

A: 媽媽在做甚麼呢？

B: 她在忙著給我們作點心吃呢。

9. 城市   **city wall; wall; city; town** (N)

他今天沒有來，他進城了。

☞ 長城   the Great Wall (PW)

弟弟上星期去長城，這星期又想去長城了。

10. 南   **south** (Adj)

☞ 南京   Nanjing (capital of Jiangsu province) (PW)

A: 是北京的人口多還是南京的人口多？

B: 北京的人口比南京多多了。

☞ 河南   Henan (province in China) (PW)

A: 你是河南人還是河北人？

B: 我是在河南出生的，可是在河北長大的。

句型練習

15.1 THE MARKER 著

The character 著 has several pronunciations. When it is used as a marker, it is pronounced in its neutral tone. 著 can function as a durative marker or as an adverbial marker.

15.1.1 著 as a durative marker

When 著 functions as a durative marker indicating an ongoing situation, the ongoing situation may be a dynamic process, a static position, or a temporary state that is the result of the action expressed by the verb. The verb to which 著 is attached determines the type of ongoing situation. The marker 呢 often comes at the end of a sentence containing 著.

When 著 is associated with a motion verb, such as 跑 "run" or 走 "walk," it indicates a dynamic ongoing situation. 著 is optional in association with motion verbs and 呢 often comes at the end of the sentence.

S	V (著)	O	呢
媽媽	說 (著)	話	呢。
Mother is talking.			

1. 馬紅跟金建跳 (著) 舞呢。

2. 他們現在喝 (著) 茶呢。

When 著 comes with verbs of activity, such as 吃 "to eat" or 寫 "to write," it also indicates an ongoing activity. The coverbs 在 and 呢 often come with 著.

S	在	V (著)	O	呢
我的朋友	在	喝 (著)	酒	呢。
My friends are drinking.				

1. A: 你在作 (著) 甚麼呢?
   B: 我在作 (著) 飯呢。

2. A: 你在寫(著)甚麼呢？
   B: 我在寫(著)信呢。

When 著 is associated with a verb of posture, such as 坐 "sit," 站 "stand" or 躺 "lie," the sentence depicts the static posture of an animate subject. 著 is required in the sentence. Without 著, the sentence is grammatically incorrect. (站 and 躺 have not been introduced in the text.)

S	在	place	V-著	呢
媽媽	在	飛機場	坐著	呢。

Mother is sitting in the airport.

1. 小美在飛機場門口站著呢。

2. 你的朋友都在飯館坐著呢。

When 著 is associated with verbs of placement, such as 放 "to put, to place," 停 "to park" or 存 "to save or deposit," it describes the state resulting from an action. 著 is required with placement verbs to indicate an ongoing situation. (停 and 存 have not been introduced in the text.)

S	在	place	V-著	呢
我的錢	在	銀行	放著	呢。

My money is in the bank.

1. 今天的報在他那兒放著呢。

2. A: 你的車在哪兒呢？
   B: 我的車在飛機場停著呢。

15.1.2 著 as an adverbial marker

When 著 appears in a complex sentence (a sentence consisting of two verbs with 著 suffixed to the first verb), it functions as an adverbial marker. It changes the first verbal expression into an adverbial phrase and modifies the following verbal expression.

When the first verb in a complex 著 sentence is a verb that describes a state, the verbal expression with 著 portrays the manner in which the main action verb is performed by the subject in the sentence.

S	Aux	V-著	(O)	V	(O)
王老師	喜歡	坐著		教	書。

Professor Wang prefers sitting while teaching.

1. 我不喜歡站著吃飯。

2. 爸爸跟朋友在那兒站著說話。

When both verbs in a complex 著 sentence are action verbs, the first verbal expression with 著 not only describes how the activity is being carried out, but also indicates that the subject is performing two activities simultaneously.

S	V-著	O	V	(O)
我們	吃著	飯	說	話。

We talked while we ate.

1. 哥哥喜歡打著電話開車。

2. 媽媽不許我跟朋友說著話作功課。

Since 著 denotes duration or process, verbs involving neither motion nor movement are not compatible with 著. Thus, verbs such as 是 "is," 知道 "know," 會 "know how," etc. cannot be combined with the marker 著.

15.2 THE ADVERBS 才 AND 就

才 is a nonmovable adverb. It has many functions. 才 and 就 share an autonomous relationship with respect to time and expectation. Without an overt time expression, 就 indicates a future event and 才 always indicates a past event, as in the following examples.

1. 金建就來。

2. 金建才來。

When there is an overt future time expression, 就 implies that the speaker feels that the matter in question will happen soon, while 才 implies that the matter in question will happen later than expected, as in the following examples.

1. 馬紅明年就可以去中國了。

2. 馬紅明年才可以去中國呢。

The combination of 才……呢 always specifies a **future** event, as in the first example, whereas the 才……的 combination always indicates a **past** event, as in the second example.

1. 我作好功課才吃飯呢。

2. 我作好功課才吃飯的。

15.3 THE ADVERBS 又 AND 再

Both the adverbs 又 and 再 mean "again" in English. However, 又 indicates that the repetition of an action has become a fact, as in the first example; whereas 再 indicates that a repetition has not yet taken place, as in the second example.

1. 林海英上學期去日本了，這學期又去了。

2. 林海英上學期去日本了，這學期要再去。

造 句

1.
等
等飛機。
等了幾個小時的飛機？
等了三個小時的飛機。

2.
又
又去了。
又去了甚麼地方？
又去了南京。

3.

機會

去中國的機會。

去中國學習的機會。

去中國學習的機會多不多？

4.

才

飛機才來。

飛機才來幾分鐘？

飛機才來十幾分鐘。

問答

1. 你們的飛機甚麼時候起飛？　　馬上就要起飛了。
2. 你們到北京的時候，有人來接你們嗎？　　我爸爸會來接我們。
3. 你們在哪兒換飛機？　　我們在日本換飛機。
4. 你們在日本等了幾個小時？　　我們等了兩個多小時。
5. 你在中國可以用美金嗎？　　不可以。我們得用中國錢"人民幣"。
6. 你們甚麼時候換錢？　　媽媽說我們到中國以後才換錢。
7. 你們到中國以後，在哪兒換錢？　　我爸爸說我們可以在飛機場換錢。
8. 在中國飛機場可以叫出租車嗎？　　當然可以。中國跟美國一樣，飛機場有很多出租車。
9. 叫出租車貴不貴？　　美國的出租車比中國的貴多了。
10. 你跟你爸爸說中國話還是說英文？　　我們有時候說中文，有時候說英文。

閱讀練習

我吃小的

從前有一個六歲的孩子,他的名字叫孔融。有一天他媽媽買了幾個梨,他叫孔融拿一個梨吃。孔融拿了一個很小的梨。他媽媽就問他:"你不喜歡吃梨嗎?怎麼拿一個最小的?"孔融說:"媽媽,不是我不喜歡吃梨,是因為我小,我應該吃小梨,哥哥比我大,大梨應該給哥哥吃。"孔融的媽媽聽了以後說:"孔融,你真是一個懂事的好孩子。"

這是中國一個很有名的故事。爸爸媽媽都說這個故事給孩子聽。為甚麼?你認為孔融是一個懂事的孩子還是一個笨孩子?

*孔融:Kǒng Róng

請查生詞

Look up the following words in a dictionary.

suì	歲	
lí	梨	
ná	拿	
dǒngshì	懂事	
bèn	笨	

第十六課　我去日本了
Lesson 16　I went to Japan

Lesson 16
Pinyin Text

CONTENTS

*T*ext   180

*V*ocabulary and Illustrative Sentences   181
   (zhù, wài, zǔ, fù, mǔ, fáng, mài, gāng, mǎi, dǒng)

*P*attern Drills   186
   (dǒng, shì ... de, yǒu and méiyǒu)

*S*entence Building
   (gāng, chūmài, yǒu, duō)   190

*Q*uestions and Responses   190

*S*upplementary Vocabulary   191

🐾 Text

Wǒ qù Rìběn le

I went to Japan

Lín Hǎiyīng :	Nǐmen dōu zhīdào wǒ fàng jià de shíhou yào qù Rìběn. Māma gēn wǒ shì xīngqīliù qù Rìběn de. Bàba méi qù, yīnwèi tā děi zuò shì. Wǒmen zhùzai wàizǔfù wàizǔmǔ jiā. Tāmen de fángzi suīrán méiyǒu wǒmen jiā de dà, kěshì hěn hǎokàn. Tāmen mài le cóngqián de fángzi, xiànzài zhù de fángzi shì zuìjìn gāng mǎi de. Tāmen jiā fùjìn yǒu yí ge hěn yǒumíng de fànguǎnr. Wǒmen cháng qù nàr chīfàn.	All of you know that I was planning to go to Japan during vacation. My mother and I left for Japan on Saturday. My father didn't go because he had to work. We stayed at our (maternal) grandparents' house. Although their house isn't as big as ours, it is very beautiful. They sold their old house and the house they are living in now has been bought recently. There is a famous restaurant near their house. We often went there to eat.
Xǔ Xiǎoměi:	Nǐ gēn nǐ wàizǔfù, wàizǔmǔ shuō nǎ guó huà?	In what language do you speak with your grandfather and grandmother?
Lín Hǎiyīng :	Wǒ wàizǔfù huì shuō Yīngwén, wǒ gēn tā shuō Yīngwén. Wǒ wàizǔmǔ bù dǒng Yīngwén, wǒ jiù huì shuō yìdiǎnr Rìběnhuà, suǒyǐ wǒmen kěyǐ shuō de huà hěn shǎo.	My grandfather can speak English, so I speak English with him. My grandmother can't speak English and I can only speak a little Japanese, so our conversations are very limited.
Mǎ Sīwén :	Nǐ zài Rìběn de shíhou yǒuméiyǒu qù lǚxíng?	Did you go traveling when you were in Japan?

Lín Hǎiyīng :	Méiyǒu. Yīnwèi wǒ māma yào wǒ gēn tā fùmǔ duō rènshi rènshi. Suīrán wǒ bú tài dǒng tāmen shuō de huà, kěshì wǒ hěn xǐhuan gēn tāmen zài yìqǐ.	No, I didn't, because my mother wanted me to get to know her parents better. Although I didn't quite understand what they said, I still enjoyed spending time with them.
Mǎ Àiwén :	Nǐmen shì shénme shíhou huí Měiguó de?	When did you come back to America?
Lín Hǎiyīng :	Wǒmen xīngqītiān xiàwǔ huílai de.	We came home on Sunday afternoon.

Vocabulary and Illustrative Sentences

1. **zhù** — **live, reside; stay; stop, cease** (V)

☞ zhùzai — live at (V)

    A: Nǐ wàizǔfù zhùzai nǎr? — Where does your maternal grandfather live?

    B: Tā zhùzai Rìběn. — He lives in Japan.

2. **wài** — **outer, outside; foreign; external** (N)

☞ wàiguó — foreign country (N)

    A: Nǐ cháng qù wàiguó lǚxíng ma? — Do you often travel to foreign countries?

    B: Bù cháng qù. Tài guì, qùbuqǐ. — I don't go very often. It's too expensive and I can't afford it.

☞ wàiguóhuà — foreign language (N)

    A: Nǐ huì shuō shénme wàiguóhuà? — What foreign languages can you speak?

    B: Wǒ huì shuō Yīngwén, yě huì shuō yìdiǎnr Rìwén. — I speak English, and also a little Japanese.

☞ wàidì   parts of the country other than where one is (N)

     A: Nǐ bàba wéishénme chángcháng bú zài jiā? — Why is your father often not at home?

     B: Tā děi qù wàidì zuò shēngyi. — He has to travel to other places for business.

☞ wàirén   stranger, outsider; foreigner (N)

     A: Míngtiān nǐ qǐng shénme rén chīfàn? — Who are you inviting for dinner tomorrow?

     B: Dōu shì jiālǐrén, méiyǒu wàirén. — They are all family members, no outsiders.

3. zǔ   **ancestor; founder** (N)

☞ zǔguó   one's country, homeland, motherland (N)

     A: Nǐ yǐhòu yào zài nǎr zuò shì? — Where do you want to work in the future?

     B: Wǒ dǎsuàn huí zǔguó zuò shì. — I intend to go back to my country to work.

☞ zǔxiān   ancestry, ancestors (N)

     A: Nǐ de zǔxiān shì nǎ guó rén? — Where are your ancestors from?

     B: Tāmen shì cóng Yīngguó lái de. Tāmen shì Yīngguórén. — They are from England. They are English.

4. fù   **father; a respectful term for an elderly man in ancient times** (N)

☞ zǔfù   (paternal) grandfather (N)

     A: Nǐ cháng qù kàn nǐ zǔfù ma? — Do you visit your (paternal) grandfather often?

     B: Wǒmen yì yǒu jīhuì jiù qù kàn tā. — We visit him whenever we can.

Lesson 16 I went to Japan
第十六課 我去日本了

☞ wàizǔfù   (maternal) grandfather (N)

    A: "Wàizǔfù" gēn "zǔfù" yǒu shénme bùtóng?

    What is the difference between "waizufu" and "zufu"?

    B: "Wàizǔfù" shì māma de bàba, "zǔfù" shì bàba de bàba.

    "Waizufu" is one's mother's father, "zufu" is one's father's father.

5. mǔ   **mother; female (animal) (N)**

☞ fùmǔ   father and mother, parents (N)

    A: "Fùmǔ" shì shénme yìsi?

    What is the meaning of "fumu"?

    B: "Fùmǔ" shì bàba māma de yìsi.

    "Fumu" means father and mother.

☞ zǔmǔ   (paternal) grandmother (N)

    A: Nǐ zǔmǔ yǒu jǐ ge érnǚ?

    How many children does your (paternal) grandmother have?

    B: Tā yǒu liǎng ge nǚ'ér, sān ge érzi.

    She has two daughters and three sons.

☞ wàizǔmǔ   (maternal) grandmother (N)

    A: Nǐ wàizǔmǔ dà háishì nǐ zǔmǔ dà?

    Who is elder? Your maternal grandmother or your paternal grandmother?

    B: Wǒ bù zhīdào. Yěxǔ shì wǒ zǔmǔ dà.

    I don't know. Maybe my paternal grandmother is elder.

6. fáng   **house; room (N)**

☞ fángzi   house, building; room (N)

    A: Nǐ wàizǔfùmǔ jiā de fángzi dà háishì zǔfùmǔ jiā de fángzi dà?

    Whose house is bigger? Your maternal grandparents' or paternal grandparents'?

    B: Zǔfùmǔ jiā de fángzi bǐ wàizǔfùmǔ de fángzi dà.

    My paternal grandparents' house is bigger than my maternal grandarents'.

	shūfáng	study (room) (N)	
		A: Nǐ jiā de fángzi yǒu shūfáng ma?	Is there a study in your house?
		B: Yǒu. Kěshì shūfáng shì wǒ fùmǔ kàn shū yòng de. Wǒmen bù kěyǐ yòng.	Yes, there is one. But only my parents read in the study. We're not allowed to use the study.
	fángzū	rent (for a house, apartment, etc.) (N)	
		A: Zài Měiguó zū fángzi fángzū guì-bu-guì?	Is it expensive to rent a house in America?
		B: Fángzū hěn guì, suǒyǐ hěn duō rén zūbuqǐ fángzi.	Rent is high. That's why many people cannot afford to rent a house.
7.	mài	**sell** (V)	
		A: Nǐmen wèishénme mài nǐmen de fángzi?	Why are you selling your house?
		B: Yīnwèi zhège fángzi tài xiǎo le.	Because this house is too small.
	chūmài	offer for sale; sell, sell out; betray (V)	
		(1) A: Zhèr yǒu fángzi yào chūmài ma?	Have you got any houses for sale here?
		B: Yǒu shì yǒu, kěshì hěn guì.	There are houses for sale here, but the prices are very high.
		(2) A: Nǐmen wèishénme bú shì hǎopéngyou le?	Why aren't you good friends anymore?
		B: Yīnwèi tā chūmài le wǒ.	Because he betrayed me.
8.	gāng	**just; exactly; barely; a short while ago** (Adv)	
		(1) A: Nǐmen shì shénme shíhou rènshi de?	When did you get to know each other?
		B: Wǒmen shì gāng rènshi de.	We got to know each other just now.

Lesson 16 I went to Japan
第十六課 我去日本了

    (2) A: Nǐ zěnme gāng lái Měiguó jiù yào huíguó? — Why do you want to go back so soon, as you have just come to the States?

        B: Yīnwèi jiālǐ yǒu yàojǐn de shìqing. — Because something important (happened) at home.

☞ **gānggāng** just, only, exactly; a moment ago, just now (Adv)

    A: Wǒ gānggāng gěi nǐ dǎ le yí ge diànhuà, kěshì méi rén jiē. — I just called you, but no one answered the phone.

    B: Nǐ zhǎo wǒ yǒu shénme shì ma? — Why were you looking for me?

☞ **gānghǎo** just; exactly; it so happened that (Adv)

    (1) Wǒ de qián gānghǎo gòu mǎi zhè běn shū. — I just have enough money to buy this book.

    (2) Wǒmen dào fēijīchǎng de shíhou, gānghǎo fēijī lái le. — Just when we arrived at the airport, the plane landed.

9. **mǎi** **buy, purchase (V)**

    A: Nǐ yào mǎi shénme? — What would you like to buy?

    B: Wǒ bù mǎi shénme, jiù kànkan. — I am not buying anything. I'm just looking around.

☞ **mǎimài** buying and selling (V); business; transaction (N)

    A: Nǐ bàba zuò shénme mǎimài? — What business is your father in?

    B: Tā mǎi fángzi yě mài fángzi. — He buys and sells houses.

    A: Tā de mǎimài hěn dà ma? — Is his business big?

    B: Bú tài dà. — Not very big.

10. **dǒng** **understand, know (V/SV/RE)**

    (1) A: Nǐ dǒng wǒ de yìsi ma? — Do you understand what I mean?

        B: Wǒ bù dǒng. — I don't understand.

(2) A: Tā **dǒng** Zhōngguóhuàr ma? — Does he understand Chinese painting?

B: Tā suīrán shì Měiguórén, kěshì tā hěn **dǒng** Zhōngguóhuàr. — Although he is an American, (but) he really understands Chinese painting.

(3) A: Nǐ kànde**dǒng** kànbu**dǒng** Yīngwén bào? — Can you read and understand an English newspaper?

B: Wǒ cái xué le yì nián Yīngwén, wǒ hái kànbu**dǒng** Yīngwén bào. — I've just studied English for a year. I can't read an English newspaper yet.

☞ **dǒngde**   understand, know, grasp (V)

A: Nǐ **dǒngde** zěnme yòng zhège shēngzì ma? — Do you know how to use this word?

B: Wǒ **dǒngde** zhège shēngzì de yìsi, kěshì wǒ bú huì yòng. — I understand the meaning of this word, but I don't know how to use it.

☞ **dǒngshì**   sensible; intelligent (IE)

A: Xǔ tàitai, nǐ de nǚ'ér yòu **dǒngshì** yòu kě'ài. — Mrs. Xu, your daughter is both sensible and lovely.

B: Nǎlǐ, nǎlǐ. Tā bú tài **dǒngshì**. — Not really, she is not very sensible.

Pattern Drills

16.1 THE VERB dǒng

The verb <u>dǒng</u> can function as a second element in an RVC. It can only be combined with the verbs <u>tīng</u> "listen" and <u>kàn</u> "read."

(1) A: Nǐ tīngde**dǒng** tīngbu**dǒng** Zhōngguóhuà? — Can you understand Chinese?

B: Wǒ tīngde**dǒng** yìdiǎnr Zhōngguóhuà. — I understand a little Chinese.

(2) A: Nǐ kàndedǒng kànbudǒng Yīngwén xiǎoshuō? Can you read an English novel?

B: Wǒ hái kànbudǒng ne. I can't read an English novel yet.

16.2 MORE ON THE shì ... de PATTERN

The shì ... de pattern was introduced in Lesson 6. It is time to discuss this pattern in detail. For the sake of clarity, we will divide the shì ... de pattern into two types.

16.2.1 Shì ... de with a past event

As we discussed in Lesson 6, the shì ... de pattern is used with a past occurrence. It focuses on a specific aspect of the occurrence, rather than the occurrence itself. If we want to find out the "where" or "when" of a past event, the shì ... de pattern must be used. Shì can sometimes be omitted.

(1) A: Wǒ mǎi le yì běn shū. I bought a book.

B: Nǐ de shū shì zài nǎr mǎi de? Where did you buy it?

A: Shì zài yí ge gāng kāi de shūdiàn mǎi de. I bought it at a newly opened bookstore.

(2) A: Wǒ bàba huílái le. My father came back.

B: Tā shì shénme shíhou huílái de? When did he come back?

A: Zuótiān wǎnshang huílái de. Last night.

Note that the preferred position of the object in a shì ... de pattern is at the beginning of the sentence.

(1) A: Zhège chē shì shéi gěi nǐ de? Who gave you this car?

B: Zhège chē shì wǒ māma gěi wǒ de. It was my mother who gave me this car.

(2) A: Zhè běn shū shì shéi xiě de? Who wrote this book?

B: Zhè běn shū shì wǒ lǎoshī xiě de. This book was written by my teacher.

> When the object in a <u>shì</u> ... <u>de</u> pattern is a pronoun, <u>de</u> is placed after the pronoun, as in the first example, **not** after the verb, as in the second example.

✔ (1) Zhège biǎo shì tā nǚpéngyou gěi tā de. It was his girlfriend who gave him the watch.

✘ (2) Zhège biǎo shì tā nǚpéngyou gěi de tā.

> When the object in a <u>shì</u> ... <u>de</u> pattern is a place word, <u>de</u> is placed either at the end of the sentence, as in the first example, or immediately after the verb, as in the second example.

(1) A: Nǐ nǚpéngyou shì shénme shíhou lái Měiguó de? When did your girlfriend come to the United States?

    B: Tā shì yījiǔbāqī nián lái Měiguó de. She came to the United States in 1987.

(2) A: Nǐ nǚpéngyou shì shénme shíhou lái de Měiguó? When did your girlfriend come to the United States?

    B: Tā shì yījiǔbāqī nián lái de Měiguó. She came to the United States in 1987.

16.2.2 <u>Shì</u> ... <u>de</u> with a presumption

> The <u>shì</u> ... <u>de</u> pattern can be used to affirm or deny some supposition or expectation.

(1) Nǐmen huì shì hǎo fùmǔ de. You will be good parents.

(2) Yàoshì nǐ yònggōng, nǐ shì huì kǎode hěn hǎo de. If you work hard, you will do well in your exams.

(3) Wǒ shì bú huì tóngyì nǐ de kànfǎ de. It is impossible for me to agree with your point of view.

(4) Shéi shuō míngtiān huì xiàyǔ? Míngtiān shì bú huì xiàyǔ de. Who says it's going to rain tomorrow? It won't rain tomorrow.

Lesson 16 I went to Japan
第十六課 我去日本了

16.3 Yǒu AND méiyǒu

16.3.1 A yǒu B (nàme/zhème) SV

> If the similarity between "A" and "B" is close enough to be considered equivalent, the word yǒu "have" is placed between "A" and "B". Nàme or zhème "so, such, to this or that extent" as an adverbial expression of degree may be added along with the appropriate predicate.

A	yǒu	B	(nàme/zhème)	SV
Tā	yǒu	tā	māma nàme	hǎokàn.
She is as pretty as her mother.				

(1) A: Tā zuò de fàn yǒu nǐ zuò de zhème hǎo ma?
    Is her cooking as good as yours?

   B: Tā zuò de fàn yǒu wǒ zuò de yíyàng hǎo.
    Her cooking is as good as mine.

(2) A: Zhōngwén yǒu Yīngwén nàme nán ma?
    Is Chinese as difficult as English?

   B: Shì. Zhōngwén yǒu Yīngwén yíyàng nán.
    Yes. Chinese is as difficult as English.

16.3.2 A méiyǒu B (nàme/zhème) SV

> To express "A" is not equivalent to or less than "B", the A méiyǒu B (nàme/zhème) SV pattern is used.

A	méiyǒu	B	(nàme/zhème)	SV
Wǒ	méiyǒu	nǐ	nàme	máng.
I am not as busy as you are.				

(1) A: Jīntiān yǒu-méiyǒu zuótiān lěng?
    Is the weather today as cold as that of yesterday?

   B: Jīntiān méiyǒu zuótiān nàme lěng.
    The weather today is not as cold as that of yesterday.

(2) A: Rìběn de rénkǒu yǒu-méiyǒu
   Zhōngguó nàme duō?

   B: Rìběn de rénkǒu yídìng méiyǒu
   Zhōngguó de duō.

Is Japan's population as big as China's?

Japan's population is definitely not as big as China's.

Sentence Building

1.
Gāng
Gāng rènshi de.
Gāng rènshi de péngyou.
Tā shì wǒ gāng rènshi de péngyou.

2.
Chūmài
Chūmài le wǒ.
Shéi chūmài le nǐ?
Wǒ zuìhǎo de péngyou chūmài le wǒ.

3.
Yǒu
Yǒu-méiyǒu?
Tā yǒu-méiyǒu nǐ yònggōng?
Tā yǒu-méiyǒu nǐ nàme yònggōng?

4.
Duō
Duō xué yìdiǎnr.
Duō xué yìdiǎnr shénme?
Duō xué yìdiǎnr wàiguóhuà.

Questions and Responses

1. Lín Hǎiyīng, nǐmen fàngjià qù nǎr le?
   Lin Haiying, where did you go on your vacation?

   Wǒmen qù Rìběn le.
   We went to Japan.

2. Rìběn de tiānqì zěnmeyàng?
   What was the weather like in Japan?

   Hěn hǎo, bù lěng yě bú rè.
   Very good. It was neither too cold nor too hot.

3. Nǐmen qù Rìběn zuò shénme?
   Why did you go to Japan?

   Wǒmen qù kàn wàizǔfùmǔ.
   We went to visit our maternal grandparents.

4. Nǐmen zài Rìběn de shíhou, zhùzai lǚguǎn háishì zhùzai wàizǔfùmǔ jiā?
   When you were in Japan, did you stay in a hotel or with your maternal grandparents?

   Wǒmen zhùzai wàizǔfùmǔ jiā.

   We stayed with our maternal grandparents.

5. Tāmen de fángzi yǒu nǐmen de dà ma?   Tāmen de fángzi méiyǒu wǒmen de dà, kěshì yě bù xiǎo.

   Is their house as big as yours?   Their house isn't as big as ours, nor is it too small.

6. Nǐ wàizǔfùmǔ dǒng-bu-dǒng Yīngwén?   Wǒ wàizǔfù dǒng yìdiǎnr, wàizǔmǔ bù dǒng.

   Do your maternal grandparents understand English?   My maternal grandfather understands a little. My maternal grandmother doesn't understand (any).

7. Nǐ huì shuō Rìběnhuà ma?   Yìdiǎnr dōu bú huì.

   Do you know how to speak Japanese?   I don't know any Japanese at all.

8. Nǐ wàizǔfù zuò shénme shì?   Tā cóngqián zuò mǎimài, xiànzài lǎo le, bú zuò shì le.

   What does your maternal grandfather do?   He used to be in business. Now he's getting old, he doesn't work anymore.

9. Nǐmen shì jǐ yuè jǐ hào huílai de?   Wǒmen shì jiǔyuè bā hào huílai de.

   When did you come back?   We came back on 8 September.

10. Nǐ hái huì qu Rìběn ma?   Wǒmen yī yǒu jīhuì jiù qù.

    Will you go to Japan again?   As soon as there is such an opportunity, we will go.

Supplementary Vocabulary

wòfáng/wòshì	(MW: jiān)	bedroom
chuáng	(MW: zhāng)	bed
yǐzi	(MW: bǎ)	chair
shūzhuō	(MW: zhāng)	desk
fàntīng	(MW: jiān)	dinner room
chēfáng	(MW: ge)	garage
chúfáng	(MW: jiān)	kitchen
kètīng	(MW: jiān)	living room
shūfáng	(MW: jiān)	study
zhuōzi	(MW: zhāng)	table

第十六課
漢字本

內容

課文　　　　　　　　　　　　　　　　　　　　　194

生詞及例句　　　　　　　　　　　　　　　　　195
(住、外、祖、父、母、房、賣、剛、買、懂)

句型練習　　　　　　　　　　　　　　　　　　199
(懂、是……的、有和沒有)

造句　　　　　　　　　　　　　　　　　　　　202
(剛、出賣、有、多)

問答　　　　　　　　　　　　　　　　　　　　202

閱讀練習　　　　　　　　　　　　　　　　　　203
　　日本的湯不好喝

課文

我去日本了

林海英：你們都知道我放假的時候要去日本。媽媽跟我是星期六去日本的。爸爸沒去，因為他得作事。我們住在外祖父外祖母家。他們的房子雖然沒有我們家的大，可是很好看。他們賣了從前的房子，現在住的房子是最近剛買的。他們家附近有一個很有名的飯館兒。我們常去那兒吃飯。

許小美：你跟你外祖父，外祖母說哪國話？

林海英：我外祖父會說英文，我跟他說英文。我外祖母不懂英文，我就會說一點兒日本話，所以我們可以說的話很少。

馬思文：你在日本的時候有沒有去旅行？

林海英：沒有。因為我媽媽要我跟她父母多認識認識。雖然我不太懂他們說的話，可是我很喜歡跟他們在一起。

馬愛文：你們是甚麼時候回美國的？

林海英：我們星期天下午回來的。

生詞及例句

1. **住** zhù **live, reside; stay; stop, cease** (V)

    住在   live at (V)
    A: 你外祖父住在哪兒?
    B: 他住在日本。

2. **外** wài **outer, outside; foreign; external** (N)

    外國   foreign country (N)
    A: 你常去外國旅行嗎?
    B: 不常去。太貴,去不起。

    外國話   foreign language (N)
    A: 你會說甚麼外國話?
    B: 我會說英文,也會說一點兒日文。

    外地   parts of the country other than where one is (N)
    A: 你爸爸為甚麼常常不在家?
    B: 他得去外地作生意。

    外人   stranger, outsider; foreigner (N)
    A: 明天你請甚麼人吃飯?
    B: 都是家裏人,沒有外人。

3. **祖** zǔ **ancestor; founder** (N)

    祖國   one's country, homeland, motherland (N)
    A: 你以後要在哪兒作事?
    B: 我打算回祖國作事。

☞ 祖先　　ancestry, ancestors (N)

A: 你的祖先是哪國人？

B: 他們是從英國來的。他們是英國人。

4. 父 fù　　**father; a respectful term for an elderly man in ancient times (N)**

☞ 祖父　　(paternal) grandfather (N)
（爺爺）
yé ye

A: 你常去看你祖父嗎？

B: 我們一有機會就去看他。

☞ 外祖父　　(maternal) grandfather (N)
wài ye

A: "外祖父"跟"祖父"有甚麼不同？

B: "外祖父"是媽媽的爸爸，"祖父"是爸爸的爸爸。

5. 母 mǔ　　**mother; female (animal) (N)**

☞ 父母　　father and mother, parents (N)

A: "父母"是甚麼意思？

B: "父母"是爸爸媽媽的意思。

☞ 祖母　　(paternal) grandmother (N)
（奶奶）
nǎi nai

A: 你祖母有幾個兒女？

B: 她有兩個女兒，三個兒子。

☞ 外祖母　　(maternal) grandmother (N)
姥姥
lǎo lao

A: 你外祖母大還是你祖母大？

B: 我不知道。也許是我祖母大。

6. 房 fáng　　**house; room (N)**

☞ 房子　　house, building; room (N)

A: 你外祖父母家的房子大還是祖父母的房子大？

B: 祖父母的房子比外祖父母的房子大。

Lesson 16 I went to Japan
第十六課 我去日本了

☞ 書房　　　study (room) (N)

　　　　　　A: 你家的房子有書房嗎？

　　　　　　B: 有。可是書房是我父母看書用的。我們不可以用。

☞ 房租　　　rent (for a house, apartment, etc.) (N)

　　　　　　A: 在美國租房子房租貴不貴？

　　　　　　B: 房租很貴，所以很多人租不起房子。

7. 賣　　　　**sell** (V)

　　　　　　A: 你們為甚麼賣你們的房子？

　　　　　　B: 因為這個房子太小了。

☞ 出賣　　　offer for sale; sell, sell out; betray (V)

　　　(1) A: 這兒有房子要出賣嗎？

　　　　　B: 有是有，可是很貴。

　　　(2) A: 你們為甚麼不是好朋友了？

　　　　　B: 因為他出賣了我。

8. 剛　　　　**just; exactly; barely; a short while ago** (Adv)

　　　(1) A: 你們是甚麼時候認識的？

　　　　　B: 我們是剛認識的。

　　　(2) A: 你怎麼剛來美國就要回國？

　　　　　B: 因為家裏有要緊的事情。

☞ 剛剛　　　just, only, exactly; a moment ago, just now (Adv)

　　　　　　A: 我剛剛給你打了一個電話，可是沒人接。

　　　　　　B: 你找我有甚麼事嗎？

☞ 剛好　　　just; exactly; it so happened that (Adv)

　　　(1) 我的錢剛好夠買這本書。

　　　(2) 我們到飛機場的時候，剛好飛機來了。

9. 買 buy, purchase (V)

A: 你要買甚麼？

B: 我不買甚麼，就看看。

☞ 買賣 buying and selling (V); business; transaction (N)

A: 你爸爸作甚麼買賣？

B: 他買房子也賣房子。

A: 他的買賣很大嗎？

B: 不太大。

10. 懂 understand, know (V/SV/RE)

(1) A: 你懂我的意思嗎？

B: 我不懂。

(2) A: 他懂中國畫兒嗎？

B: 他雖然是美國人，可是他很懂中國畫兒。

(3) A: 你看得懂看不懂英文報？

B: 我才學了一年英文，我還看不懂英文報。

☞ 懂得 understand, know, grasp (V)

A: 你懂得怎麼用這個生字嗎？

B: 我懂得這個生字的意思，可是我不會用。

☞ 懂事 sensible; intelligent (SV)

A: 許太太，你的女兒又懂事又可愛。

B: 哪裏，哪裏。她不太懂事。

句型練習

16.1 THE VERB 懂

The verb 懂 can function as a second element in an RVC. It can only be combined with the verbs 聽 "listen" and 看 "read."

(1) A: 你聽得懂聽不懂中國話？
    B: 我聽得懂一點兒中國話。

(2) A: 你看得懂看不懂英文小說？
    B: 我還看不懂呢。

16.2 MORE ON THE 是……的 PATTERN

The 是……的 pattern was introduced in Lesson 6. It is time to discuss this pattern in detail. For the sake of clarity, we will divide the 是……的 pattern into two types.

16.2.1 是……的 with a past event

As we discussed in Lesson 6, the 是……的 pattern is used with a past occurrence. It focuses on a specific aspect of the occurrence, rather than the occurrence itself. If we want to find out the "where" or "when" of a past event, the 是……的 pattern must be used. 是 can sometimes be omitted.

(1) A: 我買了一本書。
    B: 你的書是在哪兒買的？
    A: 是在一個剛開的書店買的。

(2) A: 我爸爸回來了。
    B: 他是甚麼時候回來的？
    A: 昨天晚上回來的。

Note that the preferred position of the object in a 是……的 pattern is at the beginning of the sentence.

(1) A: 這個車是誰給你的？

　　B: 這個車是我媽媽給我的。

(2) A: 這本書是誰寫的？

　　B: 這本書是我老師寫的。

> When the object in a 是……的 pattern is a pronoun, 的 is placed after the pronoun, as in the first example, **not** after the verb, as in the second example.

✔ (1) 這個錶是他女朋友給他的。

✘ (2) 這個錶是他女朋友給的他。

> When the object in a 是……的 pattern is a place word, 的 is placed either at the end of the sentence, as in the first example, or immediately after the verb, as in the second example.

(1) A: 你女朋友是甚麼時候來美國的？

　　B: 她是一九八七年來美國的。

(2) A: 你女朋友是甚麼時候來的美國？

　　B: 她是一九八七年來的美國。

16.2.2 是……的 with a presumption

> The 是……的 pattern can be used to affirm or deny some supposition or expectation.

(1) 你們會是好父母的。

(2) 要是你用功，你是會考得很好的。

(3) 我是不會同意你的看法的。

(4) 誰說明天會下雨？明天是不會下雨的。

16.3 有 AND 沒有

16.3.1 A 有 B (那麼/這麼) SV

If the similarity between "A" and "B" is close enough to be considered equivalent, the word 有 "have" is placed between "A" and "B". 那麼 or 這麼 "so, such, to this or that extent" as an adverbial expression of degree may be added along with the appropriate predicate.

A	有	B	(那麼/這麼)	SV
她	有	她媽媽	那麼	好看。

She is as pretty as her mother.

(1) A: 她作的飯有你作的這麼好嗎？
    B: 她作的飯有我作的一樣好。

(2) A: 中文有英文那麼難嗎？
    B: 是。中文有英文一樣難。

16.3.2 A 沒有 B (那麼/這麼) SV

To express "A" is not equivalent to or less than "B", the A 沒有 B (那麼/這麼) SV pattern is used.

A	沒有	B	(那麼/這麼)	SV
我	沒有	你	那麼	忙。

I am not as busy as you are.

(1) A: 今天有沒有昨天冷？
    B: 今天沒有昨天那麼冷。

(2) A: 日本的人口有沒有中國那麼多？
    B: 日本的人口一定沒有中國的多。

🌸 造 句

1.
剛
剛認識的。
剛認識的朋友。
他是我剛認識的朋友。

2.
出賣
出賣了我。
誰出賣了你？
我最好的朋友出賣了我。

3.
有
有沒有？
他有沒有你用功？
他有沒有你那麼用功？

4.
多
多學一點兒。
多學一點兒甚麼？
多學一點兒外國話。

🌸 問 答

1. 林海英，你們放假去哪兒了？   我們去日本了。
2. 日本的天氣怎麼樣？   很好，不冷也不熱。
3. 你們去日本作甚麼？   我們去看外祖父母。
4. 你們在日本的時候，住在旅館還是住在外祖父母家？   我們住在外祖父母家。
5. 他們的房子有你們的大嗎？   他們的房子沒有我們的大，可是也不少。
6. 你外祖父母懂不懂英文？   我外祖父懂一點兒，外祖母不懂。
7. 你會說日本話嗎？   一點兒都不會。
8. 你外祖父作甚麼事？   他從前作買賣，現在老了，不作事了。
9. 你們是幾月幾號回來的？   我們是九月八號回來的。
10. 你還會去日本嗎？   我們一有機會就去。

閱讀練習

日本的湯不好喝

有一天許小美到一個日本飯館去吃飯。她不懂日本話，可是有的日本字跟中國字一樣，所以她認識。她看了看菜單，就寫了一個"湯"跟兩個菜。飯館兒的小姐給她拿來了她要的湯跟菜。她吃完了以後就回家了。媽媽問她："今天你去飯館兒吃飯，那兒的菜怎麼樣？"小美說："他們的菜很好吃，可是他們的湯不好喝，一點兒味道都沒有。"媽媽問她要的甚麼湯。她說："我不知道甚麼湯好，所以我就寫了一個"湯"字。"媽媽笑著說："難怪你的湯不好喝。你喝的是"熱水"。"湯"字雖然中文跟日文一樣寫，可是意思不一樣；中文的"湯"是soup可是日文"湯"是熱水的意思。熱水當然沒有味道了。"小美說："我今天得到了一個好經驗。"

許小美得到了甚麼經驗？看外國菜單難嗎？要是你看不懂中文菜單你作甚麼？

請查生詞

Look up the following words in a dictionary.

菜單　càidān
拿　　ná
難怪　nánguài
味道　wèidào
經驗　jīngyàn
笑　　xiào

填 空

Fill in the blanks with the appropriate words from the story.

1. 中文的 _____ _____ 很難懂。我看_____ 懂，請你幫我叫兩個 _____ 。

2. 小美不知道有的<u>中國</u>字跟日文的意思不一樣，_____ _____ 她叫的 _____ 沒_____ _____ 。

3. 你有沒有過<u>小美</u>那樣的 _____ _____ ？

4. 這個菜的 _____ _____ 真好，叫甚麼名字？

第十七課　給爸爸過生日
Lesson 17　Celebrating father's birthday

Lesson 17
Pinyin Text

CONTENTS

Text   208

Vocabulary and Illustrative Sentences   209
(suì, qìng, tǎo, lùn, lǐ, wù, kè, jīng, bǎi, kuài)

Pattern Drills   214
(suì, nián and suìshu, búlùn ... dōu/yě/hái, kèqi, búkèqi, yíkuàir, gěi)

Sentence Building   217
(búlùn, kèqi, lǐwù, yìbǎi)

Questions and Responses   218

Supplementary Vocabulary   219

Cultural Notes   220

Text

Gěi bàba guò shēngrì
Celebrating father's birthday

Mǎ Àiwén: Wǒ yǐjīng gàosuguo nǐmen zhè yuè sān hào shì wǒ bàba de shēngrì. Bàba niánnián dōu gěi wǒmen guò shēngrì, kěshì tā cónglái méi guòguo shēngrì. Jīnnián tā wǔshí suì le. Wǒmen yídìng yào gěi tā qìngzhù qìngzhù. Wǒ gēn Sīwén yī huí jiā jiù gēn māma tǎolùn zěnme gěi bàba guò shēngrì: sòng tā shénme lǐwù, qǐng shénme rén lái chīfàn, qǐng duōshǎo rén, shì zài jiā chī háishì chūqu chī.

I have already told you that the third of this month is my father's birthday. My father celebrates our birthdays every year but he has never celebrated his own birthday. He turned fifty this year. We had to celebrate his birthday. As soon as Siwen and I arrived home, we discussed our plans for father's birthday celebration with our mother: what presents to give him, whom to invite for dinner, how many people to invite, whether to eat at home or to eat out.

Lín Hǎiyīng: Nǐmen qǐng le duōshǎo kèrén?

How many guests did you invite?

Mǎ Àiwén: Wǒmen jiù qǐng le shí ge bàba zuìhǎo de péngyou.

We only invited ten of our father's best friends.

Xǔ Xiǎoměi: Nǐ bàba zhīdào nǐmen gěi tā guò shēngrì ma?

Did your father know that you were planning a birthday celebration for him?

Mǎ Àiwén: Tā yìdiǎnr dōu bù zhīdào. Kànzhe bàba jīngxǐ de yàngzi, wǒmen zhēn gāoxìng. Wǒmen xià yuè yě yào gěi māma yí ge jīngxǐ de shēngrì wǔhuì. Wǒ māma hěn xǐhuan tiàowǔ.

He didn't have a clue. We were very happy when we saw our father's surprised expression. We also want to throw a surprise dance party for our mother's birthday next month. My mother loves to dance.

Lesson 17 Celebrating father's birthday
第十七課 給爸爸過生日

Lín Hǎiyīng : Nǐmen sònggěi nǐmen bàba shénme lǐwù?

What presents did you give your father?

Mǎ Àiwén : Jiějie sònggěi tā hěn duō huār, dìdi sònggěi tā yì běn shū, gēge sònggěi tā yí ge shǒubiǎo, māma sònggěi tā yí ge diànnǎo. Sīwén gēn wǒ sònggěi tā yìbǎi kuài qián.

My elder sister gave him a lot of flowers, my younger brother gave him a book, my elder brother gave him a watch, and my mother gave him a computer. Siwen and I gave him a hundred dollars.

Vocabulary and Illustrative Sentences

1. suì — **year (of age)** (MW)

   A: Nǐ mèimei jǐ suì le? — How old is your younger sister?
   B: Tā jiǔ suì le. — She is nine years old.

   suìshu — age (N)

   A: Nǐ zǔmǔ duō dà suìshu le? — How old is your (paternal) grandmother?
   B: Tā liùshíwǔ suì le. — She is sixty-five.

   tóngsuì — of the same age (IE)

   A: Wǒ shì yìjiǔbāsì nián shēng de, nǐ ne? — I was born in 1984. How about you?
   B: Wǒ yě shì. Wǒmen liǎng ge rén tóngsuì. — Me too. We are of the same age.

2. qìng — **celebrate; congratulate** (V)

   qìngzhù — celebrate (V)

   A: Dàkǎo wán le de shíhou, wǒmen kāi yí ge qìngzhùhuì, hǎo ma? — When final exams are over, we'll have a celebration (party), okay?

		B: Hǎo. Wǒmen děi zhǎo yí ge hǎo de chǎngdì.	Okay. We have to find a good venue (for the party).

☞ guóqìng   National Day (N)

	A: Měiguó de guóqìng shì jǐ yuè jǐ hào?	When is America's National Day?
	B: Qīyuè sì hào.	4 July.

☞ huānqìng   celebrate joyously (V)

	A: Jīntiān wèishénme fàngjià?	Why is today a holiday?
	B: Jīntiān shì guóqìng rì. Dàjiā dōu huānqìng guóqìng.	Today is (our) National Day. Everyone is joyously celebrating our National Day.

3. tǎo **discuss; study (V)**

☞ tǎohǎo   ingratiate oneself with; have one's labor rewarded (IE)

	A: Nǐ wèishénme xué Zhōngwén?	Why are you learning Chinese?
	B: Xiǎo shíhou xué Zhōngwén shì wèi le tǎohǎo fùmǔ. Xiànzài shì yīnwèi wǒ xǐhuan Zhōngwén.	When I was young, I learned Chinese to please my parents. Now I am learning Chinese because I like it.

4. lùn **discuss, talk about, discourse; view, opinion; theory (V/N)**

☞ búlùn   no matter (what, who, how, etc.); whether ... or ...; regardless of, whether or not (Adv)

	(1) Búlùn nǐ shuō shénme, wǒ dōu bú qù.	No matter what you say, I won't go.
	(2) Búlùn nǐ xuǎn-bu-xuǎn Zhōngwén, wǒ yě yào xuǎn.	I am going to take Chinese no matter you take it or not.

☞ tǎolùn   discuss, talk over (V)

	A: Tāmen zài shuō shénme?	What are they talking about?
	B: Tāmen zài tǎolùn yí ge hěn yàojǐn de shìqing.	They are discussing a very important issue.

Lesson 17 Celebrating father's birthday
第十七課 给爸爸过生日

☞ **tǎolùnhuì**   discussion; symposium (N)

討論

A: Nǐmen bān de tóngxué shénme shíhou yào kāi tǎolùnhuì?
When will your classmates have the discussion?

B: Xià xīngqīyī. Nǐ lái ma?
Next Monday. Are you coming?

☞ **lùnwén**   thesis, dissertation (N)

論文

A: Zhè jǐ tiān wèishénme Wáng lǎoshī nàme máng?
Why has Professor Wang been so busy over the past few days?

B: Tā zài xiě lùnwén.
He has been writing a thesis.

5. **lǐ** 礼   **ceremony, rite; courtesy; etiquette; manners; gift, present (N)**

☞ **sòng lǐ**   give somebody a gift (VO)

送礼

A: Péngyou guò shēngrì, wǒ yīnggāi sòng lǐ ma?
Should I give my friend a gift on his/her birthday?

B: Wǒ xiǎng nǐ yīnggāi sòng diǎnr lǐ.
I think you should give him/her a small gift.

6. **wù** 物   **thing; matter (N)**

☞ **lǐwù**   gift, present (N)

礼物

A: Zhōngguórén guò nián de shíhou, sòng shénme lǐwù?
When Chinese people celebrate the New Year, what kind of presents do they give?

B: Nǐ kěyǐ sòng chīde, yě kěyǐ sòng cháyè, nǐ xǐhuan sòng shénme jiù sòng shénme.
You can give food or tea (leaves). You can give whatever you want to give.

☞ **wénwù**   cultural/historical relic (N)

文物

A: Zhōngguó yǒu hěn mǐngguì de wénwù. Nǐ zài Zhōngguó de shíhou, yīnggāi qù kànkan.
There are many precious historical relics in China. When you're in China, you should go take a look.

B: Hǎo. Wǒ yídìng qù.
All right. I will definitely go.

☞ shēngwù-xué   biology (N)

生物学

A: Nǐ shàng xuéqī yǒu-méiyǒu xuǎn shēngwùxué? — Did you take biology last semester?

B: Méi xuǎn. Wǒ dǎsuàn xià xuéqī xuǎn. — I didn't. I'm planning to take the course next semester.

☞ dàrénwù   important person, personage, VIP (N)

大人物

A: Nàge dàrénwù yìtiāndàowǎn zài máng shénme? — What is that personage so busy with all day long?

B: Dàrénwù dāngrán shì zài máng yàojǐn de shìqing le. — Personages are certainly preoccupied with serious issues.

☞ xiǎorénwù   an unimportant person, a nobody (N)

小人物

A: Kāi tǎolùnhuì de shíhou, nǐ wèishénme bù shuōhuà? — Why didn't you say something during the discussion?

B: Kāihuì de rén dōu shì dàrénwù, wǒ zhège xiǎorénwù yǒu shénme huà kě shuō de. — Everyone attending the meeting was a personage. I'm a nobody, (so) I have nothing remarkable to say.

7. kè 客 **visitor; guest; traveler; passenger; customer** (N)

☞ kèrén   guest; guest (at a hotel, etc.) (N)

客人

A: Nǐmen jīntiān qǐng le duōshǎo kèrén? — How many guests have you invited today?

B: Wǒmen jiā de dìfang hěn xiǎo, jiù qǐng le liù ge kèrén. — Our house is very small, (so) we have only invited six guests.

☞ kèqi   polite, courteous, modest (Adj)

客气

(1) Nàge rén zhēn kèqi. — That person is very polite.

(2) A: Wǒ de Zhōngguóhuà shuōde bù hǎo. — I don't speak Chinese very well.

B: Nǐ tài kèqi le. Nǐ shuōde hěn hǎo. — You're too modest. You speak (Chinese) very well.

Lesson 17 Celebrating father's birthday
第十七课 给爸爸过生日

☞ búkèqi   impolite, rude, blunt; you're welcome, don't mention it (IE)

不客气

(1) A: Xièxie nǐ qǐng wǒ kàn diànyǐng. — Thank you for inviting me to a movie.

    B: Búkèqi. — You're welcome.

(2) A: Nǐ shuōhuà zěnme zhème búkèqi? — Why do you speak so rudely?

    B: Yīnwèi nǐ shuōhuà búkèqi, suǒyǐ wǒ cái búkèqi. — Because you speak impolitely, (so) I speak rudely too.

☞ qǐngkè   treat somebody, invite somebody to dinner, entertain guests (VO)

请客

(1) A: Wǒmen jīntiān wǎnshang chūqu chīfàn, wǒ qǐngkè. — We are going out for dinner tonight, (and) it will be my treat.

    B: Bù, bù. Wǒ qǐng. — No, no (I can't let you do it). I will treat you.

(2) Zuótiān wǒmen jiālǐ qǐngkè, māma zuò le hěn duō hǎochī de cài. — Yesterday we had guests over, mother cooked a lot of delicious food.

8. jīng   **to be frightened or surprised** (Adj)

☞ jīngxǐ   pleasantly surprised (Adj)

惊

A: Zhōngguórén cóngqián yě gěi rén jīngxǐ de shēngrì wǎnhuì ma? — In the past, did the Chinese also throw surprise birthday parties?

B: Méiyǒu. Zhè shì gēn Měiguórén xué de. — No. This is a custom adopted from the Americans.

☞ chījīng   to be startled, shocked or amazed (V/Adj)

吃惊

Méi xiǎngdào tā huì zuòchū zhèyàng bù hǎo de shì, zhēn jiào wǒ chījīng. — I have never thought that he could do such kind of bad thing. I am really shocked.

9. **bǎi**
百

hundred; numerous (Nu/MW)

A: Jīntiān yǒu liǎngbǎi duō ge rén lái gěi nàge dàrénwù guò shēngrì.

More than two hundred people came to celebrate the personage's birthday today.

B: Zhēn de ma!

Really!

10. **kuài**
块

piece, lump, chunk; yuan (the basic unit of currency in Chinese) (MW)

A: Zhè kuài dì duōshǎo qián?

How much is this piece of land?

B: Wǒ yě bù zhīdào.

I don't know (either).

☞ **fāngkuàizì** Chinese characters (N)
方块字

A: Wèishénme Zhōngguózì jiào fāngkuàizì?

Why are Chinese characters called "fangkuaizi"?

B: Yīnwèi Zhōngguózì shì fāng de.

Because the shape of Chinese characters is square.

☞ **yíkuàir** at the same place; together (Adv)
一块儿

(1) Zhè liǎng ge lǐwù kěyǐ fàngzài yíkuàir ma?

Can these two gifts be put together?

(2) Wǒ xǐhuan gēn tóngxué yíkuàir lǚxíng.

I like to travel together with my classmates.

🌸 Pattern Drills

17.1 Suì, nián AND suìshu

Both **suì** and **nián** mean "year," but each is used differently in Chinese. **Suì** is a measure word used for one's age, whereas **nián** is used for periods of time. **Suìshu** is a noun used in asking the age of the elderly.

(1) A: Nǐ jīnnián jǐ suì le?

How old are you?

B: Wǔ suì sān ge yuè.

Five years and three months.

Lesson 17 Celebrating father's birthday
第十七課 給爸爸過生日

(2) A: Xiǎoměi, nǐ shì nǎ nián shēng de?   Xiaomei, in which year were you born?

   B: Yījiǔbāwǔ nián.   1985.

(3) A: Nǐ mǔqīn duódà suìshu le?   How old is your mother?

   B: Tā jīnnián liùshísì suì le.   She is going to be sixty-four this year.

17.2 THE PATTERN búlùn ... dōu/yě/hái

Búlùn ... dōu/yě/hái "no matter ... yet" are two adverbial linking words. Búlùn is a movable adverb — it can be placed either in the initial position of a sentence or after the subject/topic. Dōu, yě or hái are nonmovable adverbs — they are positioned at the beginning of the second clause.

(A) Subject/Topic búlùn clause,   subject dōu/yě/hái clause.
    Jīntiān   búlùn nǐ qù-bu-qù, wǒ   dōu   děi qù.
    I have to go today no matter whether you go or not.

(B) Búlùn subject/topic clause,   subject dōu/yě/hái clause.
    Búlùn nǐ gěi wǒ duōshǎo qián,   wǒ   yě   bù gěi nǐ zuò shì.
    No matter how much money you give me, I won't work for you.

(1) Búlùn Zhōngwén duó nán, wǒ hái yào xué.   I will learn Chinese no matter how difficult it is.

(2) Nǐ búlùn zěnme shuō, tā yě bú huì xǐhuan nǐ de yìjiàn de.   He won't like your idea no matter what you say.

17.3 THE EXPRESSION kèqi

Kèqi has several meanings, depending on the context in which it appears. It can mean "modest," as in the first example; "polite," as in the second example; or "don't stand on ceremony," as in the third example.

(1) Nǐ de Yīngwén shuōde zhème hǎo, hái shuō jiù huì shuō yìdiǎnr, nǐ tài kèqi le.   You speak English so well and yet you claim that you can only speak a little. You are too modest.

(2) Wǒmen yǐjīng shì lǎopéngyou le, zěnme hái zhème kèqi?   We are already old friends. Why are we still so polite to each other?

(3) Nǐ jiù zài zhèr chīfàn ba, bú yào kèqi.   You must eat with us. Don't stand on ceremony.

17.4 THE EXPRESSION búkèqi

Búkèqi has two basic meanings. It means impolite, rude, blunt, as in the first two examples. It can also be used as a polite phrase indicating that thanks are not necessary (you're welcome, don't mention it), as in the last two examples.

(1) Zhège rén zěnme zhème búkèqi.   Why is this person so impolite?

(2) Tā duì tā fùqīn hěn búkèqide shuō, cóng jīn yǐhòu wǒ bú shì nǐ de érzi le.   He said to his father bluntly, "From now on I am not your son anymore."

(3) A: Xǔ xiānsheng, xièxie nǐ gěi wǒ xiě jièshàoxìn.   Mr. Xu, thank you for writing a recommendation letter for me.

    B: Búkèqi.   You're welcome.

(4) A: Duōxiè nǐ sòng wǒ huí jiā.   Thanks for taking me home.

    B: Búkèqi.   Don't mention it.

17.5 THE EXPRESSION yíkuàir

17.5.1 Yíkuàir as a noun

Yíkuàir can be used as a noun, meaning "in the same place" or "together."

(1) A: Kèrén sònggěi nǐ bàba de lǐwù dōu fàngzài yíkuàir le ma?   Did you put all the presents that the guests gave your dad in the same place?

    B: Dōu fàngzài yíkuàir le.   Yes, they were all put in the same place.

(2) A: Xiǎoshíhou tāmen liǎng ge rén zhùzai yíkuàir ma?   Did they live together when they were kids?

B: Tāmen méi zhùzai yíkuàir. Yí ge zhùzai Zhōngguó, yí ge zhùzai Měiguó.

They didn't live together. One lived in China and one lived in the States.

17.5.2 Yíkuàir as an adverb

When yíkuàir is used as an adverb, it is placed before the verb in a sentence.

(1) Wǒmen yíkuàir qù kàn diànyǐng ba!   Let's go to the movie together!

(2) Fàng chūnjià de shíhou, wǒ gēn péngyou yíkuàir qù lǚxíng.   During spring vacation, I will travel with my friends.

17.6 Gěi AS A POSTVERB

In Lesson 8, we learned that gěi can function as a verb meaning "to give" or as a coverb meaning "for." In fact, gěi can also function as a postverb (attached to another verb) meaning "to."

(1) Tā sònggěi wǒ yí ge hěn guì de lǐwù.   She gave me a very expensive gift.

(2) Wǒmen de chē màigěi le yí ge gāng lái Měiguó de xuésheng le.   We sold our car to a student who just came to the United States.

(3) Tā de fángzi zūgěi le yí ge zuò mǎimài de rén le.   He rented his house to a businessman.

(4) Qǐng nǐ nágei wǒ jīntiān de bào.   Please bring me today's paper.

Sentence Building

1.
Búlùn
Búlùn qù-bu-qù.
Búlùn nǐ qù-bu-qù.
Búlùn nǐ qù-bu-qù, wǒ dōu qù.

2.
Kèqi
Hěn kèqi.
Tā hěn kèqi.
Tā duì rén hěn kèqi.

3.
Lǐwù
Sòng lǐwù.
Sòng lǐwù hěn nán.
Gěi péngyou sòng lǐwù hěn nán.

4.
Yìbǎi
Yìbǎi suì.
Yìbǎi suì de shēngrì.
Qìngzhù yìbǎi suì de shēngrì.

🐾 Questions and Responses

1. Mǎ Sīwén nǐ bàba duō dà suìshu le?
   Ma Siwen, how old is your father?

   Tā jīnnián wǔshí suì le.
   He will be fifty this year.

2. Nǐmen zěnme qìngzhù tā de shēngrì?
   How are you going to celebrate his birthday?

   Wǒmen hái méi tǎolùn ne.
   We haven't discussed that yet.

3. Nǐ zhīdào tā xǐhuan shénme lǐwù ma?

   Do you know what sort of present he would like to have?

   Wǒ xiǎng wǒ māma huì zhīdào tā xǐhuan shénme.
   I think my mother will know what he likes.

4. Nǐ yào gàosu nǐ bàba gěi tā guò shēngrì ma?
   Are you going to tell your father that you're celebrating his birthday?

   Wǒmen bú yào gàosu tā, wǒmen yào gěi tā yí ge jīngxǐ.
   We are not telling him. We want to give him a surprise.

5. Nǐ de shēngrì shì jǐ yuè jǐ hào?
   When is your birthday?

   Wǒ de shēngrì shì shí'èryuè sānshí hào.
   My birthday is on 30 December.

6. Nǐ jīnnián de shēngrì xiǎng dédào shénme lǐwù?
   What do you want as a birthday present this year?

   Shénme lǐwù dōu hǎo, búguò wǒ xiǎng yào yí ge diànnǎo.
   Any present is fine, but I'm really hoping for a computer.

7. Nǐ xǐhuan gēn tóngxué zài yíkuàir guò shēngrì háishì gēn fùmǔ zài yíkuàir guò shēngrì?
   Do you like to celebrate your birthday with your classmates or with your parents?

   Wǒ xiǎo de shíhou xǐhuan gēn tóngxué yíkuàir guò shēngrì, kěshì xiànzài xǐhuan gēn fùmǔ yíkuàir guò le.
   When I was younger, I liked celebrating my birthday with my classmates, but now I enjoy celebrating it with my parents.

Lesson 17 Celebrating father's birthday
第十七課 給爸爸過生日

8. Wèishénme?

   Why?

   Yīnwèi wǒ xiànzài bú zhùzai jiā, hěn shǎo gēn fùmǔ zài yíkuàir.
   Since I am not living at home now, I rarely get to see my parents.

9. Nǐ guò shēngrì de shíhou, dǎsuàn qǐng duōshǎo kèrén?
   When you celebrate your birthday, how many guests do you plan to invite?

   Wǒ děi wèn wǒ māma wǒ kěyǐ qǐng jǐ ge kèrén.
   I have to ask my mother how many guests I may invite.

10. Nǐ huì chàng "Shēngrì Kuàilè" ma?

    Do you know how to sing "Happy Birthday"?

    Dāngrán huì. Bù nán chàng, shénme rén dōu huì chàng.
    Of course I know. It's not difficult to sing (the song). Anybody can sing it.

Supplementary Vocabulary

shēngrì	birthday
dàngāo	cake
zhùshòu	congratulate an elderly person on his or her birthday
bàishòu	congratulate an elderly person on his or her birthday
shēngrì kuàilè	Happy birthday!
chángshòu	long life; longevity
shòumiàn	noodles eaten on one's birthday; birthday (or longevity) noodles
shòutáo	peaches offered as a birthday present; (peach-shaped) birthday buns
shòuxing	the god of longevity; an elderly person whose birthday is being celebrated
wànshòuwújiāng	(wish somebody) a long life

🌸 Cultural Notes

<u>Sòng</u> <u>lǐ</u> (Gift-giving)

Gift-giving is a very common practice in China. There are many occasions in which people tend to give out gifts: (1) paying visits to relatives, (2) meeting up with friends during certain Chinese festivals, (3) upon returning from a long trip, (4) dining at someone's home, (5) paying visits to someone who is ill, (6) attending birthday parties or weddings, (7) showing gratitude for someone's kindness and help, etc.

Many Chinese people tend to decline a gift at first, as a matter of politeness as well as avoiding appearing greedy. But after being pressed two to three times, they will graciously accept the gift. And unlike the Westerners, Chinese tend not to unwrap the gift right away. They normally put the gift aside, again, to avoid appearing greedy.

The Chinese especially appreciate gifts which are well-known regional products, be it of a domestic or foreign origin. But there are gifts that the Chinese will avoid giving out. For example, clocks and umbrellas are considered to be undesirable gifts. The Chinese word for clock, <u>zhōng</u>, is synonymous with the word <u>sǐ</u>, which means death. As for the Chinese word for umbrella, <u>sàn</u>, it sounds similar to the word <u>sǎn</u>, which means "to separate." Such unpleasant gifts are thought to portend misfortune.

第十七課
漢字本

內容

課文 — 222

生詞及例句 — 223
(歲、慶、討、論、禮、物、客、驚、百、塊)

句型練習 — 227
(歲、年和歲數、不論……都/也/還、客氣、
不客氣、一塊兒、給)

造句 — 229
(不論、客氣、禮物、一百)

問答 — 230

閱讀練習 — 231
你能叫我走出去嗎?

🌸 課文

給爸爸過生日

馬愛文：我已經告訴過你們這月三號是我爸爸的生日。爸爸年年都給我們過生日，可是他從來沒過過生日。今年他五十歲了。我們一定要給他慶祝慶祝。我跟思文一回家就跟媽媽討論怎麼給爸爸過生日：送他甚麼禮物，請甚麼人來吃飯，請多少人，是在家吃還是出去吃。

林海英：你們請了多少客人？

馬愛文：我們就請了十個爸爸最好的朋友。

許小美：你爸爸知道你們給他過生日嗎？

馬愛文：他一點兒都不知道。看著爸爸驚喜的樣子，我們真高興。我們下月也要給媽媽一個驚喜的生日舞會。我媽媽很喜歡跳舞。

林海英：你們送給你們爸爸甚麼禮物？

馬愛文：姐姐送給他很多花兒，弟弟送給他一本書，哥哥送給他一個手錶，媽媽送給他一個電腦。思文跟我送給他一百塊錢。

Lesson 17 Celebrating father's birthday
第十七課 給爸爸過生日

🌸 生詞及例句

1. **歲** **year (of age) (MW)**
   A: 你妹妹幾歲了？
   B: 她九歲了。

   ☞ 歲數   age (N)
   A: 你祖母多大歲數了？
   B: 她六十五歲了。

   ☞ 同歲   of the same age (IE)
   A: 我是一九八四年生的，你呢？
   B: 我也是。我們兩個人同歲。

2. **慶** **celebrate; congratulate (V)**
   ☞ 慶祝   celebrate (V)
   A: 大考完了的時候，我們開一個慶祝會，好嗎？
   B: 好。我們得找一個好的場地。

   ☞ 國慶   National Day (N)
   A: 美國的國慶是幾月幾號？
   B: 七月四號。

   ☞ 歡慶   celebrate joyously (V)
   A: 今天為甚麼放假？
   B: 今天是國慶日。大家都歡慶國慶。

3. **討** **discuss; study (V)**
   ☞ 討好   ingratiate oneself with; have one's labor rewarded (IE)

A: 你為甚麼學中文？

B: 小時候學中文是為了討好父母。現在是因為我喜歡中文。

4. 論　**discuss, talk about, discourse; view, opinion; theory (V/N)**

☞ 不論　no matter (what, who, how, etc.); whether ... or ...; regardless of, whether or not (Adv)

(1) 不論你說甚麼，我都不去。

(2) 不論你選不選中文，我也要選。

☞ 討論　discuss, talk over (V)

A: 他們在說甚麼？

B: 他們在討論一個很要緊的事情。

☞ 討論會　discussion; symposium (N)

A: 你們班的同學甚麼時候要開討論會？

B: 下星期一。你來嗎？

☞ 論文　thesis, dissertation (N)

A: 這幾天為甚麼王老師那麼忙？

B: 他在寫論文。

5. 禮　**ceremony, rite; courtesy; etiquette; manners; gift, present (N)**

☞ 送禮　give somebody a gift (VO)

A: 朋友過生日，我應該送禮嗎？

B: 我想你應該送點兒禮。

6. 物 wù　**thing; matter (N)**

☞ 禮物　gift, present (N)

A: 中國人過年的時候，送甚麼禮物？

B: 你可以送吃的，也可以送茶葉，你喜歡送甚麼就送甚麼。

Lesson 17 Celebrating father's birthday
第十七課　給爸爸過生日

☞ 文物　　cultural/historical relic (N)
　　　　A: 中國有很名貴的文物。你在中國的時候，應該去看看。
　　　　B: 好。我一定去。

☞ 生物學　biology (N)
　　　　A: 你上學期有沒有選生物學？
　　　　B: 沒選。我打算下學期選。

☞ 大人物　important person, personage, VIP (N)
　　　　A: 那個大人物一天到晚在忙甚麼？
　　　　B: 大人物當然是在忙要緊的事情了。

☞ 小人物　an unimportant person, a nobody (N)
　　　　A: 開討論會的時候，你為甚麼不說話？
　　　　B: 開會的人都是大人物，我這個小人物有甚麼話可說的。

7. 客　　　visitor; guest; traveler; passenger; customer (N)

☞ 客人　　guest; guest (at a hotel, etc.) (N)
　　　　A: 你們今天請了多少客人？
　　　　B: 我們家的地方很小，就請了六個客人。

☞ 客氣　　polite, courteous, modest (Adj)
　　　　(1) 那個人真客氣。
　　　　(2) A: 我的中國話說得不好。
　　　　　　B: 你太客氣了。你說得很好。

☞ 不客氣　impolite, rude, blunt; you're welcome, don't mention it (IE)
　　　　(1) A: 謝謝你請我看電影。
　　　　　　B: 不客氣。
　　　　(2) A: 你說話怎麼這麼不客氣？
　　　　　　B: 因為你說話不客氣，所以我才不客氣。

☞ 請客   treat somebody, invite somebody to dinner, entertain guests (VO)

(1) A: 我們今天晚上出去吃飯，我請客。
    B: 不，不。我請。

(2) 昨天我們家裏請客，媽媽作了很多好吃的菜。

8. 驚   **to be frightened or surprised** (Adj)
   驚喜   pleasantly surprised (Adj)
   A: 中國人從前也給人驚喜的生日晚會嗎？
   B: 沒有。這是跟美國人學的。

☞ 吃驚   to be startled, shocked or amazed (V/Adj)
   沒想到他會作出這樣不好的事，真叫我吃驚。

9. 百   **hundred; numerous** (Nu/MW)
   A: 今天有兩百多個人來給那個大人物過生日。
   B: 真的嗎！

10. 塊   **piece, lump, chunk; yuan** (the basic unit of currency in Chinese) (MW)
    A: 這塊地多少錢？
    B: 我也不知道。

☞ 方塊字 Chinese characters (N)
    A: 為甚麼中國字叫方塊字？
    B: 因為中國字是方的。

☞ 一塊兒 at the same place; together (Adv)
    (1) 這兩個禮物可以放在一塊兒嗎？
    (2) 我喜歡跟同學一塊兒旅行。

Lesson 17 Celebrating father's birthday
第十七課 給爸爸過生日

句型練習

17.1 歲, 年, AND 歲數

Both 歲 and 年 mean "year," but each is used differently in Chinese. 歲 is a measure word used for one's age, whereas 年 is used for periods of time. 歲數 is a noun used in asking the age of the elderly.

(1) A: 你今年幾歲了？
    B: 五歲三個月。

(2) A: 小美，你是哪年生的？
    B: 一九八五年。

(3) A: 你母親多大歲數了？
    B: 她今年六十四歲了。

17.2 THE PATTERN 不論……都/也/還

不論……都/也/還 "no matter ... yet" are two adverbial linking words. 不論 is a movable adverb — it can be placed either in the initial position of a sentence or after the subject/topic. 都, 也 or 還 are nonmovable adverbs — they are positioned at the beginning of the second clause.

(A) Subject/Topic　不論　clause,　subject　都/也/還　clause.
    今天　　　　　　不論　你去不去，我　　　　都得去。
    I have to go today no matter you go or not.

(B) 不論　subject/topic　clause,　subject　都/也/還　clause.
    不論　你　　給我多少錢，　　我　　　也不給你作事。
    No matter how much money you give me, I won't work for you.

(1) 不論中文多難，我還要學。

(2) 你不論怎麼說，他也不會喜歡你的意見的。

17.3 THE EXPRESSION 客氣

客氣 has several meanings, depending on the context in which it appears. It can mean "modest" as in the first example; "polite" as in the second example; or "don't stand on ceremony" as in the third example.

(1) 你的英文說得這麼好，還說就會說一點兒，你太客氣了。

(2) 我們已經是老朋友了，怎麼還這麼客氣？

(3) 你就在這兒吃飯吧，不要客氣。

17.4 THE EXPRESSION 不客氣

不客氣 has two basic meanings. It means impolite, rude, blunt, as in the first two examples. It can also be used as a polite phrase indicating that thanks are not necessary (you're welcome, don't mention it), as in the last two examples.

(1) 這個人怎麼這麼不客氣。

(2) 他對他父親很不客氣地說，從今以後我不是你的兒子了。

(3) A: 許先生，謝謝你給我寫介紹信。
    B: 不客氣。

(4) A: 多謝你送我回家。
    B: 不客氣。

17.5 THE EXPRESSION 一塊兒

17.5.1 一塊兒 as a noun

一塊兒 can be used as a noun, meaning "in the same place" or "together."

(1) A: 客人送給你爸爸的禮物都放在一塊兒了嗎？
    B: 都放在一塊兒了。

(2) A: 小時候他們兩個人住在一塊兒嗎？
    B: 他們沒住在一塊兒。一個住在中國，一個住在美國。

17.5.2 一塊兒 as an adverb

When 一塊兒 is used as an adverb, it is placed before the verb in a sentence.

(1) 我們一塊兒去看電影吧！

(2) 放春假的時候，我跟朋友一塊兒去旅行。

17.6 給 AS A POSTVERB

In Lesson 8, we learned that 給 can function as a verb meaning "to give" or as a coverb meaning "for." In fact, 給 can also function as a postverb (attached to another verb) meaning "to."

(1) 她送給我一個很貴的禮物。

(2) 我們的車賣給了一個剛來美國的學生了。

(3) 他的房子租給了一個作買賣的人了。

(4) 請你拿給我今天的報。

造句

1.
不論
不論去不去。
不論你去不去。
不論你去不去，我都去。

2.
客氣
很客氣。
他很客氣。
他對人很客氣。

3.
禮物
送禮物。
送禮物很難。
給朋友送禮物很難。

4.
一百
一百歲。
一百歲的生日。
慶祝一百歲的生日。

問答

1. <u>馬思文</u>你爸爸多大歲數了？　　　他今年五十歲了。
2. 你們怎麼慶祝他的生日？　　　　我們還沒討論呢。
3. 你知道他喜歡甚麼禮物嗎？　　　我想我媽媽會知道他喜歡甚麼。
4. 你要告訴你爸爸給他過生日嗎？　我們不要告訴他，我們要給他一個驚喜。
5. 你的生日是幾月幾號？　　　　　我的生日是十二月三十號。
6. 你今年的生日想得到甚麼禮物？　甚麼禮物都好，不過我想要一個電腦。
7. 你喜歡跟同學在一塊兒過生日還是跟父母在一塊兒過生日？　我小的時候喜歡跟同學一塊兒過生日，可是現在喜歡跟父母一塊兒過了。
8. 為甚麼？　　　　　　　　　　　因為我現在不住在家，很少跟父母在一塊兒。
9. 你過生日的時候，打算請多少客人？　我得問我媽媽我可以請幾個客人。
10. 你會唱"生日快樂"嗎？　　　　當然會。不難唱，甚麼人都會唱。

閱讀練習

你能叫我走出去嗎?

老金有很多朋友,在他的朋友中,別人都認為小林最聰明。可是老金不相信。他老想試小林一下,看他是不是真聰明。

有一天,小林和老金都在朋友家吃飯。老金對小林說:"現在我坐在屋子裏,你能想個辦法叫我走到外頭去嗎?"小林說:"現在外頭很冷,你當然不願意出去了。不過要是你站在外頭,我有辦法叫你走進屋裏來。"

老金說:"好。我現在就出去。看你有甚麼辦法叫我走進來?"說著就走出去了。小林大笑著說:"我這不是已經叫你走到外頭去了嗎?"

老金為甚麼要試小林?小林是怎麼叫老金出去的?你從這個小故事裏學到了甚麼句型?你能把這個故事用英文說給你的朋友聽嗎?

請查生詞

Look up the following words in a dictionary.

聰明	cōngmíng	外頭	wàitóu
只有	zhǐyǒu	願意	yuànyì
相信	xiāngxìn	站	zhàn
辦法	bànfǎ	屋	wū

第十八課　感恩節
Lesson 18　Thanksgiving

Lesson 18
Pinyin Text

CONTENTS

Text   236

Vocabulary and Illustrative Sentences   237
(gǎn, ēn, jié, duān, wǔ, qiū, chūn, nóng, lì, chū)

Pattern Drills   243
(kànqǐlai, gòu, zěnme ... cái, chū)

Sentence Building   246
(zěnme, chū, gǎnxiè, qǐchū)

Questions and Responses   246

Pronunciation Review   247

Supplementary Vocabulary   248

Cultural Notes   248

Text

Gǎn'ēnjié
Thanksgiving

Wáng lǎoshī:	Lín Hǎiyīng, Gǎn'ēnjié kuài dào le, nǐ huí jiā ma?	Lin Haiying, Thanksgiving is coming up. Are you going home?
Lín Hǎiyīng :	Huí jiā. Yí xià kè jiù huíqu. Wáng lǎoshī, nǐmen qìngzhù Gǎn'ēnjié ma?	I'm going home. As soon as class ends, I'll go home. Professor Wang, do you celebrate Thanksgiving?
Wáng lǎoshī:	Wǒmen bú guò Gǎn'ēnjié. Wǒmen guò jǐ ge Zhōngguó de jiérì: Duānwǔjié, Zhōngqiūjié gēn Chūnjié.	We don't celebrate Thanksgiving. But we do celebrate a few Chinese festivals: the Dragon Boat Festival, the Mid-Autumn Festival and the Spring Festival.
Lín Hǎiyīng :	Wáng lǎoshī, nǐ kěyǐ gàosu wǒmen zhè jǐ ge Zhōngguó jiérì shì zěnme lái de ma?	Professor Wang, could you tell us the stories behind these Chinese festivals?
Wáng lǎoshī:	Xiànzài nǐmen hái tīng bù dǒng, yīnwèi nǐmen zhīdào de shēngzì hái bú gòu duō, búguò wǒ kěyǐ gěi nǐmen kàn zhè jǐ ge jiérì de diànyǐng.	At the moment, you can't understand yet, because you haven't learnt many Chinese words. But I can let you watch movies about these festivals.
Lín Hǎiyīng :	Nà tài hǎo le. Wáng lǎoshī, nǐ kěyǐ gàosu wǒmen zhè jǐ ge jiérì shì zài shénme shíhou ma?	That's great. Professor Wang, could you tell us when these festivals are celebrated?
Wáng lǎoshī:	Dāngrán kěyǐ. Duānwǔjié zāi nónglì wǔyuè chū wǔ, Zhōngqiūjié zài bāyuè	Of course. The Dragon Boat Festival is celebrated on the 5th day of the 5th lunar month, the Mid-Autumn Festival

Lesson 18 Thanksgiving
第十八課 感恩節

	shíwǔ, Chūnjié jiù shì Zhōngguó de xīnnián.	is on the 15th day of the 8th lunar month, and the Spring Festival is the Chinese New Year.
Lín Hǎiyīng :	Wǒ zhēn xiǎng duō zhīdào diǎnr Zhōngguó de shìqing.	I really want to know more about China.
Wáng lǎoshī:	Hǎohāor xué Zhōngwén, yǐhòu jiù kěyǐ zhīdào hěn duō Zhōngguó yǒu yìsi de shìqing.	Study Chinese diligently. In the future, you'll know many interesting things about China.

Vocabulary and Illustrative Sentences

1. **gǎn** — **feel, sense; move, touch, affect; feeling** (V)

☞ gǎnqíng — emotion, feeling, sentiment; affection, attachment; love (N)

	A: Yè xiānsheng gēn Yè tàitai de gǎnqíng zěnmeyàng?	How is Mr. Ye's relationship with Mrs. Ye?
	B: Kànqǐlai tāmen liǎng ge rén de gǎnqíng hěn hǎo.	It seems that they are on good terms with each other.

☞ gǎnxiè — thank; be grateful (V)

	A: Nǐ gěi wǒ zuò le zhème duō shì, wǒ zhēn bù zhīdào zěnme gǎnxiè nǐ cái hǎo.	You've done so much for me. I don't know how to thank you.
	B: Méi shénme, bú yào kèqi.	It's nothing. Don't mention it.

☞ gǎnxiǎng — impressions; reflections, thoughts (N)

	(1) Kàn wán zhè běn xiǎoshuō yǐhòu, qǐng xiě chūlai nǐ de gǎnxiǎng.	After you finish reading this novel, please write down your reflections on the book.
	(2) A: Kàn le zhè běn shū yǐhòu, wǒ yǒu hěn duō gǎnxiǎng.	I have a lot of thoughts after reading this book.

		B: Nǐ kěyǐ gàosu wǒ nǐ de gǎnxiǎng ma?	Can you tell me your thoughts?

B: Nǐ kěyǐ gàosu wǒ nǐ de gǎnxiǎng ma?
— Can you tell me your thoughts?

A: Dāngrán kěyǐ. Wǒ yě xiǎng zhīdào nǐ de yìjiàn.
— Of course. I'd like to hear your views too.

☞ **gǎnrén** — touching, moving (Adj)

Wǒ zuótiān kàn de nàge diànyǐng zhēn gǎnrén.
— The movie I watched yesterday was very touching.

☞ **tónggǎn** — the same feeling (or impression) (N)

A: Zhège dìfang zhēn měi. Nǐ shuō ne?
— This place is really beautiful. What do you say?

B: Wǒ gēn nǐ yǒu tónggǎn.
— I feel the same as you do.

2. **ēn** 恩 **kindness; favor; grace (N)**

☞ **ēnrén** — benefactor (N)

Wǒ chūguó de shíhou méiyǒu qián, tā gěi wǒ hěn duō qián, tā shì wǒ de ēnrén. Wǒ bù zhīdào zěnyàng gǎnxiè tā.
— When I went abroad I didn't have much money. He gave me a lot of financial support. He was my benefactor. I don't know how I can thank him.

☞ **gǎn'ēn** — feel grateful; be thankful (VO)

Fùmǔ nàme ài wǒmen, wǒmen yīnggāi zhīdào gǎn'ēn.
— Our parents love us so much that we should be grateful.

☞ **Gǎn'ēnjié** — Thanksgiving (N)

Zài Měiguó guò Gǎn'ēnjié de shíhou chī shénme?
— On Thanksgiving in America, what food is served?

3. **jié** **holiday; moral integrity (N); section, length; joint (MW)**

A: Nǐ jīntiān yǒu jǐ jié kè?
— How many classes do you have today?

B: Jīntiān wǒ shàngwǔ yǒu sān jié kè, xiàwǔ méiyǒu kè.
— Today I have three classes in the morning. And I don't have any class in the afternoon.

☞ jiérì   festival; holiday (N)

     A: Jīntiān shì shénme jiérì? Zhème duō rén.
         What holiday is it today? There are a lot of people.

     B: Jīntiān shì qīyuè sì hào, Měiguó de guóqìng.
         Today is 4 July — America's National Day.

4. duān   **end (N); proper (Adj); hold something level with both hands (V)**

     A: Nǐ shǒu lǐ duān de shì shénme?
         What are you holding in your hands?

     B: Shì huāshēngtāng.
         This is peanut soup.

☞ duānzhèng   upright; proper (Adj)

     (1) Xiě zì de shíhou yídìng yào zuò de duānzhèng. Yàoburán xiě de zì bù hǎokàn.
         You have to sit upright when writing. Otherwise your characters will not look nice.

     (2) Nàge háizi duānduānzhèngzhèngde zuò zài nàr gēn dàrén shuōhuà.
         That child is sitting quite properly over there talking with the adults.

5. wǔ   **noon, midday (TW)**

☞ Duānwǔjié   the Dragon Boat Festival (the 5th day of the 5th lunar month) (N)

     Nǐ kàn le Duānwǔjié de diànyǐng yǐhòu jiù zhīdào Duānwǔjié de shìqing le.
         After you have watched the Dragon Boat Festival video, you'll know more about the festival.

☞ wǔfàn   midday meal, lunch (N)

     A: Nǐ jīntiān dǎsuàn zài nǎr chī wǔfàn?
         Where are you going to have lunch today?

     B: Kěnéng zài Xuéshēng Zhōngxīn. Nǐ yào gēn wǒ yìqǐ chī ma?
         Maybe at the Student Center. Do you want to eat with me?

	wǔhòu	afternoon (TW)	
		Hěn duō Zhōngguórén xǐhuan wǔhòu shuì yíhuìr.	Many Chinese people like to take a nap in the afternoon.
	wǔqián	before noon; morning (TW)	
		A: Nǐ míngtiān wǔqián yǒu kòngr ma?	Are you free tomorrow morning?
		B: Wǔqián méi kòngr, wǔhòu méi shì.	I'm busy in the morning, but I've got nothing to do in the afternoon.
	shàngwǔ	morning (TW)	
		A: Nǐ zhè xuéqī xuǎn de kè dōu zài shàngwǔ háishì xiàwǔ?	Are all the classes you're taking this semester in the morning or in the afternoon?
		B: Yǒude zài shàngwǔ, yǒude zài xiàwǔ.	Some are in the morning, some are in the afternoon.
	xiàwǔ	afternoon (TW)	
		A: Wǒmen hòutiān xiàwǔ jǐ diǎn zhōng jiàn?	What time in the afternoon are we meeting up the day after tomorrow?
		B: Sì diǎn yí kè.	4:15 (p.m.).
	zhōngwǔ	noon, midday (TW)	
		Wǒmen lǎoshī lǎo zài zhōngwǔ kāihuì.	Our teachers always have meetings at noon.
6.	qiū	**autumn, fall; harvest time** (N)	
	qiūtiān	autumn, fall (N)	
		Qiūtiān de hóngyè zhēn hǎokàn.	The red leaves in autumn are really pretty.
	Zhōng-qiūjié	the Mid-Autumn Festival (the 15th day of the 8th lunar month) (N)	
		(1) Zhōngqiūjié de yuèliàng yòu dà yòu liàng, zhēn hǎokàn.	The moon during the Mid-Autumn Festival is big and bright. It's really beautiful.

Lesson 18 Thanksgiving
第十八課 感恩節

      (2) Yí dào Zhōngqiūjié jiù xiǎng qǐ wǒ de nǚpéngyou le. Wǒmen shì Zhōngqiūjié nà tiān wǎnshang rènshi de.   Whenever it is the Mid-Autumn Festival, I immediately think of my girlfriend. We first met in the evening of the Mid-Autumn Festival.

7. chūn   **spring (N)**

☞ chūntiān   spring (N)

Zhōngguórén cháng shuō, yì nián zhōng zuìhǎo de shíhou shì chūntiān, yì tiān zhōng zuìhǎo de shíhou shì zǎoshang.   The Chinese often say that the best season of the year is spring and the best time of the day is morning.

☞ chūnjià   spring vacation, spring holidays (N)

A: Nǐmen chūnjià fàng jǐ tiān jià?   How many days off have you got for your spring vacation?

B: Yí xīngqī.   A week.

☞ Chūnjié   the Spring Festival (N)

Zhōngguó de xīnnián yě jiào Chūnjié.   The Chinese New Year is also called the Spring Festival.

☞ xīnchūn   the ten to twenty days following the Lunar New Year's Day (N)

Zhōngguórén cháng zài xīnchūn de shíhou qù lǚxíng.   The Chinese often go on vacation during the ten to twenty days following the Lunar New Year's Day.

8. nóng   **agriculture; farming; farmer, peasant (N)**

☞ nóngrén/nóngmín   farmer, peasant (N)

(1) Zhōngguó yǒu hěn duō nóngrén/nóngmín.   There are many peasants in China.

(2) Hěn duō Zhōngguó de nóngrén/nóngmín bú shìzì.   Many farmers in China are illiterate.

	nóngjiā	peasant family (N)	
		Tā chūshēng zài nóngjiā, suǒyǐ zhīdào bù shǎo nóngrén de shì.	He was born into a peasant family. That's why he knows quite a bit about farming life.

9. lì 曆 **calendar (N)**

	rìlì	calendar (N)	
		A: Qǐng nǐ kànkan rìlì, jīntiān shì jǐ yuè jǐ hào?	Please take a look at the calendar. What day of what month is it today?
		B: Jīntiān shì shíyuè shí hào.	Today is 10 October.
	yuèlì	monthly calendar (N)	
		Wǒ děi mǎi yí ge yuèlì.	I have to buy a monthly calendar.
	nónglì	the traditional Chinese calendar, the lunar calendar (N)	
		(1) Nóngrén duōbàn yòng nónglì.	Peasants mostly use the lunar calendar.
		(2) Wǒ de shēngrì shì nónglì sānyuè shíwǔ.	My birthday is on the 15th day of the 3rd month of the lunar calendar.

10. chū **at the beginning of; in the early part of; first (in order); for the first time; elementary (N/Adj)**

		A: Jīntiān jiǔyuè chū jǐ?	What day of the 9th month of the lunar calendar is it today?
		B: Chū wǔ.	The 5th day.
	chūqī	initial stage; early days (N)	
		Qǐng nǐ shuō-yi-shuō Měiguó chūqī de shìqing.	Please tell me something about the United States at the early stage (of its establishment).
	chūxiǎo	junior primary school (grades 1 to 4) (N)	
		Mǎ Hóng chūxiǎo shì zài Rìběn shàng de.	Ma Hong attended junior primary school in Japan.

☞ chūzhōng   middle school (N)

> Zài Měiguó, yǒude chūzhōng shì sān nián, yǒude shì sì nián.
>
> In America, some middle schools cover three years, some cover four years.

☞ qǐchū   originally; at first; at the outset (Adv)

> Wǒ qǐchū bú tài xǐhuan chī shēngcài, xiànzài hěn xǐhuan chī le.
>
> At first, I didn't really like lettuce. Now I really like it.

☞ dāngchū   at first, originally; in the first place; at that time (Adv)

> Dāngchū Hǎiyīng shì Jīn Jiàn de nǚpéngyou, hòulái Mǎ Hóng shì tā de nǚpéngyou le, kěshì xiànzài Hǎiyīng hé Jīn Jiàn háishì hǎopéngyǒu.
>
> At first, Haiying was Jin Jian's girlfriend. Later Ma Hong became his girlfriend. But now Haiying and Jin Jian are still good friends.

Pattern Drills

18.1 THE EXPRESSION kànqǐlai

18.1.1 The use of kànqǐlai

> Kànqǐlai "it seems, it looks as if" often appears in the initial position of a sentence. The subject of kànqǐlai is often the speaker.

(1) Kànqǐlai nǐmen zǎoyǐ rènshi le.   It appears to me that you two have known each other for a long time.

(2) Kànqǐlai nǐ bú tài xǐhuan chī zhège cài.   It seems to me that you don't care too much for this dish.

18.1.2 The pattern kànqǐlai ... de yàngzi

> The noun yàngzi "appearance" often comes at the end of a sentence with kànqǐlai. Kànqǐlai ... de yàngzi has the same meaning as kànqǐlai.

(1) Nǐ kànqǐlai hěn lèi de yàngzi. You look very tired.

(2) Kànqǐlai tā bù xǐhuan gēn rén shuōhuà de yàngzi. It seems to me that she doesn't like to talk to people.

18.2 MORE ON gòu

In Lesson 9 we presented gòu "enough" as a stative verb (e.g., Nǐ de qián gòu-bu-gòu? "Do you have enough money?"). In this lesson we will discuss the usage of gòu as an adverb that modifies a stative verb to indicate that a high degree has been reached. The end of such a sentence often takes a de, le, or de le. Pay special attention to the position of gòu in Chinese sentences and the various meanings of "enough" in English sentences.

(1) Wǒmen zuìjìn gòu máng de. We have been very busy lately.

(2) Jīntiān de gōngkè gòu duō de le. We sure have a lot of homework today.

Gòu can be modified by a negative word bú "not." In this form, the de, le, or de le cannot be attached to the sentence.

(1) Nǐmen de Zhōngwén hái bú gòu hǎo. Your Chinese is not good enough yet.

(2) Wǒ zuò de shì hái bú gòu duō ma? Haven't I worked enough?

18.3 THE PATTERN zěnme ... cái

Zěnme is used to ask the way to or how to do something. Cái, meaning "so that it will be ...," comes at the end of a sentence. A literal translation of this sentence pattern into English is "How should one do something so that it will be ...?"

S	zěnme	cái	SV?
Wǒ	zěnme xiě zhège zì	cái	duì?
How should I write this character (so that it will be right)?			

(1) Wǒ zěnme xièxie nǐ cái hǎo? How should I thank you so that it will be appropriate?

(2) Wǒ zěnme shuō nǐ cái dǒng wǒ de yìsi? How should I say it so that you can understand what I mean?

18.4 REDUPLICATION FORMS OF ADJECTIVES

Certain adjectives expressing manner sometimes come in reduplicated form. For instance, gāoxìng when reduplicated becomes gāogāoxìngxìng. The suffix de (地) is attached to the reduplicated form as an adverbial modifier to modify the verb which follows.

(1) Xiǎoměi xià le kè gāogāoxìngxìngde huí sùshè le. After class, Xiaomei went happily back to her dorm.

(2) Lǎoshī dōu zài nàr kuàikuàilèlède tiàowǔ. All the teachers are dancing joyfully over there.

(3) Xuésheng dōu duānduānzhèngzhèngde zuò zài nàr shàng kè. The students are all sitting attentively in class over there.

(4) Nǐ kàn, tāmen yǐjing pīngpīng'ān'ānde huílái le. Look, they have already come back safely.

(5) Nǐ yīnggāi kèkèqìqìde gēn kèrén shuōhuà. You should talk politely to the guests.

18.5 THE WORD chū

Chū has two meanings: it may mean "the early part of ...," as in the first example; or it may mean "the first ten days of a lunar month," as in the second example.

(1) Wǒmen chū rènshi de shíhou, nǐ bú huì shuō Yīngwén, xiànzài shuōde zhème hǎo le. You couldn't speak English when we first met. Now you speak it so well.

(2) A: Nǐ de shēngrì shì shénme shíhou? When is your birthday?

B: Wǒ de shēngrì shì nónglì sānyuè chū qī. My birthday is on the 7th day of the 3rd month of the lunar calendar.

🌸 Sentence Building

1.
Zěnme?
Zěnme zhème máng?
Nǐ zěnme zhème máng?
Nǐ zuìjìn zěnme zhème máng?

2.
Chū
Zuìchū
Wǒ zuìchū bù dǒng.
Wǒ zuìchū bù dǒng nǐ de yìsi.

3.
Gǎnxiè
Gǎnxiè nǐ de hǎoyì.
Dàjiā gǎnxiè nǐ de hǎoyì.
Dàjiā dōu gǎnxiè nǐ de hǎoyì.

4.
Qǐchū
Qǐchū bù xǐhuan Zhōngwén.
Wǒ qǐchū bù xǐhuan Zhōngwén.
Wǒ qǐchū bù dà xǐhuan Zhōngwén.

🌸 Questions and Responses

1. Gǎn'ēnjié shì jǐ yuè jǐ hào?
   When is Thanksgiving?

   Jīnnián shì shíyīyuè èrshíqī hào.
   This year, it's on 27 November.

2. Nǐmen xuéyuàn Gǎn'ēnjié fàng jǐ tiān jià?
   How many days of Thanksgiving vacation does your college have?

   Cóngqián fàng liǎng tiān. Cóng qùnián qǐ fàng yí ge xīngqī de jià.
   In the past, we had two days of vacation. Since last year, we have had a week off.

3. Zěnme nàme hǎo? Cóng nǎ tiān fàng dào nǎ tiān?
   Wow, that's great. From when to when?

   Cóng shíyīyuè èrshíwǔ hào fàng dào shíyīyuè sānshí hào.
   From 25 November until 30 November.

4. Nǐ shénme shíhou huí jiā?
   When are you going home?

   Shíyīyuè èrshíwǔ hào yí xià kè jiù huí jiā. Wǒ jiějie gēge yě dōu huí jiā.
   On 25 November, as soon as classes are over, I will go home. My sister and brother are also going home.

5. Nǐmen jiā zěnme qìngzhù Gǎn'ēnjié?
   How does your family celebrate Thanksgiving?

   Jiālǐ rén dōu zài yìqǐ qìngzhù. Chī huǒjī, tiàowǔ, tánhuà.
   My family celebrates Thanksgiving together. We eat turkey, dance and chat.

6. Wèishénme xiě zì de shíhou yào zuòde hěn duānzhèng?
   Why do we have to sit upright when writing?

   Lǎoshī shuō, zuòde duānzhèng zì cái néng xiěde duānzhèng.
   Our teacher says, only if we sit upright can our characters be written properly.

7. Zhōngqiūjié shì nónglì de jǐ yuè chū jǐ?
   When is the Mid-Autumn Festival according to the lunar calendar?

   Zhōngqiūjié shì nónglì de báyuè shíwǔ.
   The Mid-Autumn Festival is on the 15th day of the 8th month of the lunar calendar.

8. "Valentine's Day" Zhōngguóhuà zěnme shuō?
   How do you say Valentine's Day in Chinese?

   Qíngrénjié.
   The Chinese call it "Qingrenjie."

9. Zhōngguórén yě guò Qíngrénjié ma?
   Do the Chinese also celebrate Valentine's Day?

   Xiànzài yǒude Zhōngguórén yě qìngzhù Qíngrénjié.
   Now some Chinese also celebrate Valentine's Day.

10. Wǒ qǐng nǐ chūqu chī diǎn Zhōngguó diǎnxīn, hǎo ba?
    I'd like to ask you out to have some Chinese pastries, okay?

    Bùhǎoyìsi, háishì wǒ qǐng nǐ ba.
    I feel embarrassed. I will treat you instead, okay?

Pronunciation Review

Four-syllable Expressions

1. Tāmen de shū.
   Xuésheng de shū.
   Lǎoshī de shū.
   Mèimei de shū.

2. Tiāntiān yǒu xiǎokǎo.
   Chángcháng yǒu xiǎokǎo.
   Jīntiān yǒu xiǎokǎo.
   Zuótiān yǒu xiǎokǎo.

3. Tā hē de tāng.
   Shéi hē de tāng?
   Nǐ hē de tāng.
   Bàba hē de tāng.

4. Gēge xiě de xìn.
   Shéi xiě de xìn?
   Jiějie xiě de xìn.
   Mèimei xiě de xìn.

🌸 Supplementary Vocabulary

Major Chinese Festivals

Chūnjié	the Spring Festival (the Chinese New Year)
Duānwǔjié	the Dragon Boat Festival (the 5th day of the 5th lunar month)
Qīngmíngjié	the Grave-sweeping Festival (celebrated around 5 April); the day to pay respects to the deceased
Yuánxiāojié	the Lantern Festival (the night of the 15th of the 1st lunar month)
Zhōngqiūjié	the Mid-Autumn Festival (the 15th day of the 8th lunar month)

🌸 Cultural Notes

Rìlì (Calendar)

Taiwan and many Chinese communities in the People's Republic of China use two different calendar systems. The Western calendar, called Yánglì, is used in nearly all official and public contexts, such as school, business, publishing, civil administration, military affairs, and politics. The Yīnlì (lunar calendar) is used to mark birthdays and traditional Chinese holidays such as the Chinese New Year, the Dragon Boat Festival, the Mid-Autumn Festival, etc. Before the massive Western cultural penetration in the nineteenth century, the lunar calendar was the sole calendar in China. Nowadays, the Western calendar is far more important than the lunar calendar, especially in urban China.

第十八課
漢字本

內容

課文 250

生詞及例句 251
(感、恩、節、端、午、秋、春、農、曆、初)

句型練習 255
(看起來、夠、怎麼……才、初)

造句 257
(怎麼、初、感謝、起初)

問答 258

閱讀練習 258
　　中國也有一個情人節

課文

感恩節

王老師：林海英，感恩節快到了，你回家嗎？

林海英：回家。一下課就回去。王老師，你們慶祝感恩節嗎？

王老師：我們不過感恩節。我們過幾個中國的節日：端午節，中秋節跟春節。

林海英：王老師，你可以告訴我們這幾個中國節日是怎麼來的嗎？

王老師：現在你們還聽不懂，因為你們知道的生字還不夠多，不過我可以給你們看這幾個節日的電影。

林海英：那太好了。王老師，你可以告訴我們這幾個節日是在甚麼時候嗎？

王老師：當然可以。端午節在農曆五月初五，中秋節在八月十五，春節就是中國的新年。

林海英：我真想多知道點兒中國的事情。

王老師：好好兒學中文，以後就可以知道很多中國有意思的事情。

Lesson 18 Thanksgiving
第十八課 感恩節

生詞及例句

1. 感   **feel, sense; move, touch, affect; feeling** (V)

   ☞ 感情   emotion, feeling, sentiment; affection, attachment; love (N)

   A: 葉先生跟葉太太的感情怎麼樣?

   B: 看起來他們兩個人的感情很好。

   ☞ 感謝   thank; be grateful (V)

   A: 你給我作了這麼多事,我真不知道怎麼感謝你才好。

   B: 沒甚麼,不要客氣。

   ☞ 感想   impressions; reflections, thoughts (N)

   (1) 看完這本小說以後,請寫出來你的感想。

   (2) A: 看了這本書以後,我有很多感想。

       B: 你可以告訴我你的感想嗎?

       A: 當然可以。我也想知道你的意見。

   ☞ 感人   touching, moving (Adj)

   我昨天看的那個電影真感人。

   ☞ 同感   the same feeling (or impression) (N)

   A: 這個地方真美。你說呢?

   B: 我跟你有同感。

2. 恩   **kindness; favor; grace** (N)

   ☞ 恩人   benefactor (N)

   我出國的時候沒有錢,他給我很多錢,他是我的恩人。我不知道怎樣感謝他。

   ☞ 感恩   feel grateful; be thankful (VO)

   父母那麼愛我們,我們應該知道感恩。

☞ 感恩節　　Thanksgiving (N)
　　　　　　在美國過感恩節的時候吃甚麼？

3. 節　　　**holiday; moral integrity (N); section, length; joint (MW)**
　　　　　　A: 你今天有幾節課？
　　　　　　B: 今天我上午有三節課，下午沒有課。

☞ 節日　　festival; holiday (N)
　　　　　　A: 今天是甚麼節日？這麼多人。
　　　　　　B: 今天是七月四號，美國的國慶。

4. 端　　　**end (N); proper (Adj); hold something level with both hands (V)**
　　　　　　A: 你手裏端的是甚麼？
　　　　　　B: 是花生湯。

☞ 端正　　upright; proper (Adj)
　　　　　　1. 寫字的時候一定要坐得端正。要不然寫的字不好看。
　　　　　　2. 那個孩子端端正正地坐在那兒跟大人說話。

5. 午　　　**noon, midday (TW)**
☞ 端午節　the Dragon Boat Festival (the 5th day of the 5th lunar month) (N)
　　　　　　你看了端午節的電影以後就知道端午節的事情了。

☞ 午飯　　midday meal, lunch (N)
　　　　　　A: 你今天打算在哪兒吃午飯？
　　　　　　B: 可能在學生中心。你要跟我一起吃嗎？

☞ 午後　　afternoon (TW)
　　　　　　很多中國人喜歡午後睡一會兒。

Lesson 18 Thanksgiving
第十八課 感恩節

☞ 午前　　　before noon; morning (TW)
　　　　　　A: 你明天午前有空兒嗎？
　　　　　　B: 午前沒空兒，午後沒事。

☞ 上午　　　morning (TW)
　　　　　　A: 你這學期選的課都在上午還是下午？
　　　　　　B: 有的在上午，有的在下午。

☞ 下午　　　afternoon (TW)
　　　　　　A: 我們後天下午幾點鐘見？
　　　　　　B: 四點一刻。

☞ 中午　　　noon, midday (TW)
　　　　　　我們老師老在中午開會。

6. 秋　　　**autumn, fall; harvest time (N)**

☞ 秋天　　　autumn, fall (N)
　　　　　　秋天的紅葉真好看。

☞ 中秋節　　the Mid-Autumn Festival (the 15th day of the 8th lunar month) (N)
　　　　　　(1) 中秋節的月亮又大又亮，真好看。
　　　　　　(2) 一到中秋節就想起我的女朋友了。我們是中秋節那天晚上認識的。

7. 春　　　spring (N)

☞ 春天　　　spring (N)
　　　　　　中國人常說，一年中最好的時候是春天，一天中最好的時候是早上。

☞ 春假　　　spring vacation, spring holidays (N)
　　　　　　A: 你們春假放幾天假？
　　　　　　B: 一星期。

☞ 春節　the Spring Festival (N)
中國的新年也叫春節。

☞ 新春　the ten to twenty days following the Lunar New Year's Day (N)
中國人常在新春的時候去旅行。

8. 農　**agriculture; farming; farmer, peasant (N)**

☞ 農人/農民　farmer, peasant (N)
(1) 中國有很多農人/農民。
(2) 很多中國的農人/農民不識字。

☞ 農家　peasant family (N)
他出生在農家，所以知道不少農人的事。

9. 曆　**calendar (N)**

☞ 日曆　calendar (N)
A: 請你看看日曆，今天是幾月幾號？
B: 今天是十月十號。

☞ 月曆　monthly calendar (N)
我得買一個月曆。

☞ 農曆　the traditional Chinese calendar, the lunar calendar (N)
(1) 農人多半用農曆。
(2) 我的生日是農曆三月十五。

10. 初　**at the beginning of; in the early part of; first (in order); for the first time; elementary (N/Adj)**
A: 今天九月初幾？
B: 初五。

☞ 初期   initial stage; early days (N)

請你說一說美國初期的事情。

☞ 初小   junior primary school (grades 1 to 4) (N)

馬紅初小是在日本上的。

☞ 初中   middle school (N)

在美國，有的初中是三年，有的是四年。

☞ 起初   originally; at first; at the outset (Adv)

我起初不太喜歡吃生菜，現在很喜歡吃了。

☞ 當初   at first, originally; in the first place; at that time (Adv)

當初海英是金建的女朋友，後來馬紅是他的女朋友了，可是現在海英和金建還是好朋友。

句型練習

18.1. THE EXPRESSION 看起來

18.1.1. The use of 看起來

看起來 "it seems, it looks as if" often appears in the initial position of a sentence. The subject of 看起來 is often the speaker.

(1) 看起來你們早已認識了。

(2) 看起來你不太喜歡吃這個菜。

18.1.2 The pattern 看起來……的樣子

The noun 樣子 "appearance" often comes at the end of a sentence with 看起來. 看起來……的樣子 has the same meaning as 看起來.

(1) 你看起來很累的樣子。

(2) 看起來她不喜歡跟人說話的樣子。

18.2 MORE ON 夠

In Lesson 9 we presented 夠 "enough" as a stative verb (e.g., 你的錢夠不夠？"Do you have enough money?"). In this lesson we will discuss the usage of 夠 as an adverb that modifies a stative verb to indicate that a high degree has been reached. The end of such a sentence often takes a 的, 了, or 的了. Pay special attention to the position of 夠 in Chinese sentences and the various meanings of "enough" in English sentences.

(1) 我們最近夠忙的。

(2) 今天的功課夠多的了。

夠 can be modified by a negative word 不 "not." In this form, the 的, 了, or 的了 cannot be attached to the sentence.

(1) 你們的中文還不夠好。

(2) 我作的事還不夠多嗎？

18.3 THE PATTERN 怎麼……才

怎麼 is used to ask the way to or how to do something. 才, meaning "so that it will be ...," comes at the end of a sentence. A literal translation of this sentence pattern into English is "How should one do something so that it will be ...?"

S	怎麼	才	SV?
我	怎麼寫這個字	才	對？

How should I write this character (so that it will be right)?

(1) 我怎麼謝謝你才好？

(2) 我怎麼說你才懂我的意思？

18.4 REDUPLICATION FORMS OF ADJECTIVES

Certain adjectives expressing manner sometimes come in reduplicated form. For instance, 高興 when reduplicated becomes 高高興興. The suffix 地 is attached to the reduplicated form as an adverbial modifier to modify the verb which follows.

Lesson 18 Thanksgiving
第十八課 感恩節

(1) 小美下了課高高興興地回宿舍了。

(2) 老師都在那兒快快樂樂地跳舞。

(3) 學生都端端正正地坐在那兒上課。

(4) 你看，他們已經平平安安地回來了。

(5) 你應該客客氣氣地跟客人說話。

18.5 THE WORD 初

> 初 has two meanings: it may mean "the early part of ...," as in the first example; or it may mean "the first ten days of a lunar month," as in the second example.

(1) 我們初認識的時候，你不會說英文，現在說得這麼好了。

(2) A: 你的生日是甚麼時候？
B: 我的生日是農曆三月初七。

造句

1.
怎麼？
怎麼這麼忙？
你怎麼這麼忙？
你最近怎麼這麼忙？

2.
初
最初
我最初不懂。
我最初不懂你的意思。

3.
感謝
感謝你的好意。
大家感謝你的好意。
大家都感謝你的好意。

4.
起初
起初不喜歡中文。
我起初不喜歡中文。
我起初不大喜歡中文。

問答

1. 感恩節是幾月幾號？ 　　今年是十一月二十七號。
2. 你們學院感恩節放幾天假？ 　　從前放兩天。從去年起放一個星期的假。
3. 怎麼那麼好？從哪天放到哪天？ 　　從十一月二十五號放到十一月三十號。
4. 你甚麼時候回家？ 　　十一月二十五號一下課就回家。我姐姐哥哥也都回家。
5. 你們家怎麼慶祝感恩節？ 　　家裏人都在一起慶祝。吃火雞、跳舞、談話。
6. 為甚麼寫字的時候要坐得很端正？ 　　老師說，坐得端正字才能寫得端正。
7. 中秋節是農曆的幾月初幾？ 　　中秋節是農曆的八月十五。
8. "Valentine's Day"中國話怎麼說？ 　　情人節。
9. 中國人也過情人節嗎？ 　　現在有的中國人也慶祝情人節。
10. 我請你出去吃點中國點心，好吧？ 　　不好意思，還是我請你吧。

閱讀練習

中國也有一個情人節

西方有情人節。中國也有一個情人節。中國的情人節是在農曆七月初七。從前中國人在夏天的晚上，家裏人喜歡在院子裏乘涼。看著天上的月亮、星星、跟銀河，就有了這麼一個很美、很難過的故事。

在銀河的東邊有一個織女，她很勤勞，每天給天上織很多好看的彩霞。玉皇大帝為了獎勵她，就叫她跟銀河西邊的牛郎結婚。

他們結婚以後快快樂樂地過日子就忘了做事了。玉皇大帝很生氣，叫他們以後每年只能見一次面。那天就是七月初七。那天晚上常常下雨。那不是雨，那是他們兩個人的眼淚。

中國情人節是怎麼來的？西方的呢？這個故事說明了甚麼？你想知道中國人情人節作甚麼嗎？我想你們在電腦上一定可以找到。找到了以後請再作討論。

請查生詞

Look up the following words in a dictionary.

夏天	xiàtiān	牛郎	Niúláng
院子	yuànzi	結婚	jiéhūn
乘涼	chéngliáng	忘了	wàng le
銀河	yínhé	只	zhǐ
織女	Zhīnǚ	一次	yícì
勤勞	qínláo	面	miàn
彩霞	cǎixiá	下雨	xiàyǔ
玉皇大帝	Yùhuáng Dàdì	眼淚	yǎnlèi
獎勵	jiǎnglì		

填空

Fill in the blanks with the appropriate words from the story.

1. 從前中國人 _____ _____ 都喜歡坐在 _____ _____ 裏 _____ _____，因為屋子裏很熱。

2. 天上的 _____ _____，一邊織女，一邊有 _____ _____。他們每年_____ 能見 _____ _____ 。

3. 農曆七月初七的晚上，常常下 _____ ，那是牛郎、織女的 _____ _____ 。

4. 織女 _____ _____ 以前是一個很 _____ _____ 的人，可是 _____ _____ 以後 _____ 了工作了。

5. 西方的 _____ _____ 節是怎麼來的？

第十九課　談心
Lesson 19　Heart-to-heart talk

玩 → wán
　　→ "play"

得 gāo xìng

前天 → day before yesterday
后天 → after tomorrow
昨天 → yesterday
今
明

　　走　起

Lesson 19
Pinyin Text

CONTENTS

Text 264

Vocabulary and Illustrative Sentences 265
(lián, luò, nào, jué, yuè, shū, cōng, jiāo, ào, bǎ)

Pattern Drills 270
(yuèláiyuè, yuè ... yuè, bǎ)

Sentence Building 274
(yìjiàn, tǎolùn, juéde, xiǎngfǎ)

Questions and Responses 274

Pronunciation Review 275

Supplementary Vocabulary 276

Cultural Notes 276

🌸 Text

Tánxīn

Heart-to-heart talk

Mǎ Hóng	: Hǎiyīng, hǎojiǔ méi gēn nǐ liánluò le. Nǐ zěnmeyàng?	Haiying, I haven't been in touch with you for a long time. How are you?
Lín Hǎiyīng	: Wǒ hěn hǎo. Nǐ ne?	I'm fine. How are you?
Mǎ Hóng	: Hái hǎo, jiù shì xīnqíng bú tài hǎo.	Okay. I am just in a bad mood.
Lín Hǎiyīng	: Zěnme le?	What's wrong?
Mǎ Hóng	: Nǐ shì Jīn Jiàn de hǎopéngyou, wǒ kěyǐ gēn nǐ tántan wǒ gēn Jīn Jiàn de shì ma?	You are Jin Jian's best friend. May I tell you about the problem between Jin Jian and me?
Lín Hǎiyīng	: Dāngrán kěyǐ. Nǐmen liǎng ge nào yìjiàn le?	Of course. Have you two quarreled?
Mǎ Hóng	: Bù zhīdào wèishénme wǒmen liǎng ge rén de kànfǎ lǎo bù yíyàng. Wǒmen de àihào yě bù yíyàng. Wǒ juéde wǒ gēn tā yuèláiyuè shūyuǎn le. Huà yě yuèláiyuè shǎo le.	I don't know why our views are always different. Our interests are also different. I feel that we're drifting apart more and more. We are also talking less and less.
Lín Hǎiyīng	: Zhēn de ma! Jīn Jiàn yòu cōngmíng yòu yònggōng. Kěshì tā jiù shì bù xǐhuan shuōhuà, suǒyǐ yǒu rén juéde tā hěn jiāo'ào.	Really? Jin Jian is smart and diligent. He just doesn't like to talk, so some people think he's arrogant.

Lesson 19 Heart-to-heart talk
第十九課 談心

Mǎ Hóng	:	Wǒ yě nàme xiǎng. Tā xiǎng tā bǐ shénme rén dōu hǎo, shénme dōu dǒng. Hěn nán gēn tā tǎolùn shìqing.	I think so too. He thinks he is better than anyone else and knows everything. It's hard to discuss matters with him.
Lín Hǎiyīng	:	Yěxǔ nǐmen yīnggāi hǎohāor tántan. Bǎ nǐ de xiǎngfǎ gàosu tā.	Maybe both of you need to talk with each other. Tell him how you feel.
Mǎ Hóng	:	Hǎo, wǒ shìshi gēn tā tántan. Wǒ xiànzài juéde hǎo yìdiǎnr le. Xièxie.	All right, I'll try talking to him. I feel better now. Thanks.
Lín Hǎiyīng	:	Búkèqi. Zài liánluò.	You are welcome. Keep in touch.
Mǎ Hóng	:	Zàijiàn.	Bye.

Vocabulary and Illustrative Sentences

1. lián 聯 **unite, join** (V)

☞ liánhuān   have a get-together (V)

聯歡會

   A: Wǒmen yīnggāi gēn nǚtóngxué kāi yí ge liánhuānhuì.   We should have a get-together party with our female classmates.

   B: Hǎo zhǔyi. Shénme shíhou?   Good idea. When?

☞ liánmíng   jointly signed; jointly (V)

   A: Wǒmen liánmíng qǐng lǎoshī míngtiān bú yào kǎoshì, hǎo-bu-hǎo?   Let's petition the teacher not to give us an exam tomorrow, okay?

   B: Hǎo.   Okay.

☞ liánxiǎng   associate; connect in the mind (V)

| | | Wǒ yí kàndào hǎi jiù liánxiǎng dào wǒ de lǎojiā, yīnwèi wǒ lǎojiā fùjìn yǒu dàhǎi. | When I look at the sea, I immediately associate it with my hometown, because my hometown is near the sea. |

2. luò 络 **a net** (N)

☞ liánluò — contact, get in touch with (V)

A: Nǐ dào Zhōngguó yǐhòu, wǒmen zěnme liánluò? — After you arrive in China, how do we contact each other?

B: Wǒmen kěyǐ xiě xìn, kěyǐ dǎ diànhuà, yě kěyǐ yòng diànzǐxìn liánluò. — We can keep in touch by writing letters, making phone calls or using e-mail.

3. nào **noisy; make noise; stir up trouble** (V)

A: Nǐmen bú yào nào le, māma lái le. — You'd better stop making trouble, mother is coming.

B: Búshì wǒ gēn dìdi nào, shì tā gēn wǒ nào. — It wasn't I who provoked my younger brother, it was he who stirred up the trouble.

☞ nào yìjiàn — be on bad terms because of a difference of opinion (VO)

A: Wèishénme tāmen liǎng ge rén yòu bù shuōhuà le? — Why are the two of them not speaking to each other again?

B: Wǒ xiǎng shì tāmen yòu nào yìjiàn le. — I think they're on bad terms because of a difference of opinion again.

A: Wèishénme tāmen cháng nào yìjiàn? — Why are they always at odds with each other?

B: Yīnwèi tāmen de yìjiàn hěn bù yíyàng. — Because their ideas and opinions are very different.

☞ nàoshì — create a disturbance; make trouble (VO)

A: Yǒu hěn duō gōngrén zài nàoshì, wèishénme? — Many workers are creating a disturbance. Why?

Lesson 19 Heart-to-heart talk
第十九課 談心

	B: Yīnwèi tāmen de gōngqián tài shǎo le.	Because their wages are too low.
☞ nàozhōng	alarm clock (N)	
	A: Nǐ zěnme jīntiān yòu lái wǎn le?	Why are you late again today?
	B: Yīnwèi wǒ de nàozhōng bù zǒu le.	Because my alarm clock doesn't work.
☞ rè'nào	lively, bustling with noise and excitement; have a joyous time (Adj)	
	(1) A: Zhōngguórén dōu hěn ài rè'nào ma?	Do all Chinese people like noise and excitement?
	B: Duō bàn de Zhōngguórén ài rè'nào, kěshì yě yǒu rén bú ài rè'nào.	Most Chinese like a lively atmosphere, but there are some who don't.
	(2) Zhōngguórén guònián de shíhou hěn rè'nào.	When the Chinese celebrate the New Year, it is always bustling with noise and excitement.
4. jué	**sense, feel; become aware** (V)	
☞ juéde	feel; think (V)	
	(1) A: Nǐ zěnme le?	What's wrong with you?
	B: Wǒ juéde hěn lèi.	I feel really tired.
	(2) A: Nǐ juéde jīntiān de kǎoshì nán-bu-nán?	Do you think the test today is difficult (or not)?
	B: Yǒu diǎnr nán.	It is a bit difficult.
☞ zhījué	consciousness; perception (N)	
	Tāmen de chē chūshì le. Kāi chē de rén méi zhījué le.	They had a car accident. The driver is unconscious.
☞ bùzhī-bùjué	unconsciously, unwittingly (IE)	
	Shíjiān guòde zhēn kuài, bùzhībùjuéde yí ge xuéqī jiù yào guòqu le.	Time flies. One is hardly aware that the semester is almost over.

	xiānzhī-xiānjué	having foresight (IE)	
		Xiānzhīxiānjué de rén bù duō.	There are not many people with foresight.

5. **yuè** — **get over; jump over; exceed** (V)

Yuèguo zhè ge dàshān jiù shì Yuènán le. — Get over this big mountain and Vietnam is there.

☞ Yuènán — Vietnam (N)

Wǒ zuìhǎo de péngyou shì Yuènánrén. — My best friend is Vietnamese.

☞ yuè ... yuè ... — the more ... the more ... (Adv)

(1) Wǒ yuè gēn wàizǔmǔ zài yìqǐ, yuè xǐhuan tā. — The more time I spend with my grandmother, the more I like her.

(2) Wǒ yuè xué Zhōngwén yuè juéde Zhōngwén yǒuyìsi. — The more I study Chinese, the more I am interested in it.

☞ yuèláiyuè — more and more (Adv)

(1) Tiānqì yuèláiyuè hǎo le. — The weather is getting better.

(2) Bù zhīdào wèishénme tā yuèláiyuè bù xǐhuan shuōhuà le. — I don't know why he is getting more and more reticent.

6. **shū** — **distant; not familiar with; neglect** (V)

☞ shūyuǎn — drift apart, become estranged (Adj)

(1) Yè xiānsheng yǒu nǚpéngyou yǐhòu, jiù gēn tā tàitai yuèláiyuè shūyuǎn le. — After Mr. Ye got a girlfriend, his relationship with his wife has become increasingly estranged.

(2) Yàoshì nǐ bù cháng gēn péngyou liánluò, jiù huì yuèláiyuè shūyuǎn le. — If you don't contact your friends often, you will drift further and further apart (from them).

☞ shēngshū — not familiar; out of practice; not as close as before (Adj)

Lesson 19 Heart-to-heart talk
第十九課 談心

	(1)	Wǒ yǐjing jǐ nián méi qù Běijīng le, nàr de shìqing, wǒ hěn shēngshū le.	I have not been to Beijing for a few years. I am not familiar with what's going on there anymore.
	(2)	Wǒ bù cháng yòng diànnǎo, suǒyǐ yǒu diǎnr shēngshū.	I don't often use a computer. That's why I'm a little unfamiliar with it.

7. cōng   **faculty of hearing; acute hearing** (Adj)

☞ cōngmíng   intelligent, bright, clever (SV)

    A: Nǐ érzi zhēn cōngmíng. Shénme shìqing yì xué jiù huì. — Your son is really intelligent. He knows everything as soon as he studies it.

    B: Nǎlǐ, nǎlǐ, tā bù cōngmíng. — No, no. He's not very bright.

☞ xiǎocōng-míng   cleverness in trivial matters; petty tricks (IE)

    Nàge rén méishénme xuéwèn, jiù shì yǒu diǎnr xiǎocōngmíng. — That person is not really knowledgeable. He's just clever in trivial matters.

8. jiāo   **proud; arrogant** (Adj)

9. ào   **proud; refuse to yield to; brave** (Adj)

☞ jiāo'ào   arrogant, conceited; be proud, take pride in (SV)

    (1) Jiāo'ào de rén bú huì yǒu hěn duō hǎopéngyou. — Conceited people won't have many good friends.

    (2) Zhōngguó de wénwù shì Zhōngguórén de jiāo'ào. — Chinese people are proud of their historical relics.

10. bǎ   **hold, grasp; control** (V/CV); **bundle, bunch** (MW)

    (1) Qǐng nǐ bǎ zhè bǎ huā sòng-gěi tā. — Please give her this bouquet of flowers.

    (2) Wǒ bǎ nǐ de yìjiàn gàosu tā le. — I have told her your ideas.

    (3) Qǐng nǐ bǎ nà běn shū gěi wǒ nálai. Xièxie. — Please bring me that book. Thank you.

Pattern Drills

19.1 THE EXPRESSION yuèláiyuè

> Yuèláiyuè means "(become) more and more." It serves as an adverbial expression to indicate the degree to which an adjective applies is on an increase.

(1) Tiānqì yuèláiyuè lěng le. The weather is getting colder and colder.

(2) Wǒmen de kǎoshì yuèláiyuè nán le. Our tests are getting more and more difficult.

19.2 THE PATTERN yuè ... yuè

> The adverb yuè "more" is used twice before successive verbal expressions to mean "the more ... the more ...."

(1) Tā yuè shuō yuè kuài. She speaks faster and faster.

(2) Wǒ yuè chī Zhōngguófàn yuè xǐhuan chī. The more Chinese food I eat, the more I like it.

19.3 THE bǎ CONSTRUCTIONS

> The bǎ construction in Mandarin Chinese is one in which the direct object is placed immediately after the coverb bǎ and before the verb.

S	bǎ	DO	V
Wǒ	bǎ	bàogào	xiěhǎo le.

I have finished writing my paper.

Although the bǎ construction is easy to understand, non-native speakers find it difficult to use it correctly because there are many restrictions on its usage. For example, one needs to know (1) what kinds of verbs and what kinds of direct objects can be used in such construction; (2) what sentence elements can precede and follow the verb in such construction; and (3) what communicative function such construction serves. In this lesson, we will present only a few commonly-used bǎ forms and will discuss some general rules of using the bǎ construction.

Lesson 19 Heart-to-heart talk
第十九課 談心

A. The <u>bǎ</u> construction stresses the subject's effect on the direct object. The subject of a <u>bǎ</u> sentence is usually an animate entity. However, some force that can have an effect on the object may also be used as a subject in a <u>bǎ</u> sentence.

    (1) Zǔmǔ <u>bǎ</u> tāmen de fángzi mài le.   Grandmother sold their house.

    (2) Jīntiān <u>bǎ</u> wǒ lèisǐ le.   Today I'm dog tired (for some reason).

B. In the <u>bǎ</u> construction the direct object has to be definite or specific. Thus, determinatives such as <u>zhè</u> "this" and <u>nà</u> "that," possessive pronouns such as <u>wǒ de</u> "mine" or <u>tā de</u> "his/her," or other specific modifiers should be used to specify the object.

    (1) <u>Bǎ</u> nà běn shū nálai.   Bring that book here.

    (2) Bú yào <u>bǎ</u> wǒ de qián názǒu.   Don't take my money away.

    (3) Wǒ <u>bǎ</u> zuótiān kàn de diànyǐng gàosu tā le.   I told him about the movie that I watched yesterday.

C. The <u>bǎ</u> form is preferred in imperative sentences, which command the listener to do something, as in the first example. The second example is correct, but not a construction usually used by a native speaker.

    (1) <u>Bǎ</u> nǐ zuótiān mǎi de nà běn shū nálai.   Bring me the book that you bought yesterday.

    (2) Nálai nǐ zuótiān mǎi de nà běn shū.   Bring me the book that you bought yesterday.

D. When a sentence contains a plural object and the adverb <u>dōu</u> "all," the <u>bǎ</u> form must be used, as in the first example. The non-<u>bǎ</u> form, as in the second example, is **unacceptable**.

    ✔ (1) Tā <u>bǎ</u> māma zuò de diǎnxīn dōu chī le.   He ate all the pastries that mother made.

    ✘ (2) Tā dōu chī le māma zuò de diǎnxīn.   He ate all the pastries that mother made.

E. To negate a <u>bǎ</u> sentence, the negative marker <u>bù</u> or <u>méiyǒu</u> must be placed before the <u>bǎ</u>.

(1) Tā bú yào bǎ diànnǎo názǒu.   He doesn't want to take away the computer.

(2) Wǒ méiyǒu bǎ nǐ de qián gěi tā.   I didn't give her your money.

19.3.1 The bǎ construction with a double noun phrase

S	bǎ	DO	gàosu/gěi	IO	(le)
Mǎ Hóng	bǎ	tā de yìjiàn	gàosu	Jīn Jiàn	le.

Ma Hong told Jin Jian her point of view.

(1) Bú yào bǎ zuótiān de shì gàosu māma.   Don't tell mother what happened yesterday.

(2) Jīn Jiàn yào bǎ tā de shū dōu gěi tā de nǚpéngyou.   Jin Jian wants to give all his books to his girlfriend.

19.3.2 The bǎ construction with V-zài PW (le)

Locative bǎ construction is usually obligatory. The bǎ form must be used.

S	bǎ	DO	V-zài	PW	(le)
Tā	bǎ	qián	fàngzài	yínháng lǐ	le.

He deposited his money in the bank.

The following verbs often appear in this pattern with -zài:

fàng	to put	huà	to draw, to paint
guà	to hang	kè	to carve
dào	to pour	tíng	to park
xiě	to write	cún	to deposit, to store

(1) Wǒmen lǎoshī bǎ jīntiān yào xué de zì xiězài yì zhāng dà zhǐ shàng le.   Our teacher wrote the characters that we have to learn today on a big sheet of paper.

(2) Bú yào bǎ nǐ de diànnǎo fàngzài zhèr.   Don't put your computer here.

19.3.3 The bǎ construction with V-dào PW lái/qù (le)

S	bǎ	O	V-dào	PW	lái/qù	(le)
Tā	bǎ	chē	kāidào	fēijīchǎng	qù	le.
She drove the car to the airport.						

The following verbs often appear in this pattern with -dào:

ná	to take	jì	to mail
sòng	to send, to deliver, to escort	bān	to move
kāi	to drive		

(1) Bǎ jīntiān de bào nádào shūfáng lái.   Take today's newspaper to the study.

(2) Qǐng bǎ zhège lǐwù sòngdào Wáng jiā qù.   Please deliver this gift to the Wang's household.

19.3.4 The bǎ construction with resultative verb compounds (le)

This lesson presents some resultative verb compounds that appear most frequently in bǎ constructions.

S	bǎ	O	RV	(le)
Wǒmen dōu	bǎ	gōngkè	zuòhǎo	le.
We all finished our homework.				

The following are some verbs that serve as a second verb in an RVC:

-wán	finish, complete
-hǎo	satisfaction, completion
-huì	mastery, grasp, understanding
-dào	attain, reach
-cuò	wrong, error

(1) Kuài bǎ jīntiān de shì zuòwán!   Hurry up and finish today's work!

(2) Wǒ bǎ zuótiān de shēngzì dōu xuéhuì le.   I mastered all the characters that were introduced yesterday.

(3) Māma bǎ wǎnfàn zuòhǎo le.   Mother has finished preparing dinner.

Sentence Building

1.
Yìjiàn
Yìjiàn hěn hǎo.
Shéi de yìjiàn hěn hǎo?
Xuésheng de yìjiàn hěn hǎo.

2.
Tǎolùn
Jīngcháng tǎolùn.
Shénme rén jīngcháng tǎolùn?
Lǎoshī gēn xuésheng jīngcháng tǎolùn.

3.
Juéde
Juéde zěnmeyàng?
Juéde tā de kànfǎ zěnmeyàng?
Nǐ juéde tā de kànfǎ zěnmeyàng?

4.
Xiǎngfǎ
Shénme xiǎngfǎ?
Nǐ yǒu shénme xiǎngfǎ?
Shuō-yi-shuō nǐ yǒu shénme xiǎngfǎ.

Questions and Responses

1. Nǐ chángcháng gēn nǐ de péngyou liánluò ma?
   Do you often contact your friends?

   Wǒ gōngkè bù máng de shíhou, jiù chángcháng gēn tāmen liánluò.
   When I'm not too busy with my homework, I often contact them.

2. Nǐ zěnme gēn péngyou liánluò?

   How do you keep in touch with your friends?

   Wǒmen yǒu shíhou dǎ diànhuà, yǒu shíhou xiě diànzǐxìn.
   Sometimes we talk on the phone, sometimes we use e-mail.

3. Nǐ gāoxìng de shíhou gēn péngyou liánluò háishì nánguò de shíhou gēn péngyou liánluò?
   Do you speak to your friends when you're happy or when you're sad?

   Wǒ gāoxìng de shíhou, nánguò de shíhou dōu xǐhuan gēn péngyou liánluò.
   Whether I'm happy or sad, I still like talking with my friends.

4. Mǎ Hóng zuìjìn wèishénme xīnqíng bù hǎo?
   Why has Ma Hong been in a bad mood lately?

   Yīnwèi tā gēn Jīn Jiàn nào yìjiàn le.
   Because she got into an argument with Jin Jian.

5. Hǎiyīng shuō Jīn Jiàn shì yí ge shénmeyàng de rén?
   What kind of person does Haiying say Jin Jian is?

   Tā rènwéi tā yòu cōngmíng yòu yònggōng.
   She thinks he is smart and hardworking.

Lesson 19 Heart-to-heart talk
第十九課 談心

6. Wèishénme yǒu rén juéde Jīn Jiàn hěn jiāo'ào?
   Why do some people think that Jin Jian is very arrogant?

   Yīnwèi tā bú dà xǐhuan gēn rén shuōhuà.
   Because he doesn't really like to talk to people.

7. Jīn Jiàn gēn Mǎ Hóng de gǎnqíng zěnmeyàng?
   How is Jin Jian's relationship with Ma Hong?

   Zuìjìn yuèláiyuè shūyuǎn le.
   They have been drifting apart lately.

8. Nǐ de àihào shì shénme?
   What are your hobbies?

   Wǒ xǐhuan kàn diànyǐng, tiàowǔ, kàn shū.
   I like to watch movies, dance and read.

9. Nǐ xiǎng Mǎ Hóng xǐhuan Jīn Jiàn ma?
   Do you think Ma Hong likes Jin Jian?

   Wǒ xiǎng tā xǐhuan tā, yàoburán tā búhuì yīnwèi Jīn Jiàn xīnqíng bù hǎo.
   I think she likes him, otherwise she wouldn't get upset because of Jin Jian.

10. Yàoshì nǐ gēn péngyou yǒu yìjiàn, nǐ zuò shénme?
    If you and your friend are in disagreement, what will you do?

    Wǒ jiù gēn tā hǎohāode tántan.
    I will discuss the matter with him/her.

Pronunciation Review

1. Tā gēn wǒ jīngcháng liánluò.
   Shéi gēn nǐ jīngcháng liánluò?
   Wǒmen jīngcháng liánluò.
   Bàba gēn wǒ jīngcháng liánluò.

2. Tā bǎ diànnǎo mài le.
   Dìdi bǎ nàozhōng mài le.
   Zǔmǔ bǎ fángzi mài le.
   Māma bǎ qìchē mài le.

3. Tāmen yuèláiyuè shūyuǎn.
   Péngyou yuèláiyuè shūyuǎn.
   Lǎoshī yuèláiyuè shūyuǎn.
   Tóngxué yuèláiyuè shūyuǎn.

4. Tā juéde wǒ hěn jiāo'ào.
   Wǒ juéde tā hěn jiāo'ào.
   Tóngxué juéde nǐ hěn jiāo'ào.
   Dàjiā dōu juéde nǐ hěn jiāo'ào.

🌸 Supplementary Vocabulary

Names of fruits

píngguǒ	apple	lóngyǎn	longan
xìng	apricot	táozi	peach
xiāngjiāo	banana	lí	pear
yīngtáo	cherry	lǐzi	plum
yòuzi	grapefruit	júzi	tangerine
lìzhī	lychee	xīguā	watermelon

🌸 Cultural Notes

Expressing apology and gratitude

Traditionally, Chinese tended not to say duìbuqǐ (sorry) or xièxie (thank you) frequently. That is because the expression duìbuqǐ has the connotation that the speaker has done something wrong. Therefore, duìbuqǐ was only used when expressing a contrite apology. The expression xièxie is used to express gratitude for a favor. However, it was not used as casually as "thank you" in English in the traditional Chinese society.

第十九課
漢字本

內容

課文	278
生詞及例句 （聯、絡、鬧、覺、越、疏、聰、驕、傲、把）	279
句型練習 （越來越、越……越、把）	282
造句 （意見、討論、覺得、想法）	286
問答	286
閱讀練習 不會說話的人	287

課文

談心

馬　　紅：海英，好久沒跟你聯絡了。你怎麼樣？

林海英：我很好。你呢？

馬　　紅：還好，就是心情不太好。

林海英：怎麼了？

馬　　紅：你是金建的好朋友，我可以跟你談談我跟金建的事嗎？

林海英：當然可以。你們兩個鬧意見了？

馬　　紅：不知道為甚麼我們兩個人的看法老不一樣。我們的愛好也不一樣。我覺得我跟他越來越疏遠了。話也越來越少了。

林海英：真的嗎！金建又聰明又用功。可是他就是不喜歡說話，所以有人覺得他很驕傲。

馬　　紅：我也那麼想。他想他比甚麼人都好，甚麼都懂。很難跟他討論事情。

林海英：也許你們應該好好兒談談。把你的想法告訴他。

馬　　紅：好，我試試跟他談談。我現在覺得好一點兒了。謝謝。

林海英：不客氣。再聯絡。

馬　　紅：再見。

Lesson 19 Heart-to-heart talk
第十九課 談心

生詞及例句

1. **聯** unite, join (V)

   ☞ 聯歡 have a get-together (V)

   A: 我們應該跟女同學開一個聯歡會。

   B: 好主意。甚麼時候？

   ☞ 聯名 jointly signed; jointly (V)

   A: 我們聯名請老師明天不要考試，好不好？

   B: 好。

   ☞ 聯想 associate; connect in mind (V)

   我一看到海就聯想到我的老家，因為我老家附近有大海。

2. **絡** a net (N)

   ☞ 聯絡 contact, get in touch with (V)

   A: 你到中國以後，我們怎麼聯絡？

   B: 我們可以寫信，可以打電話，也可以用電子信聯絡。

3. **鬧** noisy; make noise; stir up trouble (V)

   A: 你們不要鬧了，媽媽來了。

   B: 不是我跟弟弟鬧，是他跟我鬧。

   ☞ 鬧意見 be on bad terms because of a difference of opinion (VO)

   A: 為甚麼他們兩個人又不說話了？

   B: 我想是他們又鬧意見了。

   A: 為甚麼他們常鬧意見？

   B: 因為他們的意見很不一樣。

   ☞ 鬧事 create a disturbance; make trouble (VO)

   A: 有很多工人在鬧事，為甚麼？

   B: 因為他們的工錢太少了。

☞ 鬧鐘　alarm clock (N)

　　A: 你怎麼今天又來晚了？

　　B: 因為我的鬧鐘不走了。

☞ 熱鬧　lively, bustling with noise and excitement; have a joyous time (Adj)

　(1) A: 中國人都很愛熱鬧嗎？

　　　B: 多半的中國人愛熱鬧，可是也有人不愛熱鬧。

　(2) 中國人過年的時候很熱鬧。

4. 覺　**sense, feel; become aware** (V)

☞ 覺得　feel; think (V)

　(1) A: 你怎麼了？

　　　B: 我覺得很累。

　(2) A: 你覺得今天的考試難不難？

　　　B: 有點兒難。

☞ 知覺　consciousness; perception (N)

　　他們的車出事了。開車的人已經沒知覺了。

☞ 不知不覺　unconsciously, unwittingly (IE)

　　時間過得真快，不知不覺地一個學期就要過去了。

☞ 先知先覺　having foresight (IE)

　　先知先覺的人不多。

5. 越　**get over; jump over; exceed** (V)

　　越過這個大山就是越南了。

☞ 越南　Vietnam (N)

　　我最好的朋友是越南人。

Lesson 19 Heart-to-heart talk
第十九課　談心

☞ 越……　　the more ... the more ... (Adv)
　　越……
　　　　　　(1) 我越跟外祖母在一起，越喜歡她。
　　　　　　(2) 我越學中文越覺得中文有意思。

☞ 越來越　　more and more (Adv)
　　　　　　(1) 天氣越來越好了。
　　　　　　(2) 不知道為甚麼他越來越不喜歡說話了。

6. 疏 shū　　**distant; not familiar with; neglect** (V)
☞ 疏遠 yuǎn　drift apart, become estranged (Adj)
　　　　　　(1) 葉先生有女朋友以後，就跟他太太越來越疏遠了。
　　　　　　(2) 要是你不常跟朋友聯絡，就會越來越疏遠了。
　　　　　　A 跟 B 疏遠了。　　A shū yuǎn B
☞ 生疏　　　not familiar; out of practice; not as close as before (Adj)
　　　　　　(1) 我已經幾年沒去北京了，那兒的事情，我很生疏了。
　　　　　　(2) 我不常用電腦，所以有點兒生疏。

7. 聰 cōng　**faculty of hearing; acute hearing** (Adj)
☞ 聰明　　　intelligent, bright, clever (SV)
　　　　　　A: 你兒子真聰明。甚麼事情一學就會。
　　　　　　B: 哪裏，哪裏，他不聰明。

☞ 小聰明　　cleverness in trivial matters; petty tricks (IE)
　　　　　　那個人沒甚麼學問，就是有點兒小聰明。

8. 驕　　　**proud; arrogant** (Adj)
9. 傲　　　**proud; refuse to yield to; brave** (Adj)
☞ 驕傲　　　arrogant, conceited; be proud, take pride in (SV)
　　　　　　(1) 驕傲的人不會有很多好朋友。
　　　　　　(2) 中國的文物是中國人的驕傲。

10. 把 bǎ **hold, grasp; control (V/CV); bundle, bunch (MW)**

(1) 請你把這把花送給她。

(2) 我把你的意見告訴她了。

(3) 請你把那本書給我拿來。謝謝。

[handwritten: 把 + N V. wǒ bǎ qián gěi fumu.]

❀ 句型練習

19.1 THE EXPRESSION 越來越

越來越 means "(become) more and more." It serves as an adverbial expression to indicate the degree to which an adjective applies is on an increase.

(1) 天氣越來越冷了。

(2) 我們的考試越來越難了。

19.2 THE PATTERN 越……越

The adverb 越 "more" is used twice before successive verbal expressions to mean "the more ... the more ...."

(1) 他越說越快。

(2) 我越吃中國飯越喜歡吃。

19.3 THE 把 CONSTRUCTIONS

The 把 construction in Mandarin Chinese is one in which the direct object is placed immediately after the coverb 把 and before the verb.

S	把	DO	V
我	把	報告	寫好了。

I (have) finished writing my paper.

Lesson 19 Heart-to-heart talk
第十九課 談心

Although the 把 construction is easy to understand, non-native speakers find it difficult to use it correctly because there are many restrictions on its usage. For example, one needs to know (1) what kinds of verbs and what kinds of direct objects can be used in such construction; (2) what sentence elements can precede and follow the verb in such construction; and (3) what communicative function such construction serves. In this lesson, we will present only a few commonly-used 把 forms and will discuss some general rules of using the 把 construction.

A. The 把 construction stresses the subject's effect on the direct object. The subject of a 把 sentence is usually an animate entity. However, some force that can have an effect on the object may also be used as a subject in a 把 sentence.

   (1) 祖母把他們的房子賣了。

   (2) 今天把我累死了。

B. In the 把 construction the direct object has to be definite or specific. Thus, determinatives such as 這 "this" and 那 "that," possessive pronouns such as 我的 "mine" or 他的 "his/her," or other specific modifiers should be used to specify the object.

   (1) 把那本書拿來。

   (2) 不要把我的錢拿走。

   (3) 我把昨天看的電影告訴他了。

C. The 把 form is preferred in imperative sentences, which command the listener to do something, as in the first example. The second example is correct, but not a construction usually used by a native speaker.

   (1) 把你昨天買的那本書拿來。

   (2) 拿來你昨天買的那本書。

D. When a sentence contains a plural object and the adverb 都 "all," the 把 form must be used, as in the first example. The non-把 form, as in the second example, is **unacceptable**.

   ✔ (1) 他把媽媽作的點心都吃了。

   ✘ (2) 他都吃了媽媽作的點心。

E. To negate a 把 sentence, the negative marker 不 or 沒有 must be placed before the 把.

(1) 他不要把電腦拿走。

(2) 我沒有把你的錢給她。

19.3.1 The 把 construction with a double noun phrase

S	把	DO	告訴/給	IO	(了)
馬紅	把	她的意見	告訴	金建	了。

Ma Hong told Jin Jian her point of view.

(1) 不要把昨天的事告訴媽媽。

(2) 金建要把他的書都給他的女朋友。

19.3.2 The 把 construction with V-在 PW (了)

Locative 把 construction is usually obligatory. The 把 form must be used.

S	把	DO	V-在	PW	(了)
他	把	錢	放在	銀行裏	了。

He deposited his money in the bank.

The following verbs often appear in this pattern with -在:

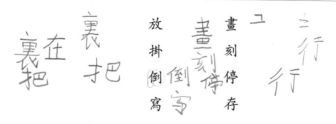

(1) 我們老師把今天要學的字寫在一張大紙上了。

(2) 不要把你的電腦放在這兒。

19.3.3 The 把 construction with V-到 PW 來/去 (了)

S	把	O	V-到	PW	來/去	(了)
他	把	車	開到	飛機場	去	了。

She drove the car to the airport.

The following verbs often appear in this pattern with -到:

拿　　寄
送　　搬
開

(1) 把今天的報拿到書房來。

(2) 請把這個禮物送到王家去。

19.3.4 The 把 construction with resultative verb compounds (了)

This lesson presents some resultative verb compounds that appear most frequently in 把 constructions.

S		把	O	RV	(了)
我們	都	把	功課	作好	了。

We all finished our homework.

The following are some verbs that serve as a second verb in an RVC:

完
好
會
到
錯

(1) 快把今天的事作完！

(2) 我把昨天的生字都學會了。

(3) 媽媽把晚飯作好了。

❀ 造 句

1.
意見
意見很好。
誰的意見很好?
學生的意見很好。

2.
討論
經常討論。
甚麼人經常討論?
老師跟學生經常討論。

3.
覺得
覺得怎麼樣?
覺得他的看法怎麼樣?
你覺得他的看法怎麼樣?

4.
想法
甚麼想法?
你有甚麼想法?
說一說你有甚麼想法。

❀ 問 答

1. 你常常跟你的朋友聯絡嗎? — 我功課不忙的時候,就常常跟他們聯絡。

2. 你怎麼跟朋友聯絡? — 我們有時候打電話,有時候寫電子信。

3. 你高興的時候跟朋友聯絡還是難過的時候跟朋友聯絡? — 我高興的時候,難過的時候都喜歡跟朋友聯絡。

4. 馬紅最近為甚麼心情不好? — 因為她跟金建鬧意見了。

5. 海英說金建是一個甚麼樣的人? — 她認為他又聰明又用功。

6. 為甚麼有人覺得金建很驕傲? — 因為他不大喜歡跟人說話。

7. 金建跟馬紅的感情怎麼樣? — 最近越來越疏遠了。

8. 你的愛好是甚麼? — 我喜歡看電影、跳舞、看書。

9. 你想馬紅喜歡金建嗎? — 我想她喜歡他,要不然她不會因為金建心情不好。

10. 要是你跟朋友有意見,你作甚麼? — 我就跟他好好地談談。

Lesson 19 Heart-to-heart talk
第十九課 談心

閱讀練習

不會說話的人

有一個人，姓湯，名字叫明。湯明不太會說話，他常常說他不應該說的話，所以會叫別人不高興。

三月七號是他的生日，他請了他的同學錢文、林木、祝貴跟馬恩來他家吃飯。已經到了吃飯的時候了，可是馬恩還沒來。湯明很不高興地說："該來的怎麼還不來？"錢文聽見了這句話，心裏想："湯明說這話的意思可能是說我是不應該來的人了。"他站起來就走了。湯明看見錢文走了，就很著急地說："怎麼不該走的走了呢？"林木一聽湯明的話，想湯明的意思是要他走了。他就甚麼話也沒說，很快地走了。湯明看見林木也走了，就馬上說："我不是說他。"祝貴聽了，心想："你不是說他，那就是說我了。"他就很生氣地走了。

湯明不知道為甚麼他的同學一個一個都走了。"我說了甚麼叫他們不高興呢？"他很難過地說。

你知道為甚麼湯明的同學都很生氣地走了嗎？從這個故事裏你學到了甚麼句型跟生詞？你可以翻譯湯明說的這幾句話嗎？

1. 該來的怎麼還不來？
2. 怎麼不該走的走了呢？
3. 我不是說他。

請查生詞

Look up the following words in a dictionary.

著急　　　zháojí　　　　　　一個一個　　yíge yíge

填　空

Fill in the blanks with the appropriate words from the story.

1. 客人 _____ _____ _____ _____ 都走了。<u>湯明</u>心裏很 _____ _____。

2. <u>湯明</u>是一個不太 _____ _____ _____ 的人。

3. <u>湯明</u>常常說他不 _____ _____ 說的話，所以叫人不 _____ _____。

4. <u>湯明</u>不知道為甚麼他的 _____ _____ 都走了。

5. <u>祝貴</u>想："你不是說他，那 _____ _____ 說我了。"

第二十課　野餐
Lesson 20　　A picnic

Lesson 20
Pinyin Text

CONTENTS

*T*ext   292

*V*ocabulary and Illustrative Sentences   293
(zhèng, gōng, yě, cān, ā, sù, shè, xiàng, wù, bié)

*P*attern Drills   300
(zhèng (zai) ... ne, shēngqì and X shēng Y de qì, bú shì ..., shì..., xiàng, yǐwéi / rènwéi)

*S*entence Building   303
(yǐwéi, rènwéi, bié, shūyuǎn)

*Q*uestions and Responses   303

*P*ronunciation Review   304

*S*upplementary Vocabulary   305

*C*ultural Notes   305

📖 Text

Yěcān
A picnic

Mǎ Hóng de diànhuà
A phone call from Ma Hong

Mǎ Hóng:	Jīn Jiàn. Nǐ hǎo ma? Nǐ zhège xīngqīliù yǒu kōngr ma?	Jin Jian, how are you? Are you free this Saturday?
Jīn Jiàn:	Yǒu kòngr. Wǒ yě zhèng xiǎng gěi nǐ dǎ diànhuà ne.	I'm free. I was just thinking of giving you a call.
Mǎ Hóng:	Zhège xīngqīliù wǒmen qù yěcān, hǎo ma?	Let's have a picnic this Saturday, okay?
Jīn Jiàn:	Hǎo a. Shàngwǔ shí diǎn wǒ kāichē qù jiē nǐ.	Great! I'll pick you up at 10:00 a.m.
Mǎ Hóng:	Hǎo. Wǒ zài sùshè děng nǐ.	Okay. I'll wait for you at my dorm.

Yěcān nà tiān
The day of the picnic

Jīn Jiàn:	Mǎ Hóng, nǐ hǎo jǐ tiān bù gěi wǒ dǎ diànhuà, nǐ yě bù jiē wǒ de diànhuà. Wèishénme? Nǐ zài shēng wǒ de qì ma?	Ma Hong, you haven't called me for a few days and you also haven't answered my calls. Why? Are you mad at me?
Mǎ Hóng:	Bú shì shēngqì, shì wǒ juéde wǒmen liǎng ge rén yuèláiyuè shūyuǎn le. Hǎoxiàng nǐ bú tài xǐhuan gēn wǒ shuōhuà de yàngzi.	I'm not mad at you. I just think we're drifting apart more and more. It seems as if you don't really like talking with me.

Lesson 20 A picnic
第二十课 野餐

Jīn Jiàn:	Méiyǒu. Zěnme huì ne? Nǐ kěnéng shì wùhuì le. Wǒ shì yí ge bú tài xǐhuan shuōhuà de rén.	That's not it. How can that be so? You are probably misunderstanding me. I'm someone who doesn't really like to talk much.
Mǎ Hóng:	Shì ma? Wǒ yǐwéi nǐ kànbuqǐ wǒ, bù xǐhuan gēn wǒ tánhuà ne.	Is that it? I thought you didn't respect me, and didn't like talking with me.
Jīn Jiàn:	Zhēnde bú shì. Bié shēngqì le. Yǐhòu yǒu shénme bù gāoxìng de shì jiù gàosu wǒ, xíng ma? Yàoburán, wùhuì jiù yuèláiyuè duō le.	That's not true. Don't get mad. From now on, if there's anything you're not happy about, please let me know, okay? Otherwise, there will be more and more misunderstandings.
Mǎ Hóng:	Hǎo ba. Chī diǎnr wǒ zuò de diǎnxīn.	Okay. (Now) try some pastries that I made.
Jīn Jiàn:	Nǐ zuò de ma? Zhēn hǎo chī.	You made them? They're delicious.

Vocabulary and Illustrative Sentences

1. **zhèng**
   正
   straight; upright; situated in the middle; punctually; chief; regular; exactly; (used to indicate an action in progress) (Adj/Adv)

   (1) Wǒ zhèng yào gěi nǐ xiěxìn, nǐ jiù dǎ diànhuà lái le. — You called me just as I was about to write to you.

   (2) Zhè běn shū zhèngshì wǒ yào zhǎo de. — This is exactly the book I was looking for.

   ☞ **zhèngcháng**
   正常
   normal; regular; routine (Adj)

   (1) Jīnnián de tiānqì bú zhèngcháng. — This year's weather is not normal.

   (2) Zhè shì wǒ zhèngcháng de gōngzuò. — This is my routine work.

☞ zhèng-dāng just when; just the time for (Adv)

Zhèngdāng wǒmen kāihuì de shíhou, tā jìnlai le. He came in just as we were having a meeting.

☞ zhènghǎo just in time; just right, just enough (Adj)

(1) Nǐ lái de zhènghǎo, wǒmen yìqǐ qù yěcān ba. You came just in time. Let's go to the picnic together.

(2) Zhè xuéqī xué Zhōngwén de rénshù zhènghǎo, bù duō yě bù shǎo. The number of students taking Chinese is just right this semester. Neither too many nor too few.

☞ zhèngzài (to indicate an action in progress), in the process of (Adv)

(1) Tāmen zhèngzài shūfáng tánhuà ne. They are talking in the study.

(2) Mǎ Hóng zhèngzài děngzhe nǐ ne. Ma Hong is waiting for you.

☞ zhēnzhèng genuine; true; real (Adj)

(1) Tā shì yí ge zhēnzhèng de hǎo rén. She is a really nice person.

(2) Zhè ge biǎo shì zhēnzhèng de míngbiǎo. This is a real famous brand of watch.

(3) Wǒ shì zhēnzhèngde ài nǐ, nǐ zěnme bú xìn ne? I truly love you. Why don't you believe me?

2. gōng **public; state-owned; collective; common; fair** (N / Adj)

☞ gōngkāi open, overt, public; make known to the public (V / Adj)

(1) Zhège shìqing bù kěyǐ gōngkāi. This matter cannot be made public.

(2) Tāmen liǎng ge rén de shìqing yǐjing gōngkāi le. Their affairs are already public knowledge.

Lesson 20   A picnic
第二十课 野餐

☞ gōnglù — highway (N)

(1) Měiguó de gōnglù hěn hǎo, shénme dìfang dōu kěyǐ qù. — The highways in America are sound. You can get to any place.

(2) Māma shuō, zài gōnglù shàng kāichē yídìng děi xiǎoxīn, yīnwèi dàjiā dōu kāide hěn kuài. — Mother says that we have to be careful when driving on the highway, since everyone drives very fast.

☞ gōngrèn — generally acknowledged (V)

Dàjiā gōngrèn, tā shì wǒmen tóngxué zhōng zuì cōngmíng de. — All of us acknowledge that he is the cleverest student among us.

☞ gōngyòng — for public use; public (Adj)

A: Qǐng wèn, nǎr yǒu gōngyòng diànhuà? — Excuse me, where can I find a public phone?

B: Wǒmen Xuéshēng Zhōngxīn yǒu yí ge. — There is one at our Student Center.

☞ gōngpíng — fair, just, impartial, equitable (SV)

Wǒ juéde zuótiān shùxué de kǎoshì bù gōngpíng, tài nán le. — I think yesterday's math exam was not fair. It was too difficult.

☞ wàigōng — (maternal) grandfather (N)

"Wàigōng" jiù shì "wàizǔfù" de yìsi. — "Waigong" and "waizufu" have the same meaning.

3. yě — **wild; open country; uncultivated; undomesticated** (Adj)

Nàge háizi zhēn yě, yìdiǎnr dōu búkèqi. — That child is wild, and he's quite impolite.

☞ yěwài — open country, field (N)

(1) Yí dào xīngqīrì wǒmen jiù qù yěwài dǎ qiú, mànpǎo. — Every Sunday, we go to the field to play ball games and to jog.

(2) Yěwài de kōngqì hěn hǎo. — The air in the country is very fresh.

☞ yěxīn   wild ambitions; ambition, big dreams (N)

(1) Wǒmen yīnggāi yǒu yěxīn, kěshì yěxīn tài dà yě bù hǎo.   We should have ambitions, but it is not very good to have vaulting ambitions.

(2) Tā de yěxīn shì yào zuò yí ge yǒumíng de míngxīng.   Her ambition is to become a famous movie star.

4. cān   food; meal (N)

Wǒmen jiā yì tiān sān cān dōu shì māma zuò de.   At home, the three meals we have each day are all prepared by our mother.

☞ yěcān   picnic (N)

(1) Jīntiān tiānqì hěn hǎo, wǒmen qù yěwài yěcān ba!   The weather is very nice today. Let's have a picnic in the countryside!

(2) Zhōngguórén yěcān de shíhou dōu chī shénme dōngxi?   What do Chinese people eat when they have a picnic?

☞ kuàicān   quick meal; fast-food (N)

(1) Xiànzài Zhōngguó yǒu hěn duō Měiguó de kuàicānguǎn.   Now, there are many American fast-food restaurants in China.

(2) Wǒ yǒu shíhou hěn máng, jiù qù kuàicānguǎn chīfàn.   Sometimes when I'm very busy, I just eat at a fast-food restaurant.

☞ zǎocān   breakfast (N)

A: Nǐ píngcháng jǐ diǎn zhōng chī zǎocān?   What time do you usually have breakfast?

B: Wǒ jīngcháng bù chī zǎocān, yīnwèi wǒ qǐde tài wǎn, méi shíjiān chī zǎocān.   I often don't have breakfast because I wake up too late and I don't have time for breakfast.

☞ zhōngcān   lunch; Chinese meal, Chinese food (N)

A: Nǐ zhōngcān huí jiā chī ma?   Do you go home for lunch?

Lesson 20 A picnic
第二十课 野餐

	B:	Bù. Wǒmen zhōngcān jiù yǒu sānshí fēnzhōng, bùnéng huí jiā chī.	No. We only have thirty minutes for lunch, (so) I can't go home to eat.
☞ wǎncān		supper, dinner (N)	
		Wǎncān wǒmen jiā duōbàn shì yí ge cài yí ge tāng.	At home, most of the time we have one dish and a soup for dinner.
☞ xīcān		Western food (N)	
	A:	Nǐ xǐhuan chī zhōngcān háishì xīcān?	Do you like to eat Chinese food or Western food?
	B:	Wǒ lái Měiguó yǐhòu, qǐchū bù xǐhuan chī xīcān, xiànzài yuèláiyuè xǐhuan le.	When I came to America, I didn't like Western food. But now I like it more and more.

5. ā   **Oh; (indicates a request or warning) (Inter)**

   Nǐ míngtiān yídìng yào lái ā!   Oh, be sure to come tomorrow!

☞ á   Eh (indicates that the speaker is pressing for an answer) (Inter)

   Nǐ qù háishì bú qù? Á? Kuài diǎnr shuō á!   Are you going or not? Well? Hurry up and answer!

☞ ǎ   What (expresses surprise) (Inter)

   Ǎ? Zěnme huì yǒu zhèyàng de shì?   What? How can that be?

☞ à   Ah; All right (expresses agreement) (Inter)

   A: Nǐmen míngtiān yìqǐ qù ba!   You'd better go together tomorrow!

   B: À. Hǎo ba.   All right. It's okay.

☞ a   (used as the end of interrogative sentences, except for those which use <u>ma</u>)

   (1) Nǐ qù nǎr a?   Where are you going?

   (2) Tā shì nǐ gēge háishì nǐ dìdi a?   Is he your elder brother or younger brother?

6. sù — **lodge for the night (V)**

☞ zhùsù — stay; to get accommodation (V)

宿

A: Nǐ shàng dàxué de shíhou, zài dàxué zhùsù ma? — When you were in college, did you live on campus?

B: Wǒ méi zhùzai dàxué sùshè, wǒ zhùzai jiālǐ. — I didn't stay in a campus dorm. I stayed at home.

7. shè — **house; shed, hut (N)**

☞ sùshè — dormitory; hostel (N)

舍

A: Nǐmen sùshè Gǎn'ēnjié de shíhou rè'nào ma? — Was your dorm very lively during Thanksgiving?

B: Hěn rè'nào, yǒu hěn duō wǔhuì. — It was very merry. There were many dance parties.

8. xiàng — **likeness (of somebody) (V); portrait, picture (N)**

像

A: Nǐ zhǎngde xiàng shéi? — Whom do you look like?

B: Yǒude dìfang xiàng bàba, yǒude dìfang xiàng māma. — In some ways I look like my father and in other ways I look like my mother.

☞ hǎoxiàng — seem; be like (V)

Wǒ hǎoxiàng zài nǎr jiànguo tā. — It seems that I have met him somewhere before.

☞ rénxiàng — portrait (N)

Nàge huàjiā huà rénxiàng huàde hěn hǎo. — That artist does portraits very well.

9. wù — **mistake, error (N); miss (V)**

误

☞ wùdiǎn — late; overdue; behind schedule (V)

A: Nǐ zěnme zhème wǎn cái lái? — Why have you come so late?

B: Huǒchē wùdiǎn le. Wǎn le èrshí fēnzhōng. — The train was behind schedule. It was late by twenty minutes.

Lesson 20 A picnic
第二十课 野餐

	wùhuì	misunderstand; mistaken (N/V)	
		(1) Nǐ wùhuì wǒ de yìsi le. Wǒ méiyǒu shuō nǐ jiāo'ào.	You have misunderstood my meaning. I never said you were conceited.
		(2) Péngyou jiān you wùhuì yīnggāi hǎohāor tántan.	If there is a misunderstanding among friends, they should talk about it.

10. bié — **don't** (IE)

    (1) Bié chī zhège! — Don't eat this!

    (2) Nǐ bié gēn wǒ shuōhuà, wǒ xiànzài hěn máng. — Please don't talk to me. I'm very busy now.

    (3) Bié zài sùshè hē jiǔ. — Don't drink alcohol in the dorm.

☞ bié rén — other people; others (Pron)

    (1) Māma bù xǔ wǒ kāi bié rén de chē. — Mother doesn't allow me to drive other people's cars.

    (2) Bié rén de jīngyàn bǐ nǐ de duōde duō. — Other people are more experienced than you are.

☞ biézì — wrongly written character (N)

    (1) Nǐ zěnme lǎo xiě biézì? — Why do you always write characters wrongly?

    (2) Tā xiě de bàogào biézì tài duō. Tā cháng bǎ "mù" zì xiě chéng "běn" zì, "jué" zì xiě chéng "xué" zì. — His report has too many wrong characters. He frequently writes "mu" as "ben" and "jue" as "xue."

☞ fēnbié — part; leave each other; distinguish; separately (V)

    (1) Wǒ gēn fùmǔ fēnbié de dì-yī tiān hěn nánguò. — I had a hard time on the first day when I parted with my parents.

    (2) Wǒ gēn nǚpéngyou yǐjing fēnbié sì ge yuè le. — My girlfriend and I have already separated for four months.

    (3) Wǒmen dōu yǒu chē, kěyǐ fēnbié qù wǔhuì. — All of us have cars. We can get to the dance party (separately) on our own.

☞ gàobié   leave; part from; bid farewell to, say good-bye to (V)

A: Wǒ yào gēn nǐmen gàobié le. Xièxie nǐmen lái sòng wǒ.   I bid farewell to you now. Thank you for coming to see me off.

B: Zàijiàn. Dào le gěi wǒmen lái xìn.   Good-bye. Write to us when you get there.

Pattern Drills

20.1 THE PATTERN zhèng(zài) ... ne

Zhèng(zài) can be rendered as "in the process of" or "in the midst of," with the particle ne often appearing at the end of the sentence. Zhèng(zài) can be used in simple sentences, as in the first two examples, and in complex sentences, as in the last two examples.

(1) Tāmen zhèng(zài) shàng kè ne.   They are in class (right now).

(2) Kèrén zhèng(zài) chīfàn ne.   The guests are eating (now).

(3) Wǒ lái de shíhou, xuésheng zhèng(zài) kǎoshì ne.   When I came in, the students were in the midst of taking a test.

(4) Wǒ tàitai lái Měiguó de shíhou, wǒ zhèng(zài) shàng dàxué ne.   I was studying in college when my wife came to the States.

20.2 Shēngqì AND X shēng Y de qì

Shēngqì means "get angry, take offense," as in the first two examples; whereas X shèng Y de qì means "X is angry with Y," as in the last two examples.

(1) Jīntiān yǒu jǐ ge xuésheng méi zuò gōngkè, lǎoshī hěn shēngqì.   Today, several students did not do their homework, so the teacher was very angry.

(2) Qǐng nǐ bú yào shēngqì.   Please don't get angry.

(3) Nǐ zài shēng shéi de qì a?   With whom are you angry?

(4) Zhè shì yí ge wùhuì, bié shēng tā de qì le.   This was a misunderstanding. Don't be mad at him anymore.

Lesson 20 A picnic
第二十課 野餐

20.3 THE PATTERN bú shì ... , shì ...

The pattern bú shì ..., shì ... is used for clarification. It explains the contrast between what is not the case and what is the case. The two clauses of this sentence pattern can be reversed.

(1) Wǒ bú shì bú yào shàng kè, shì wǒ jīntiān qǐlái wǎn le.

It wasn't that I didn't want to attend class, it was because I got up too late today.

(2) Bú shì wǒ bù gěi nǐ fángzū, shì wǒ zhēnde méiyǒu qián.

It isn't that I don't want to pay you the rent, it is because I really don't have any money.

(3) Shì wǒ bú yào tā qù de, bú shì tā bú yào qù.

It was I who didn't want him to go, not that he didn't want to go.

(4) Wǒ shì cóng Běijīng lái de, bú shì cóng Nánjīng lái de.

I came from Beijing, not from Nanjing.

20.4 THE WORD xiàng

20.4.1 The meaning of xiàng

Xiàng "resemble" is an equational verb which connects or equates two nominal expressions on either side of the verb.

(1) Hěn duō rén shuō wǒ xiàng wǒ mǔqīn.

Many people say that I look like my mother.

(2) A: Nàge rén shì Zhōngguórén háishì Rìběnrén?

Is that person a Chinese or a Japanese?

B: Tā xiàng Rìběnrén.

He looks like a Japanese.

20.4.2 Xiàng ... yíyàng expresses similarity and disparity

Xiàng ... yíyàng expresses similarity and disparity. The expression yíyàng, literally "one kind," means "be alike, similar to."

(1) Tā xiàng tā mèimei yíyàng yònggōng ma?
Does she study as diligently as her younger sister does?

(2) Jīntiān xiàng zuótiān yíyàng rè.
Today is as hot as yesterday.

20.4.3 The pattern hǎoxiàng ... de yàngzi

The expression hǎoxiàng ... de yàngzi is used to express the speaker's own sense, mind, observation, judgment, etc.

(1) Xiǎoměi jīntiān hǎoxiàng bú tài gāoxìng de yàngzi.
Xiaomei seems unhappy today.

(2) Tā hǎoxiàng hěn jiāo'ào de yàngzi.
He appears to be very arrogant.

20.5 THE WORDS yǐwéi/rènwéi

Yǐwéi/rènwéi both mean "think, consider." Each of them needs an object, usually a subject-predicate construction, as in the first two examples. However, yǐwéi, especially when it is used in a compound sentence, has another meaning. It signals that a speaker's assumption has proved incorrect, as in the last two examples.

(1) Wǒ yǐwéi/rènwéi wǒmen de xuésheng kàode hěn hǎo.
I think our students did very well in this test.

(2) Wǒ yǐwéi/rènwéi wǒmen jīntiān bù yīnggāi qù kàn diànyǐng.
I don't think we should go to a movie today.

(3) Nǐ de Zhōngguóhuà shuōde zhème hǎo, wǒ hái yǐwéi nǐ bú huì shuō ne.
You speak Chinese very well. I thought you couldn't speak it.

(4) Wǒ yǐwéi tā shì Zhōngguórén, jīntiān cái zhīdào tā shì Rìběnrén.
I thought she was Chinese. Today I have just found out that she is Japanese.

Lesson 20 A picnic
第二十课 野餐

🌸 Sentence Building

1.
Yǐwéi
Yǐwéi nǐ kànbuqǐ wǒ.
Wǒ yǐwéi nǐ kànbuqǐ wǒ.
Wǒ yǐqián yǐwéi nǐ kànbuqǐ wǒ.

2.
Rènwéi
Wǒ rènwéi
Wǒ rènwéi nǐ yīnggāi qù.
Wǒ rènwéi nǐ míngtiān yīnggāi qù.

3.
Bié
Bié hē jiǔ.
Bié hē jiǔ le.
Bié zài hē jiǔ le.

4.
Shūyuǎn
Yuèláiyuè shūyuǎn.
Wǒ gēn tā yuèláiyuè shūyuǎn.
Xiànzài wǒ gēn tā yuèláiyuè shūyuǎn le.

🌸 Questions and Responses

1. Wèishénme Mǎ Hóng yào qǐng Jīn Jiàn qù yěcān?
   Why does Ma Hong want to invite Jin Jian for a picnic?

   Tā xiǎng gēn tā hǎohāor tántan.
   She wants to have a good chat with him.

2. Wèishénme Mǎ Hóng zuìjìn bù jiē Jīn Jiàn de diànhuà?
   Why hasn't Ma Hong been answering Jin Jian's phone calls lately?

   Yīnwèi tā shēng Jīn Jiàn de qì.
   Because she has been mad at Jin Jian.

3. Jīn Jiàn zhīdào wèishénme Mǎ Hóng shēngqì ma?
   Does Jin Jian know why Ma Hong is angry?

   Wǒ xiǎng tā bù zhīdào.
   I think he doesn't know (why).

4. Yàoshì nǐ shēng nǐ péngyou de qì, nǐ huì gàosu tā ma?
   If you are angry with a friend, will you tell him/her?

   Bù yídìng. Yěxǔ wǒ bú huì gàosu tā.
   It depends. Maybe I won't tell him/her.

5. Rén gēn rén chángcháng huì yǒu wùhuì ma?
   Do people often have misunderstandings with one another?

   Wǒ xiǎng shì de.
   I think so.

6. Nǐ de sùshě zhù jǐ ge rén? Nǐmen de xiǎngfǎ yíyàng ma?
How many people are there in your dorm (room)? Do you share similar views?

Liǎng gè. Hěn bù yíyàng.
Two people. We're very different.

7. Zài Měiguó, fēijī chángcháng wùdiǎn ma?
In America, are flights often behind schedule?

Zài Měiguó, fēijī wùdiǎn shì hěn píngcháng de shì.
In America, delayed flights are very commonplace.

8. Nǐ cháng yòng gōngyòng diànhuà ma?
Do you often use the public telephone?

Bù cháng yòng. Wǒ yǒu shǒujī.
I rarely use it. I have a cellphone.

9. Nǐ xǐhuan gēn kànbuqǐ rén de rén zuò péngyou ma?
Do you like making friends with people who look down on others?

Dāngrán bù xǐhuan. Shéi huì xǐhuan gēn kànbuqǐ rén de rén zuò péngyou ne?
Of course I don't. Who likes making friends with those who scorn others?

10. Jīn Jiàn gàosu Mǎ Hóng shénme?

What did Jin Jian tell Ma Hong?

Tā shuō: "Bié shēngqì le. Yǐhòu yǒu shénme bù gāoxìng de shì jiù gàosu wǒ."
He said, "Don't get mad. From now on, if there's anything you're not happy about, please let me know."

Pronunciation Review

Question Words

1. Nǐ jīntiān qù yěcān ma?
   Nǐmen qù nǎr yěcān a?
   Wǒmen qù nǎr yěcān ne?

2. Nǐ de sùshè zài nǎr?
   Shéi zài sùshè ne?
   Nǐ de diànhuà jǐ hào?
   Nǐ zhùzai něi ge sùshè?

3. Gǎn'ēnjié zài jǐ yuè?
   Zhè shì shéi de dìtú?
   Nǐ jīnnián jǐ suì le?
   Nǐmen de fángzi dà-bu-dà?

4. Jīntiān jǐ yuè jǐ hào?
   Zhè shì nǎ guó de dìtú?
   Nǐ yào chī shénme cài?
   Wǒmen gēn shéi yìqǐ qù tiàowǔ?

Supplementary Vocabulary

Seasons and Weather

tiānqì yùbào	weather forecast	xiàtiān/xiàjì	summer
wēndù	temperature	qiūtiān/qiūjì	autumn/fall
qìhòu	climate	dōngtiān/dōngjì	winter
tiānqì	weather	yīntiān	cloudy day
sì jì	four seasons	yǔtiān	rainy day
chūntiān/chūnjì	spring	qíngtiān	sunny day

Cultural Notes

Qǐng kè (To invite a guest)

Chinese people are famous for their hospitality. Friends and relatives often get together for feasts which cost more than they can afford. When one is invited to a dinner, as a rule, one should decline the invitation at first and saying something like "Nà tài máfán nǐ le" (That will cause you too much trouble) so as to show courtesy and appreciation. But after being pressed two to three times, one can accept the invitation graciously. Such kind of "decline-accept" scenario sounds hypocritical to Westerners, but it is considered good manners in Chinese society.

During dinner, your host or hostess may say something like "Méiyǒu shénme cài" (There is not much food), even if ten dishes are lain on the table. That is only polite talk (kèqihuà). In response, the guest is expected to say something like "Nǐ tài kèqi le, cái tài fēngfù le" (You're too humble. There's plenty of food.).

第二十課
漢字本

內容

課文 　　　　　　　　　　　　　　　　　　　　　　308

生詞及例句 　　　　　　　　　　　　　　　　　　　309
（正、公、野、餐、啊、宿、舍、像、誤、別）

句型練習 　　　　　　　　　　　　　　　　　　　　314
（正(在)……呢、生氣和Ｘ生Ｙ的氣、不是……，是……、
像、以為/認為）

造句 　　　　　　　　　　　　　　　　　　　　　　316
（以為、認為、別、疏遠）

問答 　　　　　　　　　　　　　　　　　　　　　　316

閱讀練習 　　　　　　　　　　　　　　　　　　　　317
　　猜謎語

課文

野餐

馬紅的電話

馬紅： 金建。你好嗎？你這個星期六有空兒嗎？

金建： 有空兒。我也正想給你打電話呢。

馬紅： 這個星期六我們去野餐，好嗎？

金建： 好啊。上午十點我開車去接你。

馬紅： 好。我在宿舍等你。

野餐那天

金建： 馬紅，你好幾天不給我打電話，你也不接我的電話。為甚麼？你在生我的氣嗎？

馬紅： 不是生氣，是我覺得我們兩個人越來越疏遠了。好像你不太喜歡跟我說話的樣子。

金建： 沒有。怎麼會呢？你可能是誤會了。我是一個不太喜歡說話的人。

馬紅： 是嗎？我以為你看不起我，不喜歡跟我談話呢。

金建： 真的不是。別生氣了。以後有甚麼不高興的事就告訴我，行嗎？要不然，誤會就越來越多了。

馬紅： 好吧，吃點兒我作的點心。

金建： 你作的嗎？真好吃。

Lesson 20　A picnic
第二十課　野餐

🌸 生詞及例句

1. **正**　straight; upright; situated in the middle; punctually; chief; regular; exactly (used to indicate an action in progress) (Adj/Adv)

   (1) 我正要給你寫信，你就打電話來了。

   (2) 這本書正是我要找的。

   ☞ **正常**　normal; regular; routine (Adj)

   (1) 今年的天氣不正常。

   (2) 這是我正常的工作。

   ☞ **正當**　just when; just the time for (Adv)

   正當我們開會的時候，他進來了。

   ☞ **正好**　just in time; just right, just enough (Adj)

   (1) 你來得正好，我們一起去野餐吧。

   (2) 這學期學中文的人數正好，不多也不少。

   ☞ **正在**　(to indicate an action in progress), in the process of (Adv)

   (1) 他們正在書房談話呢。

   (2) 馬紅正在等著你呢。

   ☞ **真正**　genuine; true; real (Adj)

   (1) 他是一個真正的好人。

   (2) 這個錶是真正的名錶。

   (3) 我是真正地愛你，你怎麼不信呢？

2. **公**　public; state-owned; collective; common; fair (N/Adj)

   ☞ **公開**　open, overt, public; make known to the public (V/Adj)

   (1) 這個事情不可以公開。

   (2) 他們兩個人的事情已經公開了。

☞ 公路　highway (N)
(1) 美國的公路很好，甚麼地方都可以去。
(2) 媽媽說，在公路上開車一定得小心，因為大家都開得很快。

☞ 公認　generally acknowledged (V)
大家公認，他是我們同學中最聰明的。

☞ 公用　for public use; public (Adj)
A: 請問，哪兒有公用電話？
B: 我們學生中心有一個。

☞ 公平　fair, just, impartial, equitable (SV)
我覺得昨天數學的考試不公平，太難了。

☞ 外公　(maternal) grandfather (N)
"外公"就是外祖父的意思。

3. 野　**wild; open country; uncultivated; undomesticated (Adj)**
那個孩子真野，一點兒都不客氣。

☞ 野外　open country, field (N)
(1) 一到星期日我們就去野外打球，慢跑。
(2) 野外的空氣很好。

☞ 野心　wild ambitions; ambition, big dreams (N)
(1) 我們應該有野心，可是野心太大也不好。
(2) 她的野心是要作一個有名的明星。

4. 餐　**food; meal (N)**
我們家一天三餐都是媽媽作的。

☞ 野餐　picnic (N)
(1) 今天天氣很好，我們去野外野餐吧！
(2) 中國人野餐的時候都吃甚麼東西？

Lesson 20 A picnic
第二十課 野餐

☞ 快餐   quick meal; fast-food (N)

(1) 現在中國有很多美國的快餐館。

(2) 我有時候很忙，就去快餐館吃飯。

☞ 早餐   breakfast (N)

A: 你平常幾點鐘吃早餐？

B: 我經常不吃早餐，因為我起得太晚，沒時間吃早餐。

☞ 中餐   lunch; Chinese meal, Chinese food (N)

A: 你中餐回家吃嗎？

B: 不。我們中餐就有三十分鐘，不能回家吃。

☞ 晚餐   supper, dinner (N)

晚餐我們家多半是一個菜一個湯。

☞ 西餐   Western food (N)

A: 你喜歡吃中餐還是西餐？

B: 我來美國以後，起初不喜歡吃西餐，現在越來越喜歡了。

5. 啊   **Oh; (indicates a request or warning) (Inter)**

你明天一定要來啊！

☞ 啊   Eh (indicates that the speaker is pressing for an answer) (Inter)

（第二聲）   你去還是不去？啊？快點兒說啊！

☞ 啊   What (expresses surprise) (Inter)

（第三聲）   啊？怎麼會有這樣的事？

☞ 啊   Ah; All right (expresses agreement) (Inter)

（第四聲）   A: 你們明天一起去吧！

B: 啊。好吧。

☞ 啊
（輕聲）

(used at the end of interrogative sentences, except for those which use <u>ma</u>)

(1) 你去哪兒啊？

(2) 他是你哥哥還是你弟弟啊？

6. 宿 **lodge for the night** (V)

☞ 住宿　stay; to get accommodation (V)

A: 你上大學的時候，在大學住宿嗎？

B: 我沒住在大學宿舍，我住在家裏。

7. 舍 **house; shed, hut** (N)

☞ 宿舍　dormitory; hostel (N)

A: 你們宿舍感恩節的時候熱鬧嗎？

B: 很熱鬧，有很多舞會。

8. 像 **likeness (of somebody)** (V); **portrait, picture** (N)

A: 你長得像誰？

B: 有的地方像爸爸，有的地方像媽媽。

☞ 好像　seem; be like (V)

我好像在哪兒見過他。

☞ 人像　portrait (N)

那個畫家畫人像畫得很好。

9. 誤 **mistake, error** (N); **miss** (V)

☞ 誤點　late; overdue; behind schedule (V)

A: 你怎麼這麼晚才來？

B: 火車誤點了。晚了二十分鐘。

Lesson 20 A picnic
第二十課 野餐

☞ 誤會 misunderstand; mistaken (N/V)

(1) 你誤會我的意思了。我沒有說你驕傲。

(2) 朋友間有誤會應該好好兒談談。

10. 別 bié **don't** (IE)

(1) 別吃這個！

(2) 你別跟我說話，我現在很忙。

(3) 別在宿舍喝酒。

☞ 別人 other people; others (Pron)

(1) 媽媽不許我開別人的車。

(2) 別人的經驗比你的多得多。

☞ 別字 wrongly written character (N)

(1) 你怎麼老寫別字？

(2) 他寫的報告別字太多。他常把"木"字寫成"本"字，"覺"字寫成"學"字。

☞ 分別 part; leave each other; distinguish; separately (V)

(1) 我跟父母分別的第一天很難過。

(2) 我跟女朋友已經分別四個月了。

(3) 我們都有車，可以分別去舞會。

☞ 告別 leave; part from; bid farewell to, say good-bye to (V)

A. 我要跟你們告別了。謝謝你們來送我。

B. 再見。到了給我們來信。

句型練習

20.1 THE PATTERN 正(在)……呢

正(在) can be rendered as "in the process of" or "in the midst of," with the particle 呢 often appearing at the end of the sentence. 正(在) can be used in simple sentences, as in the first two examples, and in complex sentences, as in the last two examples.

(1) 他們正(在)上課呢。

(2) 客人正(在)吃飯呢。

(3) 我來的時候,學生正(在)考試呢。

(4) 我太太來美國的時候,我正(在)上大學呢。

20.2 生氣 AND X 生 Y 的氣

生氣 means "get angry, take offense," as in the first two examples; whereas X 生 Y 的氣 means "X is angry with Y," as in the last two examples.

(1) 今天有幾個學生沒作功課,老師很生氣。

(2) 請你不要生氣。

(3) 你在生誰的氣啊?

(4) 這是一個誤會,別生他的氣了。

20.3 THE WORDS 不是……,是……

The pattern 不是……,是…… is used for clarification. It explains the contrast between what is not the case and what is the case. The two clauses of this sentence pattern can be reversed.

(1) 我不是不要上課,是我今天起來晚了。

(2) 不是我不給你房租,是我真的沒有錢。

(3) 是我不要他去的,不是他不要去。

(4) 我是從北京來的，不是從南京來的。

20.4 THE WORD 像

20.4.1 The meaning of 像

> 像 "resemble" is an equational verb which connects or equates two nominal expressions on either side of the verb.

(1) 很多人說我像我母親。

(2) A: 那個人是中國人還是日本人？
   B: 他像日本人。

20.4.2 像……一樣 expresses similarity and disparity

> 像……一樣 expresses similarity and disparity. The expression 一樣, literally "one kind," means "be alike, similar to."

(1) 她像她妹妹一樣用功嗎？

(2) 今天像昨天一樣熱。

20.4.3 The pattern 好像……的樣子

> The expression 好像……的樣子 is used to express the speaker's own sense, mind, observation, judgment, etc.

(1) 小美今天好像不太高興的樣子。

(2) 他好像很驕傲的樣子。

20.5 THE WORDS 以為/認為

> 以為/認為 both mean "think, consider." Each of them needs an object, usually a subject-predicate construction, as in the first two examples. However, 以為, especially when it is used in a compound sentence, has another meaning. It signals that a speaker's assumption has proved incorrect, as in the last two examples.

(1) 我以為/認為我們的學生考得很好。

(2) 我以為/認為我們今天不應該去看電影。

(3) 你的中國話說得這麼好，我還以為你不會說呢。

(4) 我以為他是中國人，今天才知道他是日本人。

造 句

1.
以為
以為你看不起我。
我以為你看不起我。
我以前以為你看不起我。

2.
認為
我認為
我認為你應該去。
我認為你明天應該去。

3.
別
別喝酒。
別喝酒了。
別再喝酒了。

4.
疏遠
越來越疏遠。
我跟他越來越疏遠。
現在我跟他越來越疏遠了。

問 答

1. 為甚麼馬紅要請金建去野餐？　　她想跟他好好兒談談。
2. 為甚麼馬紅最近不接金建的電話？　因為她生金建的氣。
3. 金建知道為甚麼馬紅生氣嗎？　　我想他不知道。
4. 要是你生你朋友的氣，你會告訴　不一定。也許我不會告訴他。
   他嗎？
5. 人跟人常常會有誤會嗎？　　　　我想是的。
6. 你的宿舍住幾個人？你們的想法　兩個。很不一樣。
   一樣嗎？

7. 在<u>美國</u>，飛機常常誤點嗎？	在<u>美國</u>，飛機誤點是很平常的事。
8. 你常用公用電話嗎？	不常用。我有手機。
9. 你喜歡跟看不起人的人作朋友嗎？	當然不喜歡。誰會喜歡跟看不起人的人作朋友呢？
10. <u>金建</u>告訴<u>馬紅</u>甚麼？	他說："別生氣了。以後有甚麼不高興的事就告訴我。"

閱讀練習

猜謎語 (Riddle games)

(一)

東邊一個，西邊一個

東邊的看不見西邊的、西邊的也看不見東邊的。

(這兩個東西甚麼人都有，你猜得出來是甚麼嗎？)

(二)

一個人是甚麼字？

兩個人是甚麼字？

一加一不是二，是甚麼字？

一撇、一捺是甚麼字？

請查生詞

Look up the following words in a dictionary.

加	jiā
減	jiǎn
撇	piě
捺	nà

第二十一課　我生病了
Lesson 21　　I got sick

Lesson 21
Pinyin Text

CONTENTS

*T*ext   322

*V*ocabulary and Illustrative Sentences   323
(bìng, shuì, jiào, tóu, téng/tòng, fā, shāo, dōng, xī, yī)

*P*attern Drills   331
(yíhuìr..., yíhuìr..., zài, tóu, V-lái-V-qù, zháo, xià)

*S*entence Building   335
(pǎoláipǎoqù, dōngxi, chūfā, yīxué)

*Q*uestions and Responses   335

*P*ronunciation Review   336

*S*upplementary Vocabulary   337

*C*ultural Notes   337

Text

Wǒ shēngbìng le
I got sick

Zuìjìn tiānqì bù hǎo, yíhuìr lěng, yíhuìr rè. Hěn duō tóngxué dōu shēngbìng le. Zuótiān wǎnshang wǒ shuìbuzháo jiào, tóu yě hěn téng, juéde yǒu diǎnr fāshāo, shénme dōngxi dōu bù xiǎng chī, hěn lèi. Wǒ xiǎng wǒ shēngbìng le. Wǒ yīnggāi qù kàn yīshēng. Zǎoshang qǐlái yǐhòu, wǒ jiù mǎshàng qù yīyuàn kàn yīshēng le. Cóng yīyuàn huílái yǐhòu, wǒ gěi lǎoshī fā le yí ge diànzǐxìn qǐng bìngjià.

The weather has not been very good recently. One moment it is cold and the next it is hot. Many of my classmates have been ill. Last night, I couldn't sleep. And I got a splitting headache. I felt a bit feverish. I didn't want to eat anything and I was very tired. I thought I was getting sick. I really had to see a doctor. After I woke up this morning, I went to the hospital to see the doctor at once. After coming back from the hospital, I sent an e-mail to my teacher to ask for a sick leave.

Wáng lǎoshī:

Wǒ jīntiān méiyǒu néng lái shàng kè. Yīnwèi wǒ zuótiān wǎnshang bìng le, tóu hěn téng, yǒu yìdiǎnr fāshāo, yě chībuxià dōngxi. Suǒyǐ jīntiān yì zǎo jiù qù kàn yīshēng le. Yīshēng shuō wǒ méi shénme dà bìng, tā gěi le wǒ yào, jiào wǒ chī yào, duō hē shuǐ, duō shuìjiào. Wǒ yěxǔ hěn kuài jiù huì hǎo le. Wǒ xiǎng wǒ míngtiān yídìng kěyǐ lái shàng kè. Qǐng nǐ bǎ jīntiān gēn míngtiān yīnggāi zuò de gōngkè gàosu Sīwén. Hǎo ma? Xièxie.

            Zhù
kuàilè!

                 Xuéshēng
                 Mǎ Àiwén
                 Sìyuè liù rì

Lesson 21 I got sick
第二十一课 我生病了

> Professor Wang,
>
> I am not able to come to class today. I fell ill last night. I had a headache and a slight fever, and I couldn't eat. So as soon as I woke up this morning, I went to see a doctor. The doctor said that I was not seriously ill. He gave me some medicine, and asked me to take my medication, drink a lot of water and take a good rest. I should be able to recover quickly. I think I'll definitely be able to attend class tomorrow. Could you please let Siwen know what my homework is for today and tomorrow? Is that okay? Thank you.
>
> Happy all the time!
>
> > Your student,
> > Ma Aiwen
> > 6 April

Vocabulary and Illustrative Sentences

1. **bìng**   **ill, sick; disease; fault, defect (N)**

☞ shēngbìng   get ill (V/VO)

	(1) Zuìjìn tiānqì bù hǎo, shēngbìng de rén hěn duō.	The weather has been bad recently, many people have got ill.
	(2) Qùnián wǒ shēng le sān ge xīngqī de bìng.	Last year, I was ill for three weeks.

☞ bìngrén   patient (N)

	(1) Zhège yīshēng de bìngrén hěn duō.	This doctor has many patients.
	(2) Lín yīshēng, yǒu hěn duō bìngrén zài děngzhe nǐ ne.	Dr. Lin, there are many patients waiting to see you.

☞ bìngfáng   ward (of a hospital) (N)

	(1) A: Nǐ de péngyou zhù jǐ hào bìngfáng?	Which ward is your friend in?
	B: Tā zhù sānlíngqī bìngfáng.	He is in ward 307.

		(2) Nàge bìngfáng hěn dà.	That ward is very big.
☞	bìngjià	sick leave (N)	
		(1) Yàoshì nǐ yǒu bìng, bù néng lái shàng kè, zuìhǎo gēn lǎoshī qǐng bìngjià.	If you are ill and cannot attend class, you should ask the teacher for a sick leave.
		(2) Jīntiān nǐmen méiyǒu kè, yīnwèi Wáng lǎoshī qǐng bìngjià le.	You have no class today because Professor Wang is on sick leave.
☞	bìngqíng	state of an illness; patient's condition (N)	
		A: Lín yīshēng, qǐng nǐ gàosu wǒ wǒ tàitai de bìngqíng.	Dr. Lin, please tell me about my wife's condition.
		B: Tā xiànzài hǎo duō le. Tā zài shuìjiào ne.	She is much better now. She's sleeping right now.
☞	bìngcóng-kǒurù	disease goes in via one's mouth (IE)	
		Zhōngguórén shuō "bìngcóngkǒurù," suǒyǐ nǐ chī dōngxi de shíhou děi xiǎoxīn.	The Chinese believe that illnesses are transmitted orally, so one must be careful about what one eats.
2.	shuì	**sleep** (V)	
		A: Zhème wǎn le, nǐ zěnme hái méi shuì?	It's so late already. Why haven't you gone to bed yet?
		B: Wǒ de gōngkè hái méi zuò wán ne.	I haven't finished my homework yet.
3.	jiào	**sleep** (N)	
☞	shuìjiào	to sleep (V/VO)	
		(1) A: Nǐ píngcháng shénme shíhou shuìjiào?	What time do you usually go to bed?
		B: Wǒ píngcháng wǎnshang shíyī diǎn shuìjiào.	I usually go to bed at 11:00 p.m.

Lesson 21 I got sick
第二十一课 我生病了

	(2) A: Nǐ zuótiān wǎnshang shuì le jǐ ge xiǎoshí de jiào?	How many hours did you sleep last night?
	B: Wǒ jiù shuì le sì ge xiǎoshí, yīnwèi jīntiān yǒu kǎoshì.	I only slept for four hours because I have an exam today.
4. tóu	**head; top; chief** (N); **first** (prefix for ordinal numbers)	
	(1) Zhōngguórén shuō tóu dà de rén hěn cōngmíng. Nǐ xìn ma?	The Chinese say that people with big heads are intelligent. Do you believe that?
	(2) Xìnzhǐ zài nà běn shū de shàngtou.	The letter sheet is on top of that book.
	(3) Zuótiān tā tóu yí gè kǎo wán, zhēn cōngmíng.	Yesterday he was the first to finish the exam. He's really smart.
☞ wàitou	outside (PW)	
	Wèishénme wàitou yǒu rén pǎoláipǎoqù?	Why are people running around outside?
☞ lǐtou	inside; interior (PW)	
	Wàitou bǐ lǐtou lěng, nǐ hái fāshāo, zuìhǎo zài lǐtou, bú yào chūqu.	It's colder outside (than inside). You still have a fever. It's best if you stay inside. Don't go outside.
☞ diǎntóu	nod one's head (VO)	
	Yàoshì nǐmen bù xiǎng shuō-huà, dǒng le jiù diǎndiǎntóu yě kěyǐ.	If you don't want to speak, you can also nod your head to let me know that you have understood.
5. téng/ tòng	**ache, pain, sore** (Adj); **love dearly** (V)	
	Wǒ de shǒu hěn téng.	I feel a sharp pain in my hands.
☞ tóuténg/ tóutòng	(have a) headache (N)	
	(1) Zhōngwén shuō, wǒ de tóu hěn tòng, bù shuō wǒ yǒu yí ge tóuténg.	In Chinese one says "my head hurts". One doesn't say "I have a headache."

	(2) Tāmen liǎng ge rén de shì zhēn jiào wǒ tóutòng.	Their problem becomes my headache.
☞ téng'ài	be very fond of, love dearly (V)	
	Fùmǔ dōu hěn téng'ài tāmen de érnǚ.	All parents love their children dearly.
☞ xīnténg	love dearly (V); feel sorry; be distressed (SV)	
	(1) Nàme hǎo de dōngxi bújiàn le, zhēn jiào wǒ xīnténg.	Such a valuable item is lost. That really distresses me.
	(2) Wàizǔmǔ xīnténg wǒ, bú yào wǒ chūqu zuò shì.	My (maternal) grandmother loves me dearly. She doesn't want me to go out to work.
6. fā	**send out; issue, deliver; distribute; open up, discover** (V)	
	Wǒ děi chūqu fā xìn.	I have to go out to mail a letter.
☞ fāchū	issue, send out, give out (V)	
	A: Wǒ gěi nǐ jiějie xiě de xìn, nǐ shì shénme shíhou fāchū de?	When did you mail the letter that I wrote to your elder sister?
	B: Sān tiān yǐqián fāchūqù de.	I sent it out three days ago.
☞ chūfā	set out, start off (V)	
	A: Míngtiān wǒmen qù Cháng-Chéng, shénme shíhou chūfā?	We are going to visit the Great Wall tomorrow. What time are we setting out?
	B: Bā diǎn yí kè chūfā.	We are setting out at 8:15.
☞ fāshēng	happen, occur, take place (V)	
	A: Wǒ bú zài jiā de shíhou, yǒu shénme shìqing fāshēng le ma?	When I wasn't home, did anything happen?
	B: Shénme shì dōu méi fāshēng.	Nothing happened at all.

Lesson 21 I got sick
第二十一课 我生病了

☞ fāqǐ   initiate; sponsor; start, launch (V)

Wáng lǎoshī yào huíguó le, wǒmen tóngxué zuótiān fāqǐ le yí ge huānsònghuì huānsòng tā. — Professor Wang is returning to his homeland soon. Our classmates threw a farewell party for him yesterday.

☞ fāgěi   issue, distribute (V)

Wǒmen qù Zhōngguó lǚxíng yǐqián, lǎoshī fāgěi wǒmen yì zhāng Zhōngguó dìtú. — Before we went to China, our teacher distributed a map of China to each of us.

☞ fāmíng   invent; invention (V/N)

(1) Nǐ zhīdào diànhuà shì shéi fāmíng de ma? — Do you know who invented the telephone?

(2) Zhōngguó zǎoqí yǒu hěn duō fāmíng. — There were many inventions in ancient China.

☞ fāxiàn   find, discover (V)

Shì shéi xiān fāxiàn zhème hǎokàn de dìfang de? — Who first discovered this beautiful place?

7. shāo   **burn; cook, roast; run a temperature** (V)

(1) Nà tiān de dàhuǒ, bǎ tā de shū dōu shāo le. — The big fire that day destroyed all his books.

(2) Wǒ māma hěn huì shāo cài. — My mom cooks very well.

(3) Nàge fànguǎn hóngshāo de cài dōu hěn hǎochī. — All the dishes braised in soy sauce at that restaurant are very delicious.

☞ fāshāo   have a fever, have (or run) a temperature (V/VO)

(1) Wǒ bìng le, hái hǎo méi fāshāo. — I'm ill. (But) it's lucky that I don't have a temperature.

(2) Zhège bìngrén yǐjing fā le liǎng tiān shāo le. — This patient has had a fever for two days already.

☞ gāoshāo high fever (N)

    Yīshēng, qǐng nǐ xiān kàn nàge fā gāoshāo de bìngrén ba. — Doctor, please attend to the patient having a high fever first.

8. dōng **east; master; owner; host** (N)

☞ dōngfāng east (direction); the East (N)

    Cóngqián hěn duō rén bú tài dǒng dōngfāng de shìqing. — In the past, many people did not have much knowledge about the East.

☞ Dōngběi northeast; Northeast China (including the three provinces of Jilin, Liaoning and Heilongjiang) (N)

    Zhōngguó Dōngběi de tiānqì hěn lěng. — The weather in Northeast China is very cold.

☞ Shāndōng Shandong (province) (N)

    A: Qǐng nǐmen zài dìtú shàng zhǎo-yi-zhǎo Shāndōng zài nǎr. — Please look for Shandong on the map.

    B: Wǒ zhǎodào le, zài Héběi de xiàtou. — I've found it. It's below Hebei.

☞ Jìndōng the Near East (N)

    Wǒ zhēn xiǎng dào Jìndōng de guójiā qù lǚxíng. — I really want to visit the countries in the Near East.

☞ Yuǎndōng the Far East (N)

    A: Nǐ qùguo Yuǎndōng shénme guójiā? — Which countries in the Far East have you been to?

    B: Wǒ jiù qùguo Zhōngguó gēn Rìběn. — I've only been to China and Japan.

☞ Zhōngdōng the Middle East (N)

    A: Zuìjìn Zhōngdōng yǒu-méiyǒu yòu nàoshì? — Has the Middle East been in turmoil again lately?

Lesson 21   I got sick
第二十一课 我生病了

      B: Zuìjìn Zhōngdōng cháng- There has been constant
         cháng nàoshì.   upheaval in the Middle East
                                         recently.

☞ **fángdōng**   landlord or landlady (N)

      A: Nǐ de fángdōng zěnmeyàng?   What is your landlord like?

      B: Yàoshi nǐ gěi tā fángqián, tā   If you pay the rent, he is very
         jiù hěn kèqi.   polite.

9. **xī**   **west (N)**

☞ **xīfāng**   west (direction); the West (N)

      A: Xīfāng rén gēn dōngfāng rén   Are the ideas and perspectives of
         de xiǎngfǎ yíyàng ma?   Westerners and Easterners the
                                         same?

      B: Yǒu hěn duō bùtóng de   They are different in many
         dìfang.   respects.

☞ **dōngxi**   thing; a person or animal (derogatory) (N)

    (1) A: Zhège dōngxi néng-bu-   Can I eat this thing?
           néng chī?

        B: Néng chī shì néng chī,   You can eat it, but it doesn't taste
           kěshì bù hǎochī.   very good.

    (2) A: Zhège dōngxi, Zhōngguóhuà   What is this thing called in
           jiào shénme?   Chinese?

☞ **xīběi**   northwest (N)

      Zhōngguó xīběi yǒu hěn duō   There are many high mountains
      gāoshān.   in northwestern China.

10. **yī**   **doctor (of medicine); medicine (N); treat (V)**

      A: Nǐ néng yī hǎo tā de bìng ma?   Can you cure his illness?

      B: Wǒ kěyǐ shìshi.   I will give it a try.

☞ yīshēng   doctor (N)

    (1) Yàoshì nǐ bìng le, nǐ děi qù kàn yīshēng.   If you are ill, you have to see a doctor.

    (2) Zuò yīshēng yídìng děi yǒu àixīn.   To be a doctor, you must have compassion.

☞ yīyuàn   hospital (N)

    A: Zhège yīyuàn zěnmeyàng?   How is this hospital?

    B: Zhège yīyuàn shì xīn de, hěn dà, yīshēng yě hěn hǎo.   This hospital is new and is very big. The doctors are very good too.

☞ yīxué   medical science (N)

    Wǒ juéde yīxué hěn yǒuyìsi. Wǒ xiǎng yǐhòu xué yī.   I think medical science is really interesting. I'd like to study medicine in the future.

☞ xīyī   Western medicine; a doctor trained in Western medicine (N)

☞ zhōngyī   traditional Chinese medical science; a doctor trained in traditional Chinese medicine (N)

    A: Yǒude rén xìn xīyī, yǒude rén xìn zhōngyī. Nǐ ne?   Some people believe in Western medicine, some believe in Chinese medicine. How about you?

    B: Wǒ dōu xìn. Yǒude bìng kàn xīyī hǎo, yǒude bìng kàn zhōngyī hǎo.   I believe in both. For some illnesses, it is better to see a doctor trained in Western medicine, and for other illnesses, it is better to see a doctor of traditional Chinese medicine.

Lesson 21   I got sick
第二十一课 我生病了

🌸 Pattern Drills

21.1 THE PATTERN yíhuìr ..., yíhuìr ...

Yíhuìr ..., yíhuìr ... "one moment ..., the next ... " indicates alternation between two or more actions or situations. Verbs, stative verbs or other elements can be placed after yíhuìr.

(1) Tāmen yíhuìr tiàowǔ, yíhuìr hē jiǔ, zhēn gāoxìng.

They were so happy, one moment dancing, and the next drinking.

(2) Bù zhīdào wèishénme nàge bìngrén de bìng yíhuìr hǎo, yíhuìr bù hǎo.

We don't know why this patient is fine one moment and very sick the next moment.

(3) Nǐ yíhuìr yào chī Zhōngguófàn, yíhuìr yào chī Měiguófàn, wǒ bù zhīdào yīnggāi zuò shénme fàn le.

One moment you want to have Chinese food, the next moment you want to have American food. I really don't know what I should prepare.

21.2 MORE ON zài

Zài has multiple functions. The context in which it appears determines its meaning. In Lesson 3, pattern 3.10, we learned that zài can function as a verb; in pattern 3.10.1, zài functions as a durative marker. In this lesson, we present some more usages of zài.

21.2.1 Zài with (zhe) ... (ne)

The marker zhe may come after a verb with ne at the end of the sentence, to stress that the action is in progress.

S	zài	V-zhe	O	ne
Wǒ	zài	zuòzhe	fàn	ne.
I am (in the midst of) cooking.				

(1) Tāmen zài tǎolùnzhe yí ge yàojǐn de shìqing ne. Bú yào shuōhuà.

They are (in the midst of) discussing an important issue. Don't talk.

(2) Xuésheng zài shàngzhe kè ne, bié jìnqu.

The students are having a class. Don't barge in.

21.2.2 Zài as a coverb

When zài comes before a place word and the main verb in a sentence, it functions as a coverb which specifies the location where the subject is/was engaging in an activity.

S	zài	PW	V-(zhe)	O	(ne)
Tā	zài	sùshè	děngzhe	nǐ	ne.
She is waiting for you at the dormitory.					

(1) Qùnián zhège shíhou, wǒ hái zài Zhōngguó xué Zhōngwén ne.
I was still studying Chinese in China at this time last year.

(2) Yīshēng dōu zài yīyuàn kàn bìngrén ne.
All of the doctors are in the hospital taking care of patients.

21.2.3 Zài as a postverb

When zài comes after a verb, it functions as a postverb which specifies the location of the subject or the direct object as a result of the action.

O	V-zài	PW	le
Nà běn shū	fàngzài	shūfáng	le.
That book has been put in the study.			

(1) Jīn Jiàn hé Mǎ Hóng zuòzài nàr yěcān ne.
Jin Jian and Ma Hong are sitting there having a picnic.

(2) Jīntiān wǒ yào bǎ qián dōu fàngzài yínháng lǐ.
Today, I'll deposit all my money in the bank.

(3) Shéi bǎ diànnǎo fàngzài zhèr le?
Who put the computer here?

21.3 Tóu AS A LOCALIZER

Tóu "head, top, beginning, or end" can function as a localizer. It can be placed at the end of a noun of locality to make it a place word. Tóu is pronounced in its neutral tone when it is used as a localizer.

Tóu can be placed after the following nouns of locality:

shàng	above	shàngtou	surface or top of an object
xià	below	xiàtou	underneath, under, below
wài	outside	wàitou	outside
lǐ	inside	lǐtou	inside
qián	front	qiántou	front
hòu	back, behind	hòutou	back, rear

(1) Bǎ nǐ de shǒu fàngzài tóu shàngtou.   Put your hands on your head!

(2) Bǎ nǐ de bǐ fàngzài nà běn Zhōngwén shū xiàtou.   Put your pen under that Chinese book.

(3) Bǎ nǐ de běnzi ná dào wàitou qu!   Take your notebook outside!

(4) Nǐ de shǒu lǐtou názhe shénme dōngxi?   What is in your hand?

(5) Nǐmen kěyǐ zài túshūguǎn qiántou děng wǒ.   You can wait for me in front of the library.

21.4 V-lái-V-qù

The V-lái-V-qù expression is used to stress the repetition of an action. In this pattern, the verbs before lái and qù have to be identical. The adverb yě "also" or hái "still" often appears in such sentences.

(1) Wǒ xiǎngláixiǎngqù yě xiǎngbuchūlai zěnme xiě zhège zì.   I've thought about it over and over, yet I still don't know how to write this character.

(2) Lǎoshī shuōláishuōqù, wǒ háishì bù dǒng tā de yìsi.   I still don't understand what the teacher meant, even though she said it over and over again.

(3) Tā zhǎoláizhǎoqù yě méi zhǎodào tā de nàozhōng.   He searched back and forth and still couldn't find his alarm clock.

21.5 Zháo AS A RESULTATIVE VERB

The character zháo was introduced in Lesson 15 as a durative or adverbial marker. In this lesson, zháo functions as a second verb in an RVC, indicating an accomplishment or result, and is pronounced in its second tone.

(1) Wǒ zuótiān dào tā jiā qù, kěshì méi jiànzháo tā.
I went to his home yesterday, but I didn't get to see him.

(2) Zài zhèr chībuzháo hǎo de Zhōngguófàn.
You can't get good Chinese food here.

(3) Wǒ zhǎoláizhǎoqù hái méi zhǎozháo tā yào mǎi de dōngxi.
I have visited many places, but still I can't find the things she wanted to buy.

21.6 MORE ON xià

> Xià as a second element in an RVC means "have room to, have space to." Review these special expressions which have already been introduced in Lesson 12.

zuòdexià	room to sit
chīdexià	room to eat
zhùdexià	room to live
fàngdexià	space to fit

(1) A: Nǐ de qìchē zuòdexià zuòbuxià wǔ ge rén?
Can five people fit into your car?

B: Wǒ de chē hěn xiǎo, zuòbuxià wǔ ge rén.
My car is so small that five people can't fit into it.

(2) A: Zài duō chī diǎnr!
Eat some more!

B: Wǒ zhēnde chībuxià le.
I really can't eat anymore.

(3) A: Zhège fángzi zhùdexià shí ge rén ma?
Does this house have enough room for ten people?

B: Wǒ xiǎng zhùdexià.
I think so.

(4) A: Wǒmen de sùshè fàngdexià zhème duō dōngxi ma?
Can we put so much stuff in our dormitory?

B: Yídìng fàngbuxià.
No. There will not be enough space for them.

Lesson 21 *I got sick*
第二十一课 我生病了

🌸 Sentence Building

1.
Pǎoláipǎoqù
Pǎoláipǎoqù zuò shénme?
Nǐ pǎoláipǎoqù zuò shénme?
Wǒ zhǎo yīshēng gěi wǒ de yào.

2.
Dōngxi
Shénme dōngxi?
Zhèshì shénme dōngxi?
Zhèshì yí ge hěn mínguì de dōngxi.

3.
Chūfā
Shénme shíhou chūfā?
Xiàwǔ yì diǎn sān kè chūfā.

4.
Yīxué
Xīfāng guójiā de yīxué jìnbù ma?
Xīfāng guójiā de yīxué hěn jìnbù.

🌸 Questions and Responses

1. Mǎ Àiwén wèishénme jīntiān méi lái shàng kè?
   Why didn't Ma Aiwen attend class today?

   Yīnwèi tā bìng le.
   Because she is ill.

2. Tā yǒu-méiyǒu qù kàn yīshēng?
   Did she see a doctor?

   Tā zǎoshang qǐlái yǐhòu jiù qù kàn yīshēng le.
   As soon as she got up this morning, she went to see the doctor.

3. Tā yǒu-méiyǒu fāshāo?
   Does she have a fever?

   Yǒu yìdiǎnr, kěshì bú tài gāo.
   She has a slight fever, but her temperature isn't too high.

4. Tā zuótiān wǎnshang shuìde hǎo-bu-hǎo?
   Did she sleep well last night?

   Shuìde bú tài hǎo.
   She didn't sleep very well.

5. Yīshēng jiào Mǎ Àiwén zuò shénme?
   What did the doctor ask Ma Aiwen to do?

   Yīshēng jiào tā chī yào, duō hē shuǐ, duō shuìjiào.
   The doctor asked her to take her medicine, to have more water and to rest more.

6. Mǎ Àiwén wèishénme gěi lǎoshī xiě diànzǐxìn?

   Why did Ma Aiwen e-mail her teacher?

   Tā yào gàosu lǎoshī tā jīntiān bù néng lái shàng kè. Tā yě qǐng lǎoshī gàosu tā míngtiān yīnggāi zuò de gōngkè.
   She wanted to let the teacher know that she would not be able to attend class today. She also asked the teacher about the homework due tomorrow.

7. Yàoshì nǐ bù néng lái shàng kè, nǐ zěnme gàosu lǎoshī?
   If you were not able to attend class, how would you let the teacher know?

   Wǒ yěxǔ huì gěi lǎoshī xiě diànzǐxìn, yěxǔ huì gěi lǎoshī dǎ diànhuà.
   I might e-mail my teacher or I might phone him/her.

8. Zhōngguó hěn zǎo yǐqián, jiù yǒu hěn duō fāmíng. Nǐ zhīdào dōu shì shénme ma?
   There were already a lot of inventions in ancient China. Do you know what they all are?

   Wǒ xiànzài hái bù zhīdào. Wǒ yǐhòu yídìng huì zhīdào de.
   Right now I don't know. I will definitely know in the future.

9. Nǐ de péngyou shénme shíhou lái?
   When is your friend coming?

   Tā yíhuìr jiù lái.
   He will come in a while.

10. Nǐ bǎ wǒ zuótiān mǎi de shū fàngzài nǎr le?
    Where did you put the book I bought yesterday?

    Fàngzài nǐ de shūfáng lǐ le.
    I put it in your study.

🌸 Pronunciation Review

1. Wǒmen shénme shíhou chūfā?
   Nǐmen cóng nǎr chūfā?
   Nǐmen dào nǎr qù?

2. Yīsheng yǒu-méiyǒu gěi nǐ yàofāng?
   Zhèr yǒu-méiyǒu yàofāng?
   Zhège yīyuàn yǒu duōshǎo bìngfáng?

3. Bìngrén yǒu-méiyǒu fāshāo?
   Bìngrén xiǎng-bu-xiǎng chī dōngxi?
   Bìngrén néng-bu-néng shuìjiào?

4. Nǐ shì nǎr de rén?
   Tā shì nǎ guó rén?
   Tāmen shì shénme rén?

Supplementary Vocabulary

Some terms of illness

dùzi tòng/dùzi téng	bellyache
gǎnmào/shàngfēng	catch a cold
késou	cough
lā dùzi	diarrhea
tóuyūn	feel dizzy
yǎng	itch
wèi tòng/wèi téng	stomach ache
hóulóng tòng/hóulóng téng	sore throat

Cultural Notes

Chinese Dining Etiquette

It is not uncommon for Chinese dining guests to arrive well ahead of the set time, as a matter of courtesy.

In a smaller group, it is usual for the host to begin the meal by serving the guests. In other words, the guests are expected to wait until the host serves them. For a larger group, the guests wait until the host invites them to help themselves.

Some hosts expect their guests to serve themselves after the first serving. Some hosts insist on doing the initial serving each time a new dish is brought out, to show courtesy.

第二十一課
漢字本

內容

課文   340

生詞及例句   341
(病、睡、覺、頭、疼、發、燒、東、西、醫)

句型練習   346
(一會兒……，一會兒……、在、頭、V-來-V去、著、下)

造句   350
(跑來跑去、東西、出發、醫學)

問答   350

閱讀練習   351
　　小氣的人

課文

我生病了

最近天氣不好,一會兒冷,一會兒熱。很多同學都生病了。昨天晚上我睡不著覺,頭也很疼、覺得有點兒發燒、甚麼東西都不想吃,很累。我想我生病了。我應該去看醫生。早上起來以後,我就馬上去醫院看醫生了。從醫院回來以後,我給老師發了一個電子信請病假。

王老師:

　　我今天沒有能來上課。因為我昨天晚上病了,頭很疼,有一點兒發燒,也吃不下東西。所以今天一早就去看醫生了。醫生說我沒甚麼大病,他給了我藥,叫我吃藥、多喝水、多睡覺。我也許很快就會好了。我想我明天一定可以來上課。請你把今天跟明天應該作的功課告訴思文。好嗎?謝謝。

　　　　　　　　　　祝

　　　　　　快樂!

　　　　　　　　　　　　學生
　　　　　　　　　　　　馬愛文
　　　　　　　　　　　　四月六日

Lesson 21   I got sick
第二十一課 我生病了

🌸 生詞及例句

1. **病**   **ill, sick; disease; fault, defect (N)**

   ☞ 生病   get ill (V/VO)

   (1) 最近天氣不好，生病的人很多。

   (2) 去年我生了三個星期的病。

   ☞ 病人   patient (N)

   (1) 這個醫生的病人很多。

   (2) 林醫生，有很多病人在等著你呢。

   ☞ 病房   ward (of a hospital) (N)

   (1) A: 你的朋友住幾號病房？
       B: 他住三〇七病房。

   (2) 那個病房很大。

   ☞ 病假   sick leave (N)

   (1) 要是你有病，不能來上課，最好跟老師請病假。

   (2) 今天你們沒有課，因為王老師請病假了。

   ☞ 病情   state of an illness; patient's condition (N)

   A: 林醫生，請你告訴我我太太的病情。
   B: 她現在好多了。她在睡覺呢。

   ☞ 病從口入   disease goes in via one's mouth (IE)

   中國人說"病從口入"，所以你吃東西的時候得小心。

2. **睡**   **sleep (V)**

   A: 這麼晚了，你怎麼還沒睡？
   B: 我的功課還沒作完呢。

3. **覺** sleep (N)

☞ 睡覺 to sleep (V/VO)

(1) A: 你平常甚麼時候睡覺？
    B: 我平常晚上十一點睡覺。

(2) A: 你昨天晚上睡了幾個小時的覺？
    B: 我就睡了四個小時，因為今天有考試。

4. **頭** head; top; chief (N); first (prefix for ordinal numbers)

(1) 中國人說頭大的人很聰明。你信嗎？

(2) 信紙在那本書的上頭。

(3) 昨天他頭一個考完，真聰明。

☞ 外頭 outside (PW)

為甚麼外頭有人跑來跑去？

☞ 裏頭 inside; interior (PW)

外頭比裏頭冷，你還發燒，最好在裏頭，不要出去。

☞ 點頭 nod one's head (VO)

要是你們不想說話，懂了就點點頭也可以。

5. **疼** ache, pain, sore (Adj); love dearly (V)

我的手很疼。

☞ 頭疼 (have a) headache (N)

(1) 中文說，我的頭很疼，不說我有一個頭疼。

(2) 他們兩個人的事真叫我頭疼。

☞ 疼愛 be very fond of, love dearly (V)

父母都很疼愛他們的兒女。

Lesson 21 I got sick
第二十一課 我生病了
343

☞ 心疼　　love dearly (V); feel sorry; be distressed (SV)

(1) 那麼好的東西不見了，真叫我心疼。

(2) 外祖母心疼我，不要我出去作事。

6. 發　发　send out; issue, deliver; distribute; open up, discover (V)
　 发　发　我得出去發信。

☞ 發出　　issue, send out, give out (V)

A: 我給你姐姐寫的信，你是甚麼時候發出的？

B: 三天以前發出去的。

☞ 出發　　set out, start off (V)

A: 明天我們去長城，甚麼時候出發？

B: 八點一刻出發。

☞ 發生　　happen, occur, take place (V)

A: 我不在家的時候，有甚麼事情發生了嗎？

B: 甚麼事都沒發生。

☞ 發起　　initiate; sponsor; start, launch (V)

王老師要回國了，我們同學昨天發起了一個歡送會歡送他。

☞ 發給　　issue, distribute (V)

我們去中國旅行以前，老師發給我們一張中國地圖。

☞ 發明　　invent; invention (V/N)

(1) 你知道電話是誰發明的嗎？

(2) 中國早期有很多發明。

☞ 發現　　find, discover (V)

是誰先發現這麼好看的地方的？

7. 燒 **burn; cook, roast; run a temperature** (V)

(1) 那天的大火，把他的書都燒了。

(2) 我媽媽很會燒菜。

(3) 那個飯館紅燒的菜都很好吃。

☞ 發燒 have a fever, have (or run) a temperature (V/VO)

(1) 我病了，還好沒發燒。

(2) 這個病人已經發了兩天燒了。

☞ 高燒 high fever (N)

醫生，請你先看那個發高燒的病人吧。

8. 東 **east; master; owner; host** (N)

☞ 東方 east (direction); the East (N)

從前很多人不太懂東方的事情。

☞ 東北 northeast; Northeast China (including the three provinces of Jilin, Liaoning and Heilongjiang) (N)

中國東北的天氣很冷。

☞ 山東 Shandong (province) (N)

A: 請你們在地圖上找一找山東在哪兒。

B: 我找到了，在河北的下頭。

☞ 近東 the Near East (N)

我真想到近東的國家去旅行。

☞ 遠東 the Far East (N)

A: 你去過遠東甚麼國家？

B: 我就去過中國跟日本。

Lesson 21   I got sick
第二十一課 我生病了

☞ 中東   the Middle East (N)

A: 最近中東有沒有又鬧事？

B: 最近中東常常鬧事。

☞ 房東   landlord or landlady (N)

A: 你的房東怎麼樣？

B: 要是你給他房錢，他就很客氣。

9. 西   **west (N)**

☞ 西方   west (direction); the West (N)

A: 西方人跟東方人的想法一樣嗎？

B: 有很多不同的地方。

☞ 東西   thing; a person or animal (derogatory) (N)

(1) A: 這個東西能不能吃？

B: 能吃是能吃，可是不好吃。

(2) 這個東西，中國話叫甚麼？

☞ 西北   northwest (N)

中國西北有很多高山。

10. 醫 [医]   **doctor (of medicine); medicine (N); treat (V)**

A: 你能醫好他的病嗎？

B: 我可以試試。

☞ 醫生   doctor (N)

(1) 要是你病了，你得去看醫生。

(2) 作醫生一定得有愛心。

☞ 醫院   hospital (N)

A: 這個醫院怎麼樣？

B: 這個醫院是新的，很大，醫生也很好。

☞ 醫學   medical science (N)

我覺得醫學很有意思。我想以後學醫。

☞ 西醫   Western medicine; a doctor trained in Western medicine (N)

☞ 中醫   traditional Chinese medical science; a doctor trained in traditional Chinese medicine (N)

A: 有的人信西醫，有的人信中醫。你呢？

B: 我都信。有的病看西醫好，有的病看中醫好。

句型練習

21.1 THE PATTERN 一會兒……，一會兒……

> 一會兒……，一會兒…… "one moment ..., the next ..." indicates alternation between two or more actions or situations. Verbs, stative verbs or other elements can be placed after 一會兒.

(1) 他們一會兒跳舞，一會兒喝酒，真高興。

(2) 不知道為甚麼那個病人的病一會兒好，一會兒不好。

(3) 你一會兒要吃中國飯，一會兒要吃美國飯，我不知道應該作甚麼飯了。

21.2 MORE ON 在

> 在 has multiple functions. The context in which it appears determines its meaning. In Lesson 3, pattern 3.10, we learned that 在 can function as a verb; in pattern 3.10.1, 在 functions as a durative marker. In this lesson, we present some more usages of 在.

21.2.1 在 WITH (著) …… (呢)

The marker 著 may come after a verb with 呢 at the end of the sentence, to stress that the action is in progress.

S	在	V-著	O	呢
我	在	作著	飯	呢。

I am (in the midst of) cooking.

(1) 他們在討論著一個要緊的事情呢。不要說話。

(2) 學生在上著課呢，別進去。

21.2.2 在 as a coverb

When 在 comes before a place word and the main verb in a sentence, it functions as a coverb which specifies the location where the subject is/was engaging in an activity.

S	在	PW	V-(著)	O	(呢)
她	在	宿舍	等著	你	呢。

She is waiting for you at the dormitory.

(1) 去年這個時候，我還在中國學中文呢。

(2) 醫生都在醫院看病人呢。

21.2.3 在 as a postverb

When 在 comes after a verb, it functions as a postverb which specifies the location of the subject or the direct object as a result of the action.

O	V-在	PW	了
那本書	放在	書房	了。

That book has been put in the study.

(1) 金建和馬紅坐在那兒野餐呢。

(2) 今天我要把錢都放在銀行裏。

(3) 誰把電腦放在這兒了？

21.3 頭 AS A LOCALIZER

頭 "head, top, beginning, or end" can function as a localizer. It can be placed at the end of a noun of locality to make it a place word. 頭 is pronounced in its neutral tone when it is used as a localizer.

頭 can be placed after the following nouns of locality:

上	上頭
下	下頭
外	外頭
裏	裏頭
前	前頭
後	後頭

(1) 把你的手放在頭上頭！

(2) 把你的筆放在那本中文書下頭！

(3) 把你的本子拿到外頭去！

(4) 你的手裏頭拿著甚麼東西？

(5) 你們可以在圖書館前頭等我。

21.4 V-來-V-去

The V-來-V-去 expression is used to stress the repetition of an action. In this pattern, the verbs before 來 and 去 have to be identical. The adverb 也 "also" or 還 "still" often appears in such sentences.

(1) 我想來想去也想不出來怎麼寫這個字。

(2) 老師說來說去，我還是不懂她的意思。

(3) 他找來找去也沒找到他的鬧鐘。

Lesson 21   I got sick
第二十一課 我生病了

21.5 著 AS A RESULTATIVE VERB

The character 著 was introduced in Lesson 15 as a durative or adverbial marker. In this lesson, 著 functions as a second verb in an RVC, indicating an accomplishment or result, and is pronounced in its second tone.

(1) 我昨天到他家去，可是沒見著他。

(2) 在這兒吃不著好的中國菜。

(3) 我找來找去還沒找著她要買的東西。

21.6 MORE ON 下

下 as a second element in an RVC means "have room to, have space to." Review these special expressions which have already been introduced in Lesson 12.

坐得下
吃得下
住得下
放得下

(1) A: 你的汽車坐得下坐不下五個人？
    B: 我的車很小，坐不下五個人。

(2) A: 再多吃點兒。
    B: 我真的吃不下了。

(3) A: 這個房子住得下十個人嗎？
    B: 我想住得下。

(4) A: 我們的宿舍放得下這麼多東西嗎？
    B: 一定放不下。

造句

1.
跑來跑去
跑來跑去作甚麼？
你跑來跑去作甚麼？
我找醫生給我的藥。

2.
東西
甚麼東西？
這是甚麼東西？
這是一個很名貴的東西。

3.
出發
甚麼時候出發？
下午一點三刻出發。

4.
醫學
西方國家的醫學進步嗎？
西方國家的醫學很進步。

問答

1. 馬愛文為甚麼今天沒來上課？　　因為她病了。
2. 她有沒有去看醫生？　　她早上起來以後就去看醫生了。
3. 她有沒有發燒？　　有一點兒，可是不太高。
4. 她昨天晚上睡得好不好？　　睡得不太好。
5. 醫生叫馬愛文作甚麼？　　醫生叫她吃藥、多喝水、多睡覺。
6. 馬愛文為甚麼給老師寫電子信？　　她要告訴老師她今天不能來上課。她也請老師告訴她明天應該作的功課。
7. 要是你不能來上課，你怎麼告訴老師？　　我也許會給老師寫電子信，也許會給老師打電話。
8. 中國很早以前，就有很多發明。你知道都是甚麼嗎？　　我現在還不知道。我以後一定會知道的。
9. 你的朋友甚麼時候來？　　他一會兒就來。
10. 你把我昨天買的書放在哪兒了？　　放在你的書房裏了。

閱讀練習

小氣的人

從前,有個人非常小氣。他家裏的房子很大,可是他從來不請客。有一天他的朋友要借他家請客。他想,朋友在他家請客,他也可以跟著大家吃一頓飯,就答應了。他的朋友在他家作了很多菜。別人看見了,就問那個小氣人的傭人:"你們主人要請客了嗎?"他的傭人說:"不是我的主人請客,要想我們主人請客,得等到他死了以後。"主人聽到了他傭人的話,就打了傭人一頓,說:"誰叫你給我定了請客的日期的?"

那個主人是一個很小氣的人,為甚麼要把他的房子借給朋友請客?那個主人為甚麼打他的傭人?他的傭人給他定了請客的日子嗎?從這個小氣人的故事,你學到了甚麼句型?你可以把這個小故事說給朋友聽嗎?

請查生詞

Look up the following words in a dictionary.

借	jiè	答應	dāying
頓	dùn	死	sǐ

填空

Fill in the blanks with the appropriate words from the story.

1. 從前有一個人很 _____ _____ ，他 _____ _____ 不請人吃飯。

2. 他的朋友要 _____ 他的家請客，因為他家的 _____ _____ 很大。

3. 他的傭人說："要想我的 _____ _____ 請客，得 _____ _____ 他死了以後。"

4. 聽了傭人的話後，主人就很生氣地說："誰叫你給我 _____ 了請客的 _____ _____ ？"

5. 這個 _____ _____ 的人把房子 _____ 給別人請客，是因為他可以 _____ _____ 大家吃一 _____ 飯。

第二十二課　暑假的計劃
Lesson 22　　Plans for summer vacation

Lesson 22
Pinyin Text

CONTENTS

*T*ext   356

*V*ocabulary and Illustrative Sentences   357
(shǔ, fēi, jì, huà, huà, biān, xī, wàng, duì, qù)

*P*attern Drills   364
(fēi ... bùkě, biān, yìbiān ... yìbiān ..., duì)

*S*entence Building   367
(fēiděi, lèqù, míngwàng, duìdài)

*Q*uestions and Responses   367

*P*ronunciation Review   368

*S*upplementary Vocabulary   369

*C*ultural Notes   369

🌸 Text

Shǔjià de jìhuà
Plans for summer vacation

Wáng lǎoshī: Shíjiān guòde zhēn kuài, mǎshàng jiù yào fàng shǔjià le. Nǐmen dōu yǒu shénme jìhuà ma?

Time flies. Summer vacation is coming up. Do you have any plans?

Lín Hǎiyīng: Māma shuō wǒ jīnnián shǔjià qù Rìběn fēiděi xué Rìběnhuà gēn Rìběn wénhuà bùkě. Wǒ yě juéde bùhǎoyìsi bù néng gēn wǒ wàizǔmǔ tánhuà, suǒyǐ wǒ yídìng yào hǎohāorde xué.

My mother said I must learn Japanese and Japanese culture when I go to Japan this summer. I also feel ashamed that I cannot converse with my (maternal) grandmother. Therefore, I will definitely study Japanese very diligently.

Xǔ Xiǎoměi: Wǒ dǎsuàn dào Zhōngguó qù yìbiān xué Zhōngwén yìbiān zuò shì. Xīwàng wǒ bàba néng gěi wǒ zhǎo dào yí ge jìnchūkǒu shēngyi de gōngzuò. Wǒ yào dédào yìdiǎnr zuò shēngyi de jīngyàn.

I plan to go to China to learn Chinese and work at the same time. I hope my dad can find me a job in the field of import-export business. I want to get some business experience.

Mǎ Àiwén: Wǒ duì yīxué hěn yǒu xìngqù. Zhège shǔjià wǒ gēn yí ge yǒumíng de yīshēng zuò shì. Tā yào wǒ měi xīngqī zuò èrshí ge xiǎoshí de shì, kěshì tā méi gàosu wǒ zuò shénme.

I'm very interested in medicine. This summer I'll work with a famous doctor. He asked me to work twenty hours a week, but he hasn't told me what I'll need to do yet.

Lesson 22 Plans for summer vacation
第二十二課 暑假的計劃

Wáng lǎoshī: Méi xiǎngdào nǐmen yǐjing zǎo bǎ shǔjià de jìhuà dōu dìng xiàlái le. Wǒ yě děi xiǎngxiǎng wǒ shǔjià yào zuò shénme le.	I did not expect that you all have already fixed your summer vacation plans. Now I have to think about what I am going to do this summer.

❧ Vocabulary and Illustrative Sentences

1. **shǔ**   heat; hot weather (N)

☞ shǔqī   summer vacation time (N)

A: Nǐ shǔqī yào zuò shénme?	What do you want to do during the time of your summer vacation?
B: Wǒ shǔqī yào zuò hěn duō shì: lǚxíng, kàn shū, kàn péngyou, kàn diànyǐng.	I want to do a lot of things during my summer vacation: traveling, reading, visiting friends, watching movies.

☞ shǔjià   summer vacation (N)

A: Nǐmen shǔjià yǒu duó cháng?	How long is your summer vacation?
B: Sān ge yuè.	Three months.

2. **fēi**   wrong; not; have got to, simply must (Adv)

(1) Māma bú yào dìdi kāichē, tā fēi yào kāi.	Mother didn't want little brother to drive, but he insisted on driving.
(2) Tā bú yào lái jiù suàn le, wèishénme fēi jiào tā lái?	If he doesn't want to come, forget it. Why do you insist on asking him to come?

☞ **fēiděi**   have got to, must (Adv)

(1) Yào xiǎng yǒu xuéwèn, fēiděi duō kàn shū.   If one wants to be knowledgeable, one has to read a lot of books.

(2) Nǐ jīntiān fēiděi huán wǒ qián.   You have to pay me back the money today.

☞ **fēi ... bùkě**   must, have to, will inevitably, be bound to (Adv)

(1) Wǒ míngnián fēi qù Zhōngguó bùkě.   I must go to China next year.

(2) Jīntiān de huì fēi nǐ qù bùkě.   You (are the one who) must attend today's meeting.

☞ **fēicháng**   extraordinary, unusual, special; very, extremely (Adj)

(1) Tā shì yí ge fēicháng yònggōng de xuésheng.   She is an extremely diligent student.

(2) Jīntiān tiānqì fēicháng bù hǎo, wèishénme fēi yào chūqu bùkě?   Today's weather is very bad. Why do you insist on going out?

☞ **shìfēi**   right and wrong; gossip (N/V)

(1) Wǒmen yīnggāi zhīdào shìfēi.   We should know right from wrong.

(2) Tā cónglái bù shuō bié rén de shìfēi.   He has never gossiped about other people.

☞ **kǒushì-xīnfēi**   say yes and mean no; say one thing and mean another (IE)

Nǐ zěnme néng xìn tā shuō de huà? Shéi dōu zhīdào tā shì yí ge kǒushìxīnfēi de rén.   How can you believe in what he said? Everyone knows that he is a person who says one thing and means another.

Lesson 22 Plans for summer vacation
第二十二課 暑假的計劃

3. jì   **count, calculate; plan** (V/N)

☞ jìsuàn   count, calculate; compute; consideration (V)

| Wǒ děi jìsuànjìsuàn míngnián qù lǚxíng děi huā duōshǎo qián. | I have to calculate how much I will spend on my next year's trip. |

☞ jìsuànjī   computer; calculator (N)

| Zhōngguórén yǒu shíhou bǎ diànnǎo jiào jìsuànjī. | Chinese sometimes call computers "calculator." |

4. huà   **differentiate; plan; draw; mark** (V)

☞ jìhuà   plan (V); project; program (N)

| A: Nǐ fàngjià yǐhòu, yǒu shénme jìhuà? | What plans do you have for your vacation? |
| B: Wǒ xiànzài hái méiyǒu shíjiān jìhuà shǔjià de shì. | Right now I haven't got the time to plan for my summer vacation yet. |

5. huà   **change; transform; convert; melt** (V)

| Nǐ kàn, hé lǐ de bīng dōu huà le. | Look, the ice in the river has all melted. |

☞ huàxué   chemistry (N)

| Wǒ cóng xiǎo jiù duì huàxué yǒu xìngqù. | I have been interested in chemistry since I was a child. |

☞ wénhuà   civilization; culture (N)

| (1) Zhōng-xī wénhuà hěn bù yíyàng, suǒyǐ hěn yǒuyìsi. | Chinese culture and Western culture are very different. That's why it is so interesting. |
| (2) Xué Zhōngguóhuà, yídìng děi dǒng Zhōngguó de wénhuà. | If you're learning Chinese, you definitely have to understand Chinese culture. |

☞	dàshì-huàxiǎo, xiǎoshì-huàliǎo	turn big problems into small problems, and small problems into no problem at all (IE)	
		"Dàshìhuàxiǎo, xiǎoshìhuàliǎo" shì Zhōngguórén cháng shuō de huà. Yìsi shì xīwàng rén bú yào nàoshì.	"Dashihuaxiao, xiaoshihualiao" is a saying often quoted by the Chinese. The idea is to hope that people can make concessions and avoid trouble.

6. **biān**   **side; edge; border; boundary (N)**

☞ yìbiān — one side (N); at the same time, simultaneously (Adv)

(1) Wǒ jiā fángzi de **yìbiān** shì hǎi. — On one side of my house is the sea.

(2) Tā xǐhuan **yìbiān** chīfàn **yìbiān** kàn bào. — He likes to eat and read the newspaper at the same time.

☞ zhè biān — this side; here (PW)

Qǐng nǐ dào wǒ **zhè biān** lái. Wǒ yǒu huà gēn nǐ shuō. — Please come here (to my side). I have something to tell you.

☞ nà biān — that side; there (PW)

Nà biān yǒu rén zài nàoshì, nǐ zuìhǎo bú yào qù. — People are making troubles over there. It's best if you don't go there.

☞ lǐ biān — inside; in; within (PW)

(1) **Lǐ biān** méiyǒu rén. Bié jìnqù. — There is no one inside. Don't go in.

(2) Tā de lùnwén **lǐ biān** xiě le bù shǎo yǒuyìsi de shìqing. — His thesis contains a number of interesting issues.

☞ wài biān — outside, exterior; a place other than where one lives or works (PW)

(1) Wǒmen qù **wài biān** chīfàn ba. — Let's go out to eat.

(2) Zhōngguó cóngqián nǚrén bù kěyǐ zài **wài biān** zuò shì. — In the past, women couldn't work outside the domestic sphere in China.

Lesson 22   Plans for summer vacation
第二十二課 暑假的計劃

	shàng biān	above, on top of, on the surface of (PW) ; earlier on (TW)	
		(1) Qǐng bǎ nàozhōng fàngzài diànnǎo shàng biān.	Please put the alarm clock on top of the computer.
		(2) Wǒ shàng biān shuō de huà, nǐ dōu dǒng ma?	Did you understand all I have said earlier on?
	xià biān	below, under, underneath (PW); next (TW)	
		(1) Qǐng nǐ bǎ shū xià biān de xìn gěi wǒ.	Please give me the letter under the book.
		(2) Wǒmen jīntiān jiù tǎolùn dào zhèr, xià biān de míngtiān zài tǎolùn.	Our meeting today will end here. We will discuss the following issues tomorrow.
7.	xī	**hope (V)**	
8.	wàng	**gaze into the distance; look over; hope, expect (V)**	
	xīwàng	hope, wish, expect (V); possibility (N)	
		(1) Wǒ xīwàng wǒ shēngrì de shíhou huì yǒu hěn duō hǎo lǐwù.	I hope I will get a lot of good presents on my birthday.
		(2) Wǒ fùmǔ xīwàng wǒ néng zuò yí ge yǒuyòng de rén.	My parents hope I can be a useful person.
		(3) Wǒ néng xué yī de xīwàng bú dà.	My chance of studying medicine is slim.
	míngwàng	fame and prestige, good reputation (N)	
		Tā fùqīn zài běndì shì yí ge hěn yǒu míngwàng de rén.	His father is very well known within the local society.
	kànwàng	call on, visit (V)	
		Wǒ yí dào Měiguó jiù qù kànwàng wǒ zhōngxué de Yīngwén lǎoshī le.	As soon as I arrived in America, I went to visit my high school English teacher.

☞ xǐchū-wàngwài   be pleasantly surprised (at an unexpected gain, good news, etc.) (IE)

Zhè xuéqī wǒ kǎode zhème hǎo zhēn jiào wǒ xǐchūwàngwài.	I was pleasantly surprised by my good exam results this semester.

9. duì   **correct, right (SV); face to face (V); to (CV)**

(1) Nǐ shuō de huà hěn duì.	What you said is really true.
(2) Mǎ Hóng duì wǒ shuō le hěn duō nǐmen de shìqing.	Ma Hong has told me a lot about the two of you.

☞ búduì   incorrect, wrong (SV)

(1) Yàoshì wǒ zhège zì shuō de búduì, qǐng nǐ gàosu wǒ.	If I pronounce this word wrongly, please let me know.
(2) Nǐ shuō wǒmen zhèyàng zuò, duì-bu-duì?	You said we should do it this way, right?

☞ duìbuqǐ   I'm sorry, excuse me; beg your pardon (IE)

(1) Duìbuqǐ, wǒ xiànzài méiyǒu qián gěi nǐ.	I'm sorry, I don't have any money to give you right now.
(2) Wǒmen bù yīnggāi zuò duìbuqǐ rén de shì.	We shouldn't do anything that will let other people down.

☞ duìdeqǐ   treat somebody fairly (IE)

Fùmǔ gěi nǐ zhème duō qián shàngxué, yàoshì nǐ bú yònggōng, nǐ juéde duìdeqǐ duìbuqǐ tāmen?	Your parents have paid so much for your education. If you don't study hard, do you think you're being fair to them?

☞ duìdài   treat (V)

Nǐ zěnme kěyǐ zhèyàng duìdài nǐ de lǎopéngyou?	How can you treat your old friend in such manner?

Lesson 22 Plans for summer vacation
第二十二課 暑假的計劃

☞ duìmén — (of two houses) face each other; the building or room opposite (N)

> Wǒmen jiā duìmén shì yì jiā hěn yǒu míngwàng de rén. Tiāntiān mén qián yǒu hěn duō qìchē.
>
> There is a very famous person living opposite us. There are many cars outside the house every day.

☞ zuòduì — set oneself against; oppose (V)

> A: Nǐ wèishénme lǎo yào gēn wǒ zuòduì?
> Why do you always oppose me?
>
> B: Yīnwèi wǒ bù xǐhuan nǐ.
> Because I don't like you.

10. qù — **delight; interesting (SV)**

☞ xìngqù — interest (N)

> A: Nǐ duì shénme yǒu xìngqù?
> What are you interested in?
>
> B: Wǒ duì hěn duō shìqing yǒu xìngqù.
> I'm interested in many things.

☞ yǒuqù — interesting, fascinating, amusing (SV)

> (1) Qǐng nǐ gěi wǒ shuō yí ge yǒuqù de shì.
> Please tell me an amusing story.
>
> (2) Xiǎoměi shì yí ge hěn yǒuqù de rén, gēn tā tánhuà nǐ yídìng huì hěn kāixīn.
> Xiaomei is a very interesting person. You will surely find it very enjoyable talking to her.

☞ lèqù — delight, pleasure, joy (N)

> Néng xué dào xīn de dōngxi, shì wǒ zuì dà de lèqù.
> My greatest joy is being able to learn new things.

☞ zhīqù — know how to behave in a delicate situation; tactful, sensitive (Adj)

> (1) Sīwén yào gēn nǚpéngyou shuōhuà, nǐ hái zuòzài nàr, zhēn bù zhīqù.
> Siwen wants to talk with his girlfriend. You're still sitting there, you are not sensitive.
>
> (2) Tā shì yí ge zhīqù de rén, bú huì jiào rén bù gāoxìng de.
> He is a very tactful person. He won't say anything to make anyone unhappy.

Pattern Drills

22.1 THE PATTERN fēi ... bùkě

The Chinese language often puts two negatives together to make a very strong statement or resolution. Fēi ... bùkě is a double negative pattern meaning "(if) not ..., then it is not permissible." Both fēi and bù mean "not." This pattern is best conveyed in English as "absolutely must" or through emphatic intonation. In spoken Chinese, if the word following fēi is a verb, bùkě can sometimes be omitted, as in the last example.

(1) Jīntiān de huì nǐ fēi qù bùkě. You must attend today's meeting.

(2) Wǒ fēi qù zhǎo tā bùkě. I must look for him.

(3) Wǒmen bú xiǎng tā qù, tā fēi qù bùkě. We did not want him to go, but he's determined to go.

(4) Nǐ wèishénme fēi yào xué Rìwén? Why do you insist on studying Japanese?

22.2 Biān AS A LOCALIZER

Similar to tóu (introduced in Lesson 21), biān "side, edge; border" can be placed at the end of a noun of locality to turn it into a place word. Biān, like tóu, can be attached to shàng, xià, wài, lǐ, qián or hòu. Besides, biān can also come after the following nouns:

zuǒ	left	zuǒ biān	left side
yòu	right	yòu biān	right side
dōng	east	dōng biān	east side
nán	south	nán biān	south side
xī	west	xī biān	west side
běi	north	běi biān	north side

(1) Shéi zài nǐ de zuǒ biān? Who is on your left?

(2) Qǐng nǐ dào wǒ yòu biān lái. Please come to my right.

(3) Túshūguǎn zài Hǎiyīng jiā dōng biān. The library is on the east side of Haiying's house.

Lesson 22 *Plans for summer vacation*
第二十二課 暑假的計劃

(4) Fēijīchǎng zài wǒmen xuéyuàn de nán biān.
The airport is at the south of our college.

(5) A: Xuéyuàn xī biān de fànguǎn duō háishì běi biān de duō?
Are there more restaurants on the west side or the east side of the college?

B: Xuéyuàn xī biān de fànguǎn bǐ běi biān de duō.
There are more restaurants on the west side.

Biān can also come after determinative nouns, such as the following:

zhè	this	zhè biān	this side
nà	that	nà biān	that side
nǎ	which	nǎ biān	which side

(1) Wǒmen zhè biān de fànguǎn méiyǒu nǐmen nà biān de hǎo.
The restaurant on our side is not as good as the restaurant on your side.

(2) A: Nǐ zài nǎ biān děng wǒ?
On which side will you wait for me?

B: Wǒ zài túshūguǎn zhè biān děng nǐ.
I will wait for you on this side of the library.

22.3 THE PATTERN yìbiān ... yìbiān ...

Yìbiān ... yìbiān ... is a pair of adverbs. It can be used before two verbs or verbal phrases to indicate that two actions are being performed during the same time span by the subject, or that two events happened at the same time.

S	yìbiān	V (O)	yìbiān	V (O)
Sīwén	yìbiān	kāichē	yìbiān	kàn dìtú.
Siwen drove while reading the map.				

(1) Bié yìbiān zǒulù yìbiān chī dōngxi.
Don't eat while you're walking.

(2) Zài Měiguó, hěn duō xuésheng yìbiān gōngzuò yìbiān shàngxué.
In the United States, many students work and attend school at the same time.

(3) Tāmen zài yìbiān hē chá, yìbiān chī diǎnxīn.
They're drinking tea and eating pastry.

(4) Wǒmen kěyǐ yìbiān mànpǎo, yìbiān tánhuà.
We can jog and talk at the same time.

22.4 THE WORD duì

Duì means "to, toward, in relation to" and it usually takes a noun or a noun phrase.

(1) Wǒmen xué Zhōngwén shì yīnwèi wǒmen duì Zhōngguó wénhuà yǒu xìngqù.
We study the Chinese language because we are interested in Chinese culture.

(2) A: Nǐ duì tā de kànfǎ zěnmeyàng?
What is your opinion of him?

B: Wǒ juéde tā yǒu diǎnr jiāo'ào.
I think he is a bit arrogant.

(3) Nàge xuésheng duì shénme dōu hěn rènzhēn.
That student is conscientious about everything.

Duì is often placed after the subject, as in (1) and (3), but sometimes it can be placed before the noun for emphasis, as in (2) and (4).

(1) Wǒ duì zhōngyī yìdiǎnr xìngqù dōu méiyǒu.
I am not interested in Chinese medicine at all.

(2) Duì zhōngyī, wǒ yìdiǎnr xìngqù dōu méiyǒu.
Speaking of Chinese medicine, I have no interest in it whatsoever.

(3) Wǒ duì zuòfàn yìdiǎnr xìngqù dōu méiyǒu, kěshì wǒ duì chīfàn hěn yǒu xìngqù.
I am not interested in cooking at all, but I am very interested in eating.

(4) Duì zuòfàn, wǒ yìdiǎnr xìngqù dōu méiyǒu. Kěshì duì chīfàn, wǒ hěn yǒu xìngqù.
Speaking of cooking, I have no interest at all. As for eating, however, I am very interested.

Lesson 22 Plans for summer vacation
第二十二課 暑假的計劃

🌸 Sentence Building

1.
Fēiděi
Fēiděi xué hǎo Zhōngwén.
Fēiděi xué hǎo Zhōngwén bùkě.
Wǒ fēiděi xué hǎo Zhōngwén bùkě.

2.
Lèqù
Kàn shū de lèqù.
Kàn shū de lèqù hěn duō.
Wǒ juéde kàn shū de lèqù hěn duō.

3.
Míngwàng
Yǒu míngwàng de rén.
Tā shì yí ge yǒu míngwàng de rén.
Tā shì yí ge běndì yǒu míngwàng de rén.

4.
Duìdài
Duìdài shénme rén
Duìdài shénme rén dōu hěn hǎo.
Ta duìdài shénme rén dōu hěn hǎo.

🌸 Questions and Responses

1. Wáng lǎoshī yǒu-méiyǒu shǔjià de jìhuà?
   Has Professor Wang got any summer plans?

   Tā hái méiyǒu ne.
   He hasn't got any plans yet.

2. Wèishénme?
   Why?

   Wǒmen bù zhīdào. Tā méi shuō.
   We don't know. He didn't say.

3. Lín Hǎiyīng dǎsuàn zuò shénme?
   What does Lin Haiying plan to do?

   Tā dǎsuàn qù Rìběn xué Rìběnhuà gēn Rìběn wénhuà.
   She plans to go to Japan to study Japanese and Japanese culture.

4. Xǔ Xiǎoměi xiǎng zuò shénme?
   What does Xu Xiaomei want to do?

   Tā xiǎng dédào zuò jìnchūkǒu shēngyi de jīngyàn.
   She wants to get some experience in the import-export business sector.

5. Mǎ Sīwén xīwàng shǔjià néng dédào shénme zhīshi?
   What kind of knowlege does Ma Siwen hope to obtain this summer?

   Tā xiǎng duō zhīdào yìdiǎnr diànnǎo de zhīshi.
   He wants to know a little more about computers.

6. Mǎ Àiwén yào gēn shénme rén zuòshì?

    Whom does Ma Aiwen want to work with?

    Tā yào gēn yí ge yǒumíng de yīshēng gōngzuò.

    She wants to work with a famous doctor.

7. Wǒmen wèishénme bù xǐhuan gēn kǒushìxīnfēi de rén zuò péngyou?

    Why don't we like making friends with fickle-minded people?

    Yīnwèi kǒushìxīnfēi de rén chángcháng shuōhuà bú suàn huà.

    Because a fickle-minded person tends not to keep his/her word.

8. Nǐ kěyǐ yìbiān kāichē yìbiān kàn dìtú ma?

    Can you drive and read a map at the same time?

    Kěyǐ.

    Yes, I can.

9. Nǐ duì shénme yǒu xìngqù?

    What are you interested in?

    Wǒ de xìngqù hěn duō. Wǒ xǐhuan lǚxíng, kàn diànyǐng, kàn shū.

    I have many hobbies. I like traveling, watching movies, and reading books.

10. Nǐ cháng qù kànwàng nǐ de lǎoshī ma?

    Do you often visit your teacher?

    Bù cháng qù. Yīnwèi wǒ xiànzài gōngkè tài duō. Měitiān yǒu zuòbuwán de shì.

    I don't often visit him, because I have too much work right now. Every day I have endless work to do.

🌸 Pronunciation Review

1. Nǐ duì shénme yǒu xìngqù?
    Wǒ duì huàxué yǒu xìngqù.
    Nǐ duì shénme méi xìngqù?
    Wǒ duì yīxué méi xìngqù.

2. Wǒ fēicháng xǐhuan tiàowǔ.
    Māma fēicháng bù xǐhuan hē jiǔ.
    Bàba fēicháng xǐhuan dǎ qiú.
    Dìdi fēicháng bù xǐhuan zuò gōngkè.

3. Nǐ jiānglái xīwàng zuò shénme?
    Wǒ xīwàng zuò yīshēng.
    Nǐ xīwàng dào nǎr qù lǚxíng?
    Wǒ xīwàng dào Yuǎndōng qù lǚxíng.

4. Nǐmen shénme shíhou fàng shǔjià?
    Wǔyuè èrshíliù hào fàng shǔjià.
    Nǐ shǔqī yào zuò shénme?
    Xiànzài hái méiyǒu jìhuà.

Supplementary Vocabulary

wǎn	(MW: ge)	bowls
bēizi	(MW: ge)	cups
kāfēihù	(MW: ge)	coffee pot
kuàizi	(MW: shuāng)	chopsticks
chāzi	(MW: ge)	fork
dāozi	(MW: bǎ)	knife
pánzi	(MW: ge)	plates
sháozi/tiáogēng	(MW: ge/bǎ)	spoons
cháhú	(MW: ge)	teapot

Cultural Notes

Holding hands with same-sex friends

Young people of the same sex in China and in Taiwan often appear very intimate with each other. Young women often hold hands or link arms with each other when they are walking in the street. Young people of opposite sexes, on the other hand, tend to keep some distance from one another, unless an overt boyfriend-girlfriend relationship has been established. Until recently, public displays of affection were not common, but this is not true anymore. Nowadays, it is not uncommon to see people holding hands, kissing or hugging in public in China, especially among young people in big cities.

第二十二課
漢字本

內容

課文   372

生詞及例句   373
   (暑、非、計、劃、化、邊、希、望、對、趣)

句型練習   377
   (非……不可、邊、一邊……一邊……、對)

造句   380
   (非得、樂趣、名望、對待)

問答   380

閱讀練習   381
   哪裏?哪裏?

課文

暑假的計劃

王老師：時間過得真快，馬上就要放暑假了。你們都有甚麼計劃嗎？

林海英：媽媽說我今年暑假去日本非得學日本話跟日本文化不可。我也覺得不好意思不能跟我外祖母談話，所以我一定要好好兒地學。

許小美：我打算到中國去一邊學中文一邊作事。希望我爸爸能給我找到一個進出口生意的工作。我要得到一點兒作生意的經驗。

馬愛文：我對醫學很有興趣。這個暑假我跟一個有名的醫生作事。他要我每星期作二十個小時的事，可是他沒告訴我作甚麼。

王老師：沒想到你們已經早把暑假的計劃都定下來了。我也得想想我暑假要作甚麼了。

Lesson 22 *Plans for summer vacation*
第二十二課 暑假的計劃

生詞及例句

1. 暑   **heat; hot weather** (N)

   ☞ 暑期   summer vacation time (N)

   A: 你暑期要作甚麼？

   B: 我暑期要作很多事：旅行、看書、看朋友、看電影。

   ☞ 暑假   summer vacation (N)

   A: 你們暑假有多長？

   B: 三個月。

2. 非   **wrong; not; have got to, simply must** (Adv)

   (1) 媽媽不要弟弟開車，他非要開。

   (2) 他不要來就算了，為甚麼非叫他來？

   ☞ 非得   have got to, must (Adv)

   (1) 要想有學問，非得多看書。

   (2) 你今天非得還我錢。

   ☞ 非……不可   must, have to, will inevitably, be bound to (Adv)

   (1) 我明年非去中國不可。

   (2) 今天的會非你去不可。

   ☞ 非常   extraordinary, unusual, special; very, extremely (Adj)

   (1) 她是一個非常用功的學生。

   (2) 今天天氣非常不好，為甚麼非要出去不可？

   ☞ 是非   right and wrong; gossip (N/V)

   (1) 我們應該知道是非。

   (2) 他從來不說別人的是非。

☞ 口是心非　say yes and mean no; say one thing and mean another (IE)

你怎麼能信他說的話？誰都知道他是一個口是心非的人。

3. **計**　**count, calculate; plan (V/N)**

☞ 計算　count, calculate; compute; consideration (V)

我得計算計算明年去旅行得花多少錢。

☞ 計算機　computer; calculator (N)

中國人有時候把電腦叫計算機。

4. **劃**　**differentiate; plan; draw; mark (V)**

☞ 計劃　plan (V); project; program (N)

A: 你放假以後，有甚麼計劃？

B: 我現在還沒有時間計劃暑假的事。

5. **化**　**change; transform; convert; melt (V)**

你看，河裏的冰都化了。

☞ 化學　chemistry (N)

我從小就對化學有興趣。

☞ 文化　civilization; culture (N)

(1) 中西文化很不一樣，所以很有意思。

(2) 學中國話，一定得懂中國的文化。

☞ 大事化小，小事化了　turn big problems into small problems, and small problems into no problem at all (IE)

"大事化小，小事化了"是中國人常說的話。意思是希望人不要鬧事。

6. **邊**　**side; edge; border; boundary (N)**

☞ 一邊　one side (N); at the same time, simultaneously (Adv)

Lesson 22   Plans for summer vacation
第二十二課 暑假的計劃   375

(1) 我家房子的一邊是海。

(2) 他喜歡一邊吃飯一邊看報。

☞ 這邊   this side; here (PW)

請你到我這邊來。我有話跟你說。

☞ 那邊   that side; there (PW)

那邊有人在鬧事，你最好不要去。

☞ 裏邊   inside; in; within (PW)

(1) 裏邊沒有人。別進去。

(2) 他的論文裏邊寫了不少有意思的事情。

☞ 外邊   outside, exterior; a place other than where one lives or works (PW)

(1) 我們去外邊吃飯吧。

(2) 中國從前女人不可以在外邊做事。

☞ 上邊   above, on top of, on the surface of (PW); earlier on (TW)

(1) 請把鬧鐘放在電腦上邊。

(2) 我上邊說的話，你都懂嗎？

☞ 下邊   below, under, underneath (PW); next (TW)

(1) 請你把書下邊的信給我。

(2) 我們今天就討論到這兒，下邊的明天再討論。

7. 希   **hope** (V)

8. 望   **gaze into the distance; look over; hope, expect** (V)

☞ 希望   hope, wish, expect (V); possibility (N)

(1) 我希望我生日的時候會有很多好禮物。

(2) 我父母希望我能作一個有用的人。

(3) 我能學醫的希望不大。

☞ 名望　　　fame and prestige, good reputation (N)

他父親在本地是一個很有名望的人。

☞ 看望　　　call on, visit (V)

我一到美國就去看望我中學的英文老師了。

☞ 喜出望外　be pleasantly surprised (at an unexpected gain, good news, etc.) (IE)

這學期我考得這麼好真叫我喜出望外。

9. 對　　　**correct, right** (SV); **face to face** (V); **to** (CV)

(1) 你說的話很對。

(2) 馬紅對我說了很多你們的事情。

☞ 不對　　　incorrect, wrong (SV)

(1) 要是我這個字說得不對，請你告訴我。

(2) 你說我們這樣作，對不對？

☞ 對不起　　I'm sorry, excuse me; beg your pardon (IE)

(1) 對不起，我現在沒有錢給你。

(2) 我們不應該作對不起人的事。

☞ 對得起　　treat somebody fairly (IE)

父母給你這麼多錢上學，要是你不用功，你覺得對得起對不起他們？

☞ 對待　　　treat (V)

你怎麼可以這樣對待你的老朋友？

☞ 對門　　　(of two houses) face each other; the building or room opposite (N)

我們家對門是一家很有名望的人。天天門前有很多汽車。

☞ 作對　　　set oneself against; oppose (V)

A: 你為甚麼老要跟我作對？

B: 因為我不喜歡你。

Lesson 22 *Plans for summer vacation*
第二十二課 暑假的計劃

10. 趣   **delight; interesting** (SV)

☞ 興趣   interest (N)

A: 你對甚麼有興趣？

B: 我對很多事情有興趣。

☞ 有趣   interesting, fascinating, amusing (SV)

(1) 請你給我說一個有趣的事。

(2) 小美是一個很有趣的人，跟他談話你一定會很開心。

☞ 樂趣   delight, pleasure, joy (N)

能學到新的東西，是我最大的樂趣。

☞ 知趣   know how to behave in a delicate situation; tactful, sensitive (Adj)

(1) 思文要跟女朋友說話，你還坐在那兒，真不知趣。

(2) 他是一個知趣的人，不會叫人不高興的。

句型練習

22.1 THE PATTERN 非……不可

The Chinese language often puts two negatives together to make a very strong statement or resolution. 非……不可 is a double negative pattern meaning "(if) not ..., then it is not permissible." Both 非 and 不 mean "not." This pattern is best conveyed in English as "absolutely must" or through emphatic intonation. In spoken Chinese, if the word following 非 is a verb, 不可 can sometimes be omitted, as in the last example.

(1) 今天的會你非去不可。

(2) 我非去找他不可。

(3) 我們不想他去，他非去不可。

(4) 你為甚麼非要學日文？

22.2 邊 AS A LOCALIZER

Similar to 頭 (introduced in Lesson 21), 邊 "side, edge; border" can be placed at the end of a noun of locality to turn it into a place word. 邊, like 頭, can be attached to 上, 下, 外, 裏, 前 or 後. Besides, 邊 can also come after the following nouns:

左	左邊
右	右邊
東	東邊
南	南邊
西	西邊
北	北邊

(1) 誰在你的左邊？

(2) 請你到我右邊來。

(3) 圖書館在海英家東邊。

(4) 飛機場在我們學院的南邊。

(5) A: 學院西邊的飯館多還是北邊的多？
　　B: 學院西邊的飯館比北邊的多。

邊 can also come after determinative nouns, such as the following:

這	這邊
那	那邊
哪	哪邊

(1) 我們這邊的飯館沒有你們那邊的好。

(2) A: 你在哪邊等我？
　　B: 我在圖書館這邊等你。

Lesson 22　*Plans for summer vacation*
第二十二課　暑假的計劃

22.3 THE PATTERN 一邊……一邊……

一邊……一邊…… is a pair of adverbs. It can be used before two verbs or verbal phrases to indicate that two actions are being performed during the same time span by the subject, or that two events happened at the same time.

S	一邊	V(O)	一邊	V(O)
思文	一邊	開車	一邊	看地圖。

Siwen drove while reading the map.

(1) 別一邊走路一邊吃東西。

(2) 在美國，很多學生一邊工作一邊上學。

(3) 他們在一邊喝茶，一邊吃點心。

(4) 我們可以一邊慢跑，一邊談話。

22.4 THE WORD 對

對 means "to, toward, in relation to" and it usually takes a noun or a noun phrase.

(1) 我們學中文是因為我們對中國文化有興趣。

(2) A: 你對他的看法怎麼樣？
　　B: 我覺得他有點兒驕傲。

(3) 那個學生對甚麼都很認真。

對 is often placed after the subject, as in (1) and (3), but sometimes it can be placed before the noun for emphasis, as in (2) and (4).

(1) 我對中醫一點兒興趣都沒有。

(2) 對中醫，我一點兒興趣都沒有。

(3) 我對作飯一點兒興趣都沒有，可是我對吃飯很有興趣。

(4) 對作飯，我一點兒興趣都沒有，可是對吃飯，我很有興趣。

🌸 造句

1.
非得
非得學好中文。
非得學好中文不可。
我非得學好中文不可。

2.
樂趣
看書的樂趣。
看書的樂趣很多。
我覺得看書的樂趣很多。

3.
名望
有名望的人。
他是一個有名望的人。
他是一個本地有名望的人。

4.
對待
對待甚麼人
對待甚麼人都很好。
他對待甚麼人都很好。

🌸 問答

1. 王老師有沒有暑假的計劃？ 他還沒有呢。
2. 為甚麼？ 我們不知道。他沒說。
3. 林海英打算作甚麼？ 她打算去日本學日本話跟日本文化。
4. 許小美想作甚麼？ 她想得到作進出口生意的經驗。
5. 馬思文希望暑假能得到甚麼知識？ 他想多知道一點兒電腦的知識。
6. 馬愛文要跟甚麼人作事？ 她要跟一個有名的醫生工作。
7. 我們為甚麼不喜歡跟口是心非的人作朋友？ 因為口是心非的人常常說話不算話。
8. 你可以一邊開車一邊看地圖嗎？ 可以。
9. 你對甚麼有興趣？ 我的興趣很多。我喜歡旅行、看電影、看書。
10. 你常去看望你的老師嗎？ 不常去。因為我現在功課太多。每天有作不完的事。

Lesson 22 *Plans for summer vacation*
第二十二課 暑假的計劃

🌸 閱讀練習

哪裏？哪裏？

我們都學過"哪裏"這個詞兒，也知道"哪裏"是"甚麼地方"的意思。可是"哪裏"還有一個別的意思。

你看懂了下面的笑話以後就會知道了。

有一個美國人要到飛機場去接一個有名的中國女明星。可是這個美國人不懂中文，所以他就請他一個中國朋友跟他一塊兒去接這個明星。他這個中國朋友懂一點英文，可是也不太好。他們看見這個明星的時候，美國人就對那個女明星說："How are you? You look beautiful."這個明星不懂英文，所以她看了看那個中國人。那個中國人就馬上說："他問你好，也說你很美。"這個明星一聽，馬上就說："哪裏，哪裏。"那個中國人就對那個美國人說："她說甚麼地方？甚麼地方？"這個美國人想："她真的要知道甚麼地方好看嗎？"他從上到下看了看那個明星就說："Everywhere."中國人就告訴她說："他說你甚麼地方都好看。"這個明星雖然心裏很開心，可是她覺得有點兒不好意思。

請討論

1. 現在你可以告訴我"哪裏"的第二個意思是甚麼嗎？
2. 那個明星聽到別人說她很美的時候，她為甚麼覺得不好意思？

Appendixes
附錄

VOCABULARY INDEX

Pinyin	Character	Meaning in English	Lesson	Page (P)	(C)
A					
ā	啊	Oh; (indicates a request or warning) (Inter)	20	297	311
á	啊	Eh (indicates that the speaker is pressing for an answer) (Inter)	20	297	311
ǎ	啊	What (expresses surprise) (Inter)	20	297	311
à	啊	Ah; All right (expresses agreement) (Inter)	20	297	311
a	啊	(used at the end of interrogative sentences, except for those which use <u>ma</u>)	20	297	312
àiqíng	愛情	love (romance) (N)	11	9	30
ào	傲	proud; refuse to yield to; brave (Adj)	19	269	281
B					
bǎ	把	hold, grasp; control (V/CV); bundle, bunch (MW)	19	269	282
bǎi	百	hundred; numerous (Nu/MW)	17	214	226
bānjī	班機	airline; flight (N)	15	152	168
běi	北	north (Adj)	15	154	169
Běijīng	北京	Beijing (Peking) (PW)	15	154	169
běnshi	本事	skill; ability, capability (N)	11	8	29
běnzi	本子	notebook (N)	12	47	65
bǐ	比	compare, contrast, compete (V)	12	49	67
biān	邊	side; edge; border; boundary (N)	22	360	374
biàn	便	convenient, handy (Adj)	12	48	66
biànfàn	便飯	a simple meal (N)	12	49	66
bié	別	don't (IE)	20	299	313
bié rén	別人	other people; others (Pron)	20	299	313
biézì	別字	wrongly written character (N)	20	299	313
bìng	病	ill, sick; disease; fault, defect (N)	21	323	341
bìngcóng-kǒurù	病從口入	disease goes in via one's mouth (IE)	21	324	341

Pinyin	Character	Meaning in English	Lesson	Page (P)	(C)
bìngfáng	病房	ward (of a hospital) (N)	21	323	341
bìngjià	病假	sick leave (N)	21	324	341
bìngqíng	病情	state of an illness; patient's condition (N)	21	324	341
bìngrén	病人	patient (N)	21	323	341
búduì	不對	incorrect, wrong (SV)	22	362	376
búkèqi	不客氣	impolite, rude, blunt; you're welcome, don't mention it (IE)	17	213	225
búlùn	不論	no matter (what, who, how, etc.); whether ... or ...; regardless of, whether or not (Adv)	17	210	224
búxiè	不謝	don't mention it, not at all (IE)	13	83	101
bùxíng	不行	won't do; be out of the question (IE)	14	123	139
bùxíng	步行	go on foot, walk (V)	14	123	139
bùyǐwéirán	不以為然	not approve (IE)	13	84	102
búyòng	不用	need not (IE)	13	87	104
bùzhībùjué	不知不覺	unconsciously, unwittingly (IE)	19	267	280

C

Pinyin	Character	Meaning in English	Lesson	Page (P)	(C)
càichǎng	菜場	food market (PW)	15	153	168
cān	餐	food; meal (N)	20	296	310
chádiǎn	茶點	tea and pastries, refreshments (N)	11	6	27
cháng	常	ordinary, common, normal; frequently, often (Adv)	13	85	102
chǎng	場	a level open space (PW)	15	153	168
chángcháng	常常	frequently, often, usually (Adv)	13	85	102
Chángchéng	長城	the Great Wall (PW)	13	155	170
chǎngdì	場地	space, place, site (PW)	15	153	168
chángjiàn	常見	commonplace (SV)	13	85	103
chángshí	常識	general knowledge, common sense (N)	13	86	103
chǎngsuǒ	場所	place, arena (PW)	15	153	168
chángyòng	常用	in common use, commonly-used, often use (Adj)	13	86	103
chē	車	vehicle, wheeled machine (N)	11	7	28
chéng	城	city wall; wall; city; town (N)	15	155	170
chībuxià	吃不下	do not feel like eating; be unable to eat any more (RV)	12	51	68

Vocabulary Index
索引

Pinyin	Character	Meaning in English	Lesson	Page (P)	(C)
chīdeqǐ	吃得起	can afford to eat (RV)	14	122	138
chīdexià	吃得下	be able to eat (RV)	12	51	68
chījīng	吃驚	to be startled, shocked or amazed (V/Adj)	17	213	226
chū	初	at the beginning of; in the early part of; first (in order); for the first time; elementary (N/Adj)	18	242	254
chū	出	go or come out (V)	13	88	104
chūfā	出發	set out, start off (V)	21	326	343
chū guó	出國	go abroad (VO)	13	88	105
chūkǒu	出口	exit (PW); export (V)	13	88	105
chūlai	出來	come out (V)	13	88	104
chūmài	出賣	offer for sale; sell, sell out; betray (V)	16	184	197
chūmén	出門	be away from home; go on a journey, go out (V)	13	88	104
chūn	春	spring (N)	18	241	253
chūnjià	春假	spring vacation, spring holidays (N)	18	241	253
Chūnjié	春節	the Spring Festival (N)	18	241	254
chūntiān	春天	spring (N)	18	241	253
chūqī	初期	initial stage; early days (N)	18	242	255
chūqu	出去	go out; get out (V)	13	88	104
chūxiǎo	初小	junior primary school (grades 1 to 4) (N)	18	242	255
chūzhōng	初中	middle school (N)	18	243	255
chūzū	出租	hire (V)	15	151	167
cōng	聰	faculty of hearing; acute hearing (Adj)	19	269	281
cōngmíng	聰明	intelligent, bright, clever (SV)	19	269	281

D

Pinyin	Character	Meaning in English	Lesson	Page (P)	(C)
dàfāng	大方	generous; poised and natural (SV)	12	48	66
dāng	當	just at (a time or place); serve as; should, must (V)	13	83	101
dāngchū	當初	at first, originally; in the first place; at that time (Adv)	18	243	255
dāngrán	當然	as it should be, without doubt, certainly, of course, naturally (Adv)	13	84	101
dàrénwù	大人物	important person, personage, VIP (N)	17	212	225
dàshì	大事	great (or major) event, important matter, major issue (N)	11	8	29

Pinyin	Character	Meaning in English	Lesson	Page (P)	(C)
dàshìhuà-xiǎo, xiǎoshì-huàliǎo	大事化小，小事化了	turn big problems into small problems and small problems into no problem at all (IE)	22	360	374
dǎsuàn	打算	plan; intend (V/N)	14	120	137
děngzhe	等著	waiting (V)	15	155	170
diǎn	點	dot, point; drop (of liquid) (N); o'clock (MW)	11	5	27
diǎn cài	點菜	choose dishes from a menu, order dishes (in a restaurant) (VO)	11	6	27
diànchē	電車	trolley, streetcar (N)	11	8	28
diànjī	電機	electrical engineering (N)	15	152	168
diànnǎo	電腦	computer (N)	12	50	67
diǎntóu	點頭	nod one's head (VO)	21	325	342
diǎnxīn	點心	snacks (N)	11	6	27
diànzǐxìn	電子信	electronic-mail, e-mail (N)	12	47	65
dìfang	地方	place, space (N)	12	48	65
dìtú	地圖	map (N)	13	85	102
dìxia	地下	on the ground (PW)	12	51	68
dōng	東	east; master; owner; host (N)	21	328	344
Dōngběi	東北	northeast; Northeast China (including the three provinces of Jilin, Liaoning and Heilongjiang) (N)	21	328	344
dōngfāng	東方	east (direction); the East (N)	21	328	344
dōngxi	東西	thing; a person or animal (derogatory) (N)	21	329	345
dǒng	懂	understand, know (V/SV/RE)	16	185	198
dǒngde	懂得	understand, know, grasp (V)	16	186	198
dǒngshì	懂事	sensible; intelligent (IE)	16	186	198
duān	端	end (N); proper (Adj); hold something level with both hands (V)	18	239	252
Duānwǔjié	端午節	the Dragon Boat Festival (the 5th day of the 5th lunar month) (N)	18	239	252
duānzhèng	端正	upright; proper (Adj)	18	239	252
duì	對	correct, right (SV); face to face (V); to (CV)	22	362	376
duìbuqǐ	對不起	I'm sorry, excuse me; beg your pardon (IE)	22	362	376

Vocabulary Index
索引

Pinyin	Character	Meaning in English	Lesson	Page (P)	(C)
duìdài	對待	treat (V)	22	362	376
duìdeqǐ	對得起	treat somebody fairly (IE)	22	362	376
duìfāng	對方	the other (or opposite) side; the other party (N)	12	48	66
duìmén	對門	(of two houses) face each other; the building or room opposite (N)	22	363	376
duōfāng	多方	in many ways, in every way, from various angles (Adj)	12	48	66
duōxiè	多謝	many thanks, thanks a lot (IE)	13	83	101

E

ēn	恩	kindness; favor; grace (N)	18	238	251
ēnrén	恩人	benefactor (N)	18	238	251
ér	兒	child, youngster, son; male (N); (suffix)	11	12	32
érnǚ	兒女	sons and daughters, children (N)	11	12	32
érzi	兒子	son (N)	12	47	65

F

fā	發	send out; issue, deliver; distribute; open up, discover (V)	21	326	343
fāchū	發出	issue, send out, give out (V)	21	326	343
fāgěi	發給	issue, distribute (V)	21	327	343
fāmíng	發明	invent; invention (V/N)	21	327	343
fāqǐ	發起	initiate; sponsor; start, launch (V)	21	327	343
fāshāo	發燒	have a fever, have (or run) a temperature (V/VO)	21	327	344
fāshēng	發生	happen, occur, take place (V)	21	326	343
fāxiàn	發現	find, discover (V)	21	327	343
fāng	方	square (Adj); locality (N)	12	48	65
fáng	房	house; room (N)	16	183	196
fàng	放	put, place; let go, set free; give up (V)	14	118	136
fāngbiàn	方便	convenient (Adj)	12	48	66
fángdōng	房東	landlord or landlady (N)	21	329	345
fāngkuàizì	方塊字	Chinese characters (N)	17	214	226
fàngjià	放假	have a holiday or vacation; have a day off (VO)	14	119	136
fàngxīn	放心	set one's mind at rest, be at ease, rest assured, feel relieved (SV)	14	119	136

Pinyin	Character	Meaning in English	Lesson	Page (P)	(C)
fàngxué	放學	classes are over (V)	14	119	136
fángzi	房子	house, building; room (N)	16	183	196
fángzū	房租	rent (for a house, apartment, etc.) (N)	16	184	197
fēi	非	wrong; not; have got to, simply must (Adv)	22	357	373
fēi	飛	fly (V)	15	151	167
fēi ... bùkě	非⋯⋯不可	must, have to, will inevitably, be bound to (Adv)	22	358	373
fēicháng	非常	extraordinary, unusual, special; very, extremely (Adj)	22	358	373
fēiděi	非得	have got to, must (Adv)	22	358	373
fēijī	飛機	aircraft, plane (N)	15	152	167
fēijīchǎng	飛機場	airport (PW)	15	153	168
fēikuài	飛快	very fast, at lightning speed (Adj)	15	151	167
fēiwǔ	飛舞	dance in the air; flutter (V)	15	152	167
fēn	分	divide, separate (V); minute (of time) (MW)	11	7	28
fēnbié	分別	part; leave each other; distinguish; separately (V)	20	299	313
fù	父	father; a respectful term for an elderly man in ancient times (N)	16	182	196
fù	附	get close to, be near; attach, enclose (V)	14	121	137
fùjìn	附近	nearby, neighboring, close to, in the vicinity of (PW)	14	121	137
fùmǔ	父母	father and mother, parents (N)	16	183	196
fùshàng	附上	enclosed herewith (V)	14	121	137
G					
gǎn	感	feel, sense; move, touch, affect; feeling (V)	18	237	251
gǎn'ēn	感恩	feel grateful; be thankful (VO)	18	238	251
Gǎn'ēn jié	感恩節	Thanksgiving (N)	18	238	252
gāng	剛	just; exactly; barely; a short while ago (Adv)	16	184	197
gānggāng	剛剛	just, only, exactly; a moment ago, just now (Adv)	16	185	197
gānghǎo	剛好	just; exactly; it so happened that (Adv)	16	185	197

Vocabulary Index
索引

Pinyin	Character	Meaning in English	Lesson	Page (P)	(C)
gǎnqíng	感情	emotion, feeling, sentiment; affection, attachment; love (N)	18	237	251
gǎnrén	感人	touching, moving (Adj)	18	238	251
gǎnxiǎng	感想	impressions; reflections, thoughts (N)	18	237	251
gǎnxiè	感謝	thank; be grateful (V)	18	237	251
gàobié	告別	leave; part from; bid farewell to, say good-bye to (V)	20	300	313
gāoshāo	高燒	high fever (N)	21	328	344
gōng	公	public; state-owned; collective; common; fair (N/Adj)	20	294	309
gōngkāi	公開	open, overt, public; make known to the public (V/Adj)	20	294	309
gōnglù	公路	highway (N)	20	295	310
gōngpíng	公平	fair, just, impartial, equitable (SV)	20	295	310
gōngrèn	公認	generally acknowledged (V)	20	295	310
gōngyòng	公用	for public use; public (Adj)	20	295	310
guì	貴	expensive, costly (SV)	12	49	67
guìxìng	貴姓	what is your name (lit., honorable family name) (IE)	12	50	67
guóqìng	國慶	National Day (N)	17	210	223

H

Pinyin	Character	Meaning in English	Lesson	Page (P)	(C)
hào	號	date; number; size (N)	14	122	138
hǎoxiàng	好像	seem; be like (V)	20	298	312
Héběi	河北	Hebei (province in China) (PW)	15	154	169
Hé'nán	河南	Henan (province in China) (PW)	15	156	170
huà	化	change; transform; convert; melt (V)	22	359	374
huà	劃	differentiate; plan; draw; mark (V)	22	359	374
huàn	換	exchange; change (V)	15	153	168
huàn chē	換車	change trains or buses (VO)	15	154	169
huàn fēijī	換飛機	take a connecting flight (VO)	15	154	169
huàn qián	換錢	change money (VO)	15	154	169
huānqìng	歡慶	celebrate joyously (V)	17	210	223
huàxué	化學	chemistry (N)	22	359	374
huǒchē	火車	train (N)	11	8	29

J

Pinyin	Character	Meaning in English	Lesson	Page (P)	(C)
jī	機	machine, engine (N)	15	152	167

Pinyin	Character	Meaning in English	Lesson	Page (P)	(C)
jì	計	count, calculate; plan (V/N)	22	359	374
jì	寄	send, mail (V)	12	49	66
jǐ diǎn	幾點	what time, when (QW)	11	5	27
jǐ hào	幾號	which day of the month; what number (QW)	14	122	138
jìhuà	計劃	plan (V); project; program (N)	22	359	374
jīhuì	機會	chance, opportunity (N)	15	152	167
jìsuàn	計算	count, calculate; compute; consideration (V)	22	359	374
jìsuànjī	計算機	computer; calculator (N)	22	359	374
jì xìn	寄信	mail letters (VO)	12	49	66
jìxìnrén	寄信人	sender (N)	12	49	66
jià	假	holiday, vacation; leave of absence (N)	14	119	136
jiān	間	between; among; within a definite time or space (N)	14	117	135
jiàqī	假期	vacation; period of leave (N)	14	119	136
jiàrì	假日	holiday; day off (N)	14	119	136
jiāo	驕	proud; arrogant (Adj)	19	269	281
jiào	覺	sleep (N)	21	324	342
jiāo'ào	驕傲	arrogant, conceited; be proud, take pride in (SV)	19	269	281
jié	節	holiday; moral integrity (N); section, length; joint (MW)	18	238	252
jiérì	節日	festival; holiday (N)	18	239	252
Jìndōng	近東	the Near East (N)	21	328	344
jìnchūkǒu	進出口	imports and exports; exits and entrances (Adj)	13	88	105
jīng	京	the capital of a country (PW)	15	154	169
jīng	驚	to be frightened or surprised (Adj)	17	213	226
jīngcháng	經常	daily; constantly, often (Adv)	13	86	103
jīngxǐ	驚喜	pleasantly surprised (Adj)	17	213	226
jué	覺	sense, feel; become aware (V)	19	267	280
juéde	覺得	feel; think (V)	19	267	280

K

kāichē	開車	drive or start a car, train, etc. (VO)	11	8	29
kànbuqǐ	看不起	look down upon, scorn, despise (IE)	14	122	138

Vocabulary Index
索引

Pinyin	Character	Meaning in English	Lesson	Page (P)	(C)
kànwàng	看望	call on, visit (V)	22	361	376
kànzhe	看著	see, look at (V)	15	155	169
kè	客	visitor; guest; traveler; passenger; customer (N)	17	212	225
kè	刻	a quarter of an hour; moment (MV); carve, engrave, cut (V)	11	12	32
kèqi	客氣	polite, courteous, modest (Adj)	17	212	225
kèrén	客人	guest; guest (at a hotel, etc.) (N)	17	212	225
kè zì	刻字	carve (or engrave) characters on a seal, etc. (VO)	11	12	32
kòng	空	leave empty or blank; unoccupied (Adj)	13	89	105
kòngr	空兒	free time, spare time (IE); empty space (N)	13	89	105
kǒushìxīnfēi	口是心非	say yes and mean no; say one thing and mean another (IE)	22	358	374
kuài	塊	piece, lump, chunk; yuan (the basic unit of currency in Chinese) (MW)	17	214	226
kuàicān	快餐	quick meal; fast-food (N)	20	296	311

L

lèqù	樂趣	delight, pleasure, joy (N)	22	363	377
lǐ	禮	ceremony, rite; courtesy; etiquette; manners; gift, present (N)	17	211	224
lì	曆	calendar (N)	18	242	254
lián	聯	unite, join (V)	19	265	279
liánhuān	聯歡	have a get-together (V)	19	265	279
liánluò	聯絡	contact, get in touch with (V)	19	266	279
liánmíng	聯名	jointly signed; jointly (V)	19	265	279
liánxiǎng	聯想	associate; connect in the mind (V)	19	265	279
lǐ biān	裏邊	inside; in; within (PW)	22	360	375
lǐtou	裏頭	inside; interior (PW)	21	325	342
lǐwù	禮物	gift, present (N)	17	211	224
lùn	論	discuss, talk about, discourse; view, opinion; theory (V/N)	17	210	224
lùnwén	論文	thesis, dissertation (N)	17	211	224
luò	絡	a net (N)	19	266	279
lǔ	旅	travel; stay away from home (V)	14	122	139
lǔguǎn	旅館	hotel (N)	14	122	139

Pinyin	Character	Meaning in English	Lesson	Page (P)	(C)
lǚxíng	旅行	travel; journey, tour (V)	14	123	139

M

Pinyin	Character	Meaning in English	Lesson	Page (P)	(C)
mǎi	買	buy, purchase (V)	16	185	198
mài	賣	sell (V)	16	184	197
mǎimài	買賣	buying and selling (V); business; transaction (N)	16	185	198
mángzhe	忙著	busy (SV); fully occupied (V)	15	155	170
méishì-zhǎoshì	沒事找事	ask for trouble, try hard to find fault (IE)	11	9	29
mínggui	名貴	famous and very valuable (Adj/SV)	12	50	67
míngwàng	名望	fame and prestige, good reputation (N)	22	361	376
mǔ	母	mother; female (animal) (N)	16	183	196

N

Pinyin	Character	Meaning in English	Lesson	Page (P)	(C)
nà biān	那邊	that side; there (PW)	22	360	375
nán	南	south (Adj)	15	156	170
nándiǎn	難點	difficult point, difficulty (N)	11	7	28
Nánjīng	南京	Nanjing (capital of Jiangsu province) (PW)	15	156	170
nǎo	腦	brain (N)	12	50	67
nào	鬧	noisy; make a noise; stir up trouble (V)	19	266	279
nàoshì	鬧事	create a disturbance; make trouble (VO)	19	266	279
nǎozi	腦子	brain (N)	12	50	67
nào yìjiàn	鬧意見	be on bad terms because of a difference of opinion (VO)	19	266	279
nàozhōng	鬧鐘	alarm clock (N)	19	267	280
nǎr	哪兒	where (QW)	11	13	32
nàr	那兒	there (PW)	11	12	32
niánjià	年假	New Year's holiday; winter vacation (N)	14	119	136
nóng	農	agriculture; farming; farmer, peasant (N)	18	241	254
nóngjiā	農家	peasant family (N)	18	242	254
nónglì	農曆	the traditional Chinese calendar, the lunar calendar (N)	18	242	254
nóngrén/ nóngmín	農人/ 農民	farmer, peasant (N)	18	241	254
nǚ'ér	女兒	daughter, girl (N)	11	12	32

Pinyin	Character	Meaning in English	Lesson	Page (P)	(C)
Q					
qǐ	起	rise, get up, stand up; start, begin (V)	14	121	138
qián	前	front; forward, ahead; before; preceding; former; first (Adv)	12	52	68
qiántiān	前天	the day before yesterday (TW)	12	52	68
qìchē	汽車	automobile, car (N)	11	7	28
qǐchū	起初	originally; at first; at the outset (Adv)	18	243	255
qǐjiàn	起見	for the purpose of; in order to (N)	14	121	138
qǐlai	起來	stand up, sit up, get up; get out of bed (V)	14	121	138
qíng	情	feeling, sentiment; love (V)	11	9	30
qìng	慶	celebrate; congratulate (V)	17	209	223
qǐng jià	請假	ask for leave (VO)	14	120	136
qǐngkè	請客	treat somebody, invite somebody to dinner, entertain guests (VO)	17	213	226
qíngrén	情人	sweetheart, lover (N)	11	9	30
qìngzhù	慶祝	celebrate (V)	17	209	223
qīshàngbāxià	七上八下	be agitated, be perturbed (IE)	12	52	68
qiū	秋	autumn, fall; harvest time (N)	18	240	253
qiūtiān	秋天	autumn, fall (N)	18	240	253
qǐxiān	起先	at first, in the beginning (Adv)	14	121	138
qǐyīn	起因	cause; origin (N)	14	122	138
qù	趣	delight; interesting (SV)	22	363	377
R					
rán	然	but, nevertheless, however (Conj)	13	84	101
ránhòu	然後	then, after that, afterwards (Conj)	13	84	101
rè'nào	熱鬧	lively, bustling with noise and excitement; have a joyous time (Adj)	19	267	280
rénxiàng	人像	portrait (N)	20	298	312
rìcháng	日常	daily; commonplace (Adj)	13	86	103
rìlì	日曆	calendar (N)	18	242	254
rìyòng	日用	daily expenses; for everyday use (Adj)	13	86	103
S					
Shāndōng	山東	Shandong (province) (N)	21	328	344
shàng biān	上邊	above, on top of, on the surface of (PW); earlier on (TW)	22	361	375

Pinyin	Character	Meaning in English	Lesson	Page (P)	Page (C)
shàngwǔ	上午	morning (TW)	18	240	253
shàngxiàwén	上下文	context (N)	12	51	68
shāo	燒	burn; cook, roast; run a temperature (V)	21	327	344
shè	舍	house; shed, hut (N)	20	298	312
shēngbìng	生病	get ill (V/VO)	21	323	341
shēngshū	生疏	not familiar; out of practice; not as close as before (Adj)	19	268	281
shēngwùxué	生物學	biology (N)	17	212	225
shì	事	matter, affair, thing; business; trouble; job, work (N)	11	8	29
shícháng	時常	often, frequently (Adv)	13	86	103
shìfēi	是非	right and wrong; gossip (N/V)	22	358	373
shíjī	時機	an advantageous time or opportunity (N)	15	153	168
shìjià	事假	leave of absence (to attend to private affairs) (N)	14	120	137
shíjiān	時間	(concept of) time; (duration of) time; (a point of) time (N)	14	117	135
shìqián	事前	before the event, in advance, beforehand (Adv)	12	52	69
shìqing	事情	affair; matter, thing; business (N)	11	9	30
shū	疏	distant; not familiar with; neglect (V)	19	268	281
shǔ	暑	heat; hot weather (N)	22	357	373
shūfáng	書房	study (room) (N)	16	184	197
shuì	睡	sleep (V)	21	324	341
shuìjiào	睡覺	to sleep (V/VO)	21	324	342
shǔjià	暑假	summer vacation (N)	22	357	373
shǔqī	暑期	summer vacation time (N)	22	357	373
shūyuǎn	疏遠	drift apart, become estranged (Adj)	19	268	281
sìfāng	四方	square; the four directions (north, south, east, west); all sides (Adj)	12	48	66
sòng lǐ	送禮	give somebody a gift (VO)	17	211	224
sòngxíng	送行	see somebody off; give a send-off party (V)	14	123	139
sù	宿	lodge for the night (V)	20	298	312
suàn	算	calculate, reckon; include; count; suppose (V)	14	120	137

Vocabulary Index
索引

Pinyin	Character	Meaning in English	Lesson	Page (P)	(C)
suàn le	算了	forget it; drop it (IE)	14	120	137
suànshì	算是	consider as (V)	14	120	137
suī	雖	though, although, even though (Conj)	13	84	102
suì	歲	year (of age) (MW)	17	209	223
suīrán	雖然	though, although (Conj)	13	84	102
suìshu	歲數	age (N)	17	209	223
suǒ	所	place (N); (MW for houses)	13	89	105
suǒyǐ	所以	so, therefore, as a result (Conj)	13	89	105
suǒyǒu	所有	all (Adj)	13	89	105
sùshè	宿舍	dormitory; hostel (N)	20	298	312

T

Pinyin	Character	Meaning in English	Lesson	Page (P)	(C)
tǎo	討	discuss; study (V)	17	210	223
tǎohǎo	討好	ingratiate oneself with; have one's labor rewarded (IE)	17	210	223
tǎolùn	討論	discuss, talk over (V)	17	210	224
tǎolùnhuì	討論會	discussion; symposium (N)	17	211	224
téng/tòng	疼	ache, pain, sore (Adj); love dearly (V)	21	325	342
téng'ài	疼愛	be very fond of, love dearly (V)	21	326	342
tiānrán	天然	natural (Adj)	13	84	102
tónggǎn	同感	the same feeling (or impression) (N)	18	238	251
tóngsuì	同歲	of the same age (IE)	17	209	223
tóu	頭	head; top; chief (N); first (prefix for ordinal numbers)	21	325	342
tóuténg/tóutòng	頭疼	(have a) headache (N)	21	325	342
tú	圖	picture, drawing, chart, map (N)	13	85	102
túbiǎo	圖表	chart, diagram, graph (N)	13	85	102
túshū	圖書	books (N)	13	85	102
túshūguǎn	圖書館	library (PW)	13	85	102

W

Pinyin	Character	Meaning in English	Lesson	Page (P)	(C)
wài	外	outer, outside; foreign; external (N)	16	181	195
wài biān	外邊	outside, exterior; a place othern than where one lives or works (PW)	22	360	375
wàidì	外地	parts of the country other than where one is (N)	16	182	195

Vocabulary Index
索引

Pinyin	Character	Meaning in English	Lesson	Page (P)	(C)
wàigōng	外公	(maternal) grandfather (N)	20	295	310
wàiguó	外國	foreign country (N)	16	181	195
wàiguóhuà	外國話	foreign language (N)	16	181	195
wàirén	外人	stranger, outsider; foreigner (N)	16	182	195
wàitou	外頭	outside (PW)	21	325	342
wàizǔfù	外祖父	(maternal) grandfather (N)	16	183	196
wàizǔmǔ	外祖母	(maternal) grandmother (N)	16	183	196
wán	完	use up; finish; complete; be over (V/RV)	14	118	135
wǎncān	晚餐	supper, dinner (N)	20	297	311
wàng	望	gaze into the distance; look over; hope, expect (V)	22	361	375
wǎnjiān	晚間	(in the) evening; (at) night (TW)	14	118	135
wán le	完了	come to an end, be over (V)	14	118	135
wánměi	完美	perfect, flawless (SV)	14	118	135
wènhào	問號	question mark; unknown factor; unsolved problem (N)	14	122	139
wénhuà	文化	civilization; culture (N)	22	359	374
wénwù	文物	cultural/historical relic (N)	17	211	225
wǔ	午	noon, midday (TW)	18	239	252
wù	物	thing; matter (N)	17	211	224
wù	誤	mistake, error (N); miss (V)	20	298	312
wùdiǎn	誤點	late; overdue; behind schedule (V)	20	298	312
wǔfàn	午飯	midday meal, lunch (N)	18	239	252
wǔhòu	午後	afternoon (TW)	18	240	252
wùhuì	誤會	misunderstand; mistaken (N/V)	20	299	313
wǔqián	午前	before noon; morning (TW)	18	240	253

X

Pinyin	Character	Meaning in English	Lesson	Page (P)	(C)
xī	西	west (N)	21	329	345
xī	希	hope (V)	22	361	375
xià	下	below, under, underneath (PW); to descend, to get off (V)	12	50	67
xià biān	下邊	below, under, underneath (PW); next (TW)	22	361	375
xià chē	下車	get off or out of a vehicle (VO)	12	51	68

Vocabulary Index
索引

Pinyin	Character	Meaning in English	Lesson	Page (P)	(C)
xiàfàng	下放	sent down (Cadres, etc., in Communist China, were "sent down" to work at the grassroots level or to do manual labor in the countryside or in a factory.) (V)	14	119	136
xià kè	下課	get out of class, finish class (VO)	12	50	67
xiān	先	earlier, before; first; in advance (Adv)	11	10	30
xiàng	像	likeness (of somebody) (V); portrait, picture (N)	20	298	312
xiānhòu	先後	altoghter; priority, order, successively, one after another (Adv)	11	10	30
xiānsheng	先生	teacher; mister (Mr.); gentleman, sir; husband (N)	11	10	30
xiān ... zài	先……再	first ... then (Conj)	11	10	31
xiānzhī-xiānjué	先知先覺	having foresight (IE)	19	268	280
xiǎocōngmíng	小聰明	cleverness in trivial matters; petty tricks (IE)	19	269	281
xiǎorénwù	小人物	an unimportant person, a nobody (N)	17	212	225
xiàwǔ	下午	afternoon (TW)	18	240	253
xīběi	西北	northwest (N)	21	329	345
xīcān	西餐	Western food (N)	20	297	311
xǐchū-wàngwài	喜出望外	be pleasantly surprised (at an unexpected gain, good news, etc.) (IE)	22	362	376
xiè	謝	thank (V); surname	13	83	101
xièxie	謝謝	thanks, thank you (V)	13	83	101
xīfāng	西方	west (direction); the West (N)	21	329	345
xīnbúèr-yòng	心不二用	concentrate on one thing at a time (IE)	13	87	104
xīnchūn	新春	the ten to twenty days following the Lunar New Year's Day (N)	18	241	254
xíng	行	go; travel (V); all right, ok; capable (SV)	14	123	139
xīnqíng	心情	frame of mind, mood (N)	11	9	30
xìngqù	興趣	interest (N)	22	363	377
xīnténg	心疼	love dearly (V); feel sorry; be distressed (SV)	21	326	343
xīwàng	希望	hope, wish, expect (V); possibility (N)	21	361	375
xīyī	西醫	Western medicine; a doctor trained in Western medicine (N)	21	330	346

Pinyin	Character	Meaning in English	Lesson	Page (P)	(C)
xuéfēn	學分	credit (official acceptance and record of a student's work in a particular course of study) (N)	11	7	28

Y

Pinyin	Character	Meaning in English	Lesson	Page (P)	(C)
yàoburán	要不然	otherwise, if not, or else (Conj)	13	84	102
yàodiǎn	要點	main points, essentials, gist, key point (N)	11	6	28
yě	野	wild; open country; uncultivated; undomesticated (Adj)	20	295	310
yěcān	野餐	picnic (N)	20	296	310
yěwài	野外	open country, field (N)	20	295	310
yěxīn	野心	wild ambitions; ambition, big dreams (N)	20	296	310
yī	醫	doctor (of medicine); medicine (N); treat (V)	21	329	345
yìbiān	一邊	one side (N); at the same time, simultaneously (Adv)	22	360	374
yìdiǎnr	一點兒	a bit, a little (Adv)	11	13	32
yíhuìr	一會兒	soon, a little while, a moment; one moment (TW)	11	13	33
yíkuàir	一塊兒	at the same place; together (Adv)	17	214	226
yìqǐ	一起	in the same place, together, in the company of (Adv)	14	121	138
yǐqián	以前	before; formerly, previously (Adv)	12	52	69
yīshēng	醫生	doctor (N)	21	330	345
yīyuàn	醫院	hospital (N)	21	330	346
yīxué	醫學	medical science (N)	21	330	346
yòng	用	use, employ (V)	13	86	103
yòngbuliǎo	用不了	have more than is needed, use less than, not use up (RV)	13	87	104
yònggōng	用功	hardworking, diligent, studious (SV)	13	87	103
yòng rén	用人	choose a person for a job, make use of personnel (VO)	13	87	103
yòngxīn	用心	diligently; attentively, with concentrated attention (SV)	13	87	104
yòu	又	again (Adv)	12	47	65
yǒu diǎnr	有點兒	some, a bit; somewhat (IE)	11	13	32

Pinyin	Character	Meaning in English	Lesson	Page (P)	(C)
yǒuqù	有趣	interesting, fascinating, amusing (SV)	22	363	377
yǒu shì	有事	when problems crop up (VO); busy (N)	11	9	29
yòu ... yòu	又……又	both ... and (Conj)	12	47	65
Yuǎndōng	遠東	the Far East (N)	21	328	344
yuǎnzǒu-gāofēi	遠走高飛	flee; run away (IE)	15	152	167
yuè	越	get over; jump over; exceed (V)	19	268	280
yuèláiyuè	越來越	more and more (Adv)	19	268	281
yuèlì	月曆	monthly calendar (N)	18	242	254
Yuènán	越南	Vietnam (N)	19	268	280
yuè ... yuè ...	越……越……	the more ... the more ... (Adv)	19	268	281

Z

Pinyin	Character	Meaning in English	Lesson	Page (P)	(C)
zài	再	another time, again, once more (Adv)	11	10	31
zàijiàn	再見	good-bye; see you again (V)	11	11	31
zàisān	再三	over and over again, repeatedly (Adv)	11	11	31
zàishuō	再説	put off until some time later; moreover (IE)	11	11	31
zǎocān	早餐	breakfast (N)	20	296	311
zǎodiǎn	早點	breakfast (N)	11	5	27
zhǎo shì	找事	look (or hunt) for a job (VO); pick a quarrel (V)	11	9	29
zhe	著	(indicating an action in progress; stressing the tone in an imperative sentence; used after a verb to form a preposition) (As)	15	155	169
zhè biān	這邊	this side; here (PW)	22	360	375
zhèng	正	straight; upright; situated in the middle; punctually; chief; regular; exactly; (used to indicate an action in progress) (Adj/Adv)	20	293	309
zhèngcháng	正常	normal; regular; routine (Adj)	20	293	309
zhèngdāng	正當	just when; just the time for (Adv)	20	294	309
zhènghǎo	正好	just in time; just right, just enough (Adj)	20	294	309
zhèngzài	正在	(to indicate an action in progress), in the process of (Adv)	20	294	309
zhēnzhèng	真正	genuine; true; real (Adj)	20	294	309

Pinyin	Character	Meaning in English	Lesson	Page (P)	(C)
zhèr	這兒	here (PW)	11	12	32
zhījué	知覺	consciousness; perception (N)	19	267	280
zhīqù	知趣	know how to behave in a delicate situation; tactful, sensitive (Adj)	22	363	377
zhōng	鐘	clock; hour; time (N)	11	11	31
zhōngcān	中餐	lunch; Chinese meal, Chinese food (N)	20	296	311
Zhōngdōng	中東	the Middle East (N)	21	328	345
zhōngjiān	中間	among; between; center; middle (PW)	14	118	135
Zhōngqiūjié	中秋節	the Mid-Autumn Festival (the 15th day of the 8th lunar month) (N)	18	240	253
zhōngwǔ	中午	noon, midday (TW)	18	240	253
zhōngyī	中醫	traditional Chinese medical science; a doctor trained in traditional Chinese medicine (N)	21	330	346
zhù	住	live, reside; stay; stop, cease (V)	16	181	195
zhùsù	住宿	stay; to get accommodation (V)	20	298	312
zhùzai	住在	live at (V)	16	181	195
zǐ	子	son; child; person; seed; egg (N)	12	47	65
zǐnǚ	子女	sons and daughters, children (N)	12	47	65
zū	租	rent, lease; land tax (V)	15	151	167
zǔ	祖	ancestor; founder (N)	16	182	195
zǔguó	祖國	one's country, homeland, motherland (N)	16	182	195
zǔfù	祖父	(paternal) grandfather (N)	16	182	196
zǔmǔ	祖母	(paternal) grandmother (N)	16	183	196
zuòduì	作對	set oneself against; oppose (V)	22	363	376
zuòzhe	坐著	sitting (V)	15	155	170
zǔxiān	祖先	ancestry, ancestors (N)	16	182	196

SENTENCE PATTERN INDEX

Sentence Pattern	Pattern Number	Page (P)	(C)
B			
The bǎ (把) constructions	19.3	270	282
The bǎ (把) construction with a double noun phrase	19.3.1	272	284
The bǎ (把) construction with V-zài (在) PW (le (了))	19.3.2	272	284
The bǎ (把) construction with V-dào (到) PW lái/qù (來/去) (le (了))	19.3.3	273	285
The bǎ (把) construction with resultative verb compounds (le (了))	19.3.4	273	285
The pattern bǐ (比)	12.3	54	70
A bǐ (比) B SV	12.3.1	54	70
A bǐ (比) B SV degree	12.3.3	55	71
Biān (邊) as a localizer	22.2	364	378
A bù bǐ (不比) B SV	12.3.2	54	71
The expression búkèqi (不客氣)	17.4	216	228
The pattern búlùn (不論) ... dōu/yě/hái (都/也/還)	17.2	215	227
The pattern bú shì (不是)..., shì (是)...	20.3	301	314
C			
The adverbs cái (才) and jiù (就)	15.2	159	173
The compound verb chūlai (出來)	13.3	91	107
The word chū (初)	18.5	245	257
Sentence patterns with cóng (從)	14.2	124	140
The pattern cóng (從) ... dào (到)	14.2.1	124	140
The pattern cóng (從) ... qǐ (起)	14.2.2	125	141
D			
The pattern dāng (當) ... de shíhou (的時候)	13.7	93	108
The verbs dào (到) and jiàn (見)	12.4.1	58	74
The pattern děi (得) ... yàoburán (要不然)	13.6	93	108
The verb dǒng (懂)	16.1	186	199
The word duì (對)	22.4	366	379

Sentence Pattern	Pattern Number	Page (P)	(C)
F			
The pattern fēi (非) ... bùkě (不可)	22.1	364	377
G			
Gěi (給) as a postverb	17.6	217	229
More on gòu (夠)	18.2	244	256
H			
The pattern hǎoxiàng (好像) ... de yàngzi (的樣子)	20.4.3	302	315
K			
The expression kànqǐlai (看起來)	18.1	243	255
The use of kànqǐlai (看起來)	18.1.1	243	255
The pattern kànqǐlai (看起來) ... de yàngzi (的樣子)	18.1.2	243	255
The expression kèqi (客氣)	17.3	215	228
L			
V-lái (來)-V-qù (去)	21.4	333	348
The verb liǎo (了)	13.2	90	106
M			
The pattern méiyǒu bù (沒有不) ... de (的)	13.4	92	108
A méiyǒu (沒有) B (nàme/zhème (那麼/這麼)) SV	16.3.2	189	201
Q			
The verb qǐ (起)	14.5	127	142
S			
Shèngqì (生氣) and X shèng (生) Y de qì (的氣)	20.2	300	314
More on the shì (是) ... de (的) pattern	16.2	187	199
Shì (是) ... de (的) with a past event	16.2.1	187	199
Shì (是) ... de (的) with a presumption	16.2.2	188	200
The pattern suīrán (雖然) ... kěshì (可是)	13.1	90	106
Suì (歲), nián (年), and suìshu (歲數)	17.1	214	227
T			
Tóu (頭) as a localizer	21.3	332	348

Sentence Pattern Index

Sentence Pattern	Pattern Number	Page (P)	(C)
W			
Wán (完) and hǎo (好)	14.4	126	141
Sentence patterns with wèi (為)	14.3	125	141
The verb wèi (為)	14.3.1	125	141
The pattern wèi le (為了) ... qǐjiàn (起見)	14.3.2	125	141
X			
The verb xià (下)	12.4.2	59	75
More on xià (下)	21.6	334	349
The pattern xiān (先) ... ránhòu (然後)	13.5	92	108
Xiān (先) ... zài (再) also denotes two actions in sequence	11.5.3	21	39
The word xiàng (像)	20.4	301	315
The meaning of xiàng (像)	20.4.1	301	315
Xiàng (像) ... yíyàng (一樣) expresses similarity and disparity	20.4.2	301	315
Y			
The pattern yìbiān (一邊) ... yìbiān (一邊) ...	22.3	365	379
The pattern yìdiǎnr (一點兒)	11.4	18	36
When yìdiǎnr (一點兒) comes after a verb	11.4.1	18	36
Yìdiǎnr (一點兒) may come either before or after a verb	11.4.2	19	37
Yìdiǎnr yě (一點兒也) and yìdiǎnr dōu (一點兒都)	11.4.3	19	38
The time word yìhuìr (一會兒)	14.1	123	140
The pattern yíhuìr (一會兒) ... yíhuìr (一會兒) ...	21.1	331	349
The expression yíkuàir (一塊兒)	17.5	216	228
Yíkuàir (一塊兒) as a noun	17.5.1	216	228
Yíkuàir (一塊兒) as an adverb	17.5.2	217	229
The words yǐwéi/rènwéi (以為/認為)	20.5	302	315
The linking adverbs yīnwèi (因為) ... suǒyǐ (所以)	13.8	94	109
Yǒu (有) and méiyǒu (沒有)	16.3	189	201
A yǒu (有) B (nàme/zhème (那麼/這麼)) SV	16.3.1	189	201
The differences between yòu (又) and zài (再)	12.1	52	69
The pattern yòu (又) ... yòu (又)	12.2	53	70
The adverbs yòu (又) and zài (再)	15.3	160	174
The expression yuèláiyuè (越來越)	19.1	270	282
The pattern yuè (越) ... yuè (越) ...	19.2	270	282

Sentence Pattern	Pattern Number	Page (P)	(C)
Z			
The pattern zài (再)	11.5	20	38
Zài (再) indicates a repetition of an event in the future	11.5.1	20	38
Zài (再) denotes two actions in sequence	11.5.2	20	39
The pattern zàiyěbù (再也不)	11.5.4	21	39
More on zài (在)	21.2	331	346
Zài (在) with (zhe (著)) ... (ne (呢))	21.2.1	331	347
Zài (在) as a coverb	21.2.2	332	347
Zài (在) as a postverb	21.2.3	332	347
The pattern zěnme (怎麼) ... cái (才)	18.3	244	256
Zháo (著) as a resultative verb	21.5	333	349
The marker zhe (著)	15.1	156	171
Zhe (著) as a durative marker	15.1.1	156	171
Zhe (著) as an adverbial marker	15.1.2	158	172
The pattern zhèng (zài) (正 (在)) ... ne (呢)	20.1	300	314
Miscellaneous			
Clock time	11.1	14	33
Asking and answering in clock time	11.1.1	15	34
Amounts of clock time	11.1.2	15	34
Functions of time words	11.2	15	34
As movable adverbs	11.2.1	15	34
As nouns	11.2.2	16	35
Time expressions and their positions within the sentence	11.3	16	35
A particular point of time	11.3.1	16	35
Duration I	11.3.2	17	36
Duration II	11.3.3	17	36
Comparison of manner of action between A and B	12.3.4	56	72
Comparison of an action with an object between A and B	12.3.5	56	73
Resultative verb compounds	12.4	57	73
As a second element in an RVC	13.3.1	91	107
As a complement	13.3.2	91	107
As a resultative verb ending	13.3.3	91	107
Reduplication forms of adjectives	18.4	245	256

Flash Cards

11.1 diǎn	11.2 fēn	11.3 chē	11.4 shì	11.5 qíng
黑 點	八 分	車 車	丿 事	心 情
11.6 xiān	11.7 zài	11.8 zhōng	11.9 kè	11.10 ér
儿 先	冂 再	金 鐘	刀 刻	儿 兒
12.1 zǐ	12.2 yòu	12.3 fāng	12.4 biàn	12.5 jì
子 子	又 又	方 方	亻 便	宀 寄
12.6 bǐ	12.7 guì	12.8 nǎo	12.9 xià	12.10 qián
比 比	貝 貴	月 腦	一 下	刀 前
13.1 xiè	13.2 dāng	13.3 rán	13.4 suī	13.5 tú
言 謝	田 當	火 然	隹 雖	囗 圖

13.6 cháng	13.7 yòng	13.8 chū	13.9 suǒ	13.10 kòng
巾 常	用	凵 出	厂 所	宀 空
14.1 jiān	14.2 wán	14.3 fàng	14.4 jià	14.5 suàn
門 問	宀 完	方 放	人 假	竹 算
14.6 fù	14.7 qǐ	14.8 hào	14.9 lǚ	14.10 xíng
阜 附	走 起	虍 號	方 旅	彳 行
15.1 zū	15.2 fēi	15.3 jī	15.4 chǎng	15.5 huàn
禾 租	飛	木 機	土 場	手 換
15.6 běi	15.7 jīng	15.8 zhe	15.9 chéng	15.10 nán
匕 北	亠 京	艹 著	土 城	十 南

16.1 zhù 住	16.2 wài 外	16.3 zǔ 祖	16.4 fù 父	16.5 mǔ 母
16.6 fáng 房	16.7 mài 賣	16.8 gāng 剛	16.9 mǎi 買	16.10 dǒng 懂
17.1 suì 歲	17.2 qìng 慶	17.3 tǎo 討	17.4 lùn 論	17.5 lǐ 禮
17.6 wù 物	17.7 kè 客	17.8 jīng 驚	17.9 bǎi 百	17.10 kuài 塊
18.1 gǎn 感	18.2 ēn 恩	18.3 jié 節	18.4 duān 端	18.5 wǔ 午

18.6 qiū 禾 秋	**18.7** chūn 日 春	**18.8** nóng 辰 農	**18.9** lì 日 曆	**18.10** chū 衣 初
19.1 lián 耳 聯	**19.2** luò 糸 絡	**19.3** nào 鬥 鬧	**19.4** jué 見 覺	**19.5** yuè 走 越
19.6 shū 疋 疏	**19.7** cōng 耳 聰	**19.8** jiāo 馬 驕	**19.9** ào 人 傲	**19.10** bǎ 手 把
20.1 zhèng 止 正	**20.2** gōng 八 公	**20.3** yě 里 野	**20.4** cān 食 餐	**20.5** ā 口 啊
20.6 sù 宀 宿	**20.7** shè 舌 舍	**20.8** xiàng 人 像	**20.9** wù 言 誤	**20.10** bié 刀 別

21.1 bìng	21.2 shuì	21.3 jiào	21.4 tóu	21.5 téng / tòng
疒 病	目 睡	見 覺	頁 頭	疒 疼

21.6 fā	21.7 shāo	21.8 dōng	21.9 xī	21.10 yī
癶 發	火 燒	木 東	西 西	醫

22.1 shǔ	22.2 fēi	22.3 jì	22.4 huà	22.5 huà
日 暑	非 非	言 計	刀 劃	匕 化

22.6 biān	22.7 xī	22.8 wàng	22.9 duì	22.10 qù
辶 邊	巾 希	月 望	寸 對	走 趣